POPULATION AND INDUSTRIALIZATION

Documents in Economic History

POPULATION AND INDUSTRIALIZATION N. L. Tranter

In preparation
THE AGRICULTURAL REVOLUTION G. E. Mingay, Ph.D.
THE CHALLENGE OF URBANISATION A. R. Sutcliffe
ENTREPRENEURSHIP 1750-1939 R. H. Campbell, Ph.D.
THE FREE TRADE ERA B. M. Ratcliffe and O. W. Henderson
MIGRATION Charlotte Erikson, Ph.D.
THE POPULATION REVOLUTION J. D. Chalmers
THE PRICE REVOLUTION OF THE XVIth CENTURY Harland Taylor
TECHNOLOGICAL CHANGE IN BRITAIN 1660-1800 J. D. Harris

DOCUMENTS IN ECONOMIC HISTORY
General Editor: Professor Sidney Pollard, University of Sheffield

POPULATION
and
INDUSTRIALIZATION

The evolution of a concept
and its practical application

EDITED AND WITH AN INTRODUCTION BY

N. L. TRANTER
University of East Anglia

ADAM & CHARLES BLACK
LONDON

First published 1973
A. & C. Black Ltd., Soho Square, London W1

© N. L. Tranter, 1973
ISBN 0 7136 1310 6

To My Family

Designed and produced by
Richard Sadler Ltd.
Halfpenny Furze, Chalfont St. Giles,
Buckinghamshire.

Printed in Great Britain by
The Garden City Press Limited
Letchworth, Hertfordshire SG6 1JS

ACKNOWLEDGEMENTS

I am indebted to the following for permission to reproduce extracts from their works:

George Allen and Unwin Ltd for W. H. Beveridge, *Full employment in a free society*, London, 1944:

the literary executors of J. D. Chambers, the Economic History Society and Cambridge University Press for J. D. Chambers, *The Vale of Trent, 1670-1800*, Economic History Review Supplement 3, 1957:

Staples Press Ltd and Granada Publishing Ltd for E. Cannan, *Wealth, a brief explanation of the causes of economic welfare*, 3rd ed., London, 1928:

P. Deane and W. A. Cole and Cambridge U.P. for P. Deane and W. A. Cole, *British economic growth, 1688-1959*, 2nd ed., Cambridge, 1967:

D. E. C. Eversley, E. L. Jones, G. E. Mingay, and Edward Arnold Ltd for D. E. C. Eversley, The home market and economic growth in England, 1750-1780, in E. L. Jones and G. E. Mingay eds., *Land, labour and population in the Industrial Revolution*, London, 1967:

Cambridge U.P. for G. Talbot Griffiths, *Population problems in the age of Malthus*, 2nd ed., published by Frank Cass and Co. Ltd, London, 1967:

H. J. Habakkuk and Cambridge U.P. for H. J. Habakkuk, *American and British technology in the nineteenth century*, Cambridge, 1962:

J. Jewkes and the Manchester School of Economic and Social Studies for J. Jewkes, The population scare, *Manchester School of Economic and Social Studies*, X, 2, 1939;

the executors of the Paul Mantoux estate and Jonathan Cape Ltd for P. Mantoux, *The Industrial Revolution in the eighteenth century*, London, 1966:

Macmillan Ltd for A. Marshall, *Principles of economics*, vol. I. 3rd ed., London, 1895:

the Royal Statistical Society for E. C. Snow, The limits of industrial employment (II). The influence of growth of population on the development of industry, *Journal of the Royal Statistical Society*, XCVIII, Part II, 1935, and for P. Stocks, The effects of occupation and of its accompanying environment on mortality, *Journal of the Royal Statistical Society*, CI, Part IV, 1938:

R and K. Titmuss, and Martin Secker and Warburg Ltd, for R. and K. Titmuss, *Parents' revolt*, London, 1942.

I am also deeply grateful to Mrs N. Alderson, Mrs E. Hitchburn and Mrs D. Roberts for typing an often difficult and complex manuscript so capably. Finally, I wish to thank Professor R. H. Campbell of the University of Stirling and Mr N. Miller of the University of East Anglia for their valuable advice and suggestions. They are, however, in no way responsible for the choice of extracts included in the volume nor for the views expressed in the introduction.

N. TRANTER
University of East Anglia

CONTENTS

Extract Number		Page
	Acknowledgements	6
	Introduction	9
I	ANON *Britannia Languens*, 1680.	33
II	JOSIAH TUCKER, *The Elements of Commerce*, 1755.	37
III	SIR C. D'AVENANT, *Discourses on the Public Revenues*, 1698	43
IV	D. DEFOE, *A Plan of the English Commerce*, 1728.	51
V	S. GRAY, *The Happiness of States*, 1815.	57
VI	G. K. RICKARDS, *Population and Capital*, 1854.	64
VII	T. R. MALTHUS, *Principles of Political Economy*, 1836.	69
VIII	W. H. BEVERIDGE, *Full Employment in a Free Society*, 1944.	72
IX	UNITED NATIONS, *The Determinants and Consequences of Population Trends*, 1953.	74
X	*Thirty-Ninth Annual Report*, REGISTRAR-GENERAL, 1878.	80
XI	H. SIDGWICK, *Principles of Political Economy*, 1883.	87
XII	R. TORRENS, *An Essay on the Production of Wealth*, 1821.	95
XIII	J. S. MILL, *Principles of Political Economy*, 1871.	98
XIV	A. MARSHALL, *Principles of Economics*, 1895.	107
XV	E. CANNAN, *Wealth*, 1928.	110
XVI	UNITED NATIONS, *The Determinants and Consequences of Population Trends*, 1953.	114
XVII	J. D. CHAMBERS, *The Vale of Trent*, 1957.	122
XVIII	P. DEANE AND W. A. COLE, *British Economic Growth*, 1967.	127
XIX	H. J. HABAKKUK, *American and British Technology in the Nineteenth Century*, 1962.	136
XX	D. E. C. EVERSLEY, *The Home Market and Economic Growth in England, 1750-80*, 1967.	141
XXI	E. C. SNOW, *The Limits of Industrial Employment*, 1935.	150
XXII	R. AND K. TITMUSS, *Parents' Revolt*, 1942.	155
XXIII	J. JEWKES, *The Population Scare*, 1939.	163
XXIV	UNITED NATIONS, *The Determinants and Consequences of Population Trends*, 1953.	171

XXV	A. YOUNG, *Political Arithmetic*, 1774.	187
XXVI	S. LAING, *National Distress*, 1844.	191
XXVII	P. GASKELL, *Artisans and Machinery*, 1836.	200
XXVIII	J. R. MCCULLOCH, *The Principles of Political Economy*, 1825.	202
XXIX	J. KENNEDY, *Observations on the Influence of Machinery upon the Working Classes of the Community*, 1829.	204
XXX	G. TALBOT GRIFFITH, *Population Problems in the Age of Malthus*, 1967.	208
XXXI	P. MANTOUX, *The Industrial Revolution in the Eighteenth Century*, 1966.	211
XXXII	E. C. SNOW, *The Limits of Industrial Employment*, 1935.	218
XXXIII	R. WALLACE, *A Dissertation on the Numbers of Mankind in Antient and Modern Times*, 1753.	225
XXIV	T. R. MALTHUS, *First Essay on Population*, 1798.	229
XXXV	T. R. MALTHUS, *An Essay on the Principle of Population*, 1826	235
XXXVI	A. ALISON, *The Principles of Population and their Connection with Human Happiness*, 1840.	239
XXXVII	UNITED NATIONS, *The Determinants and Consequences of Population Trends*, 1953.	244
XXXVIII	*First Annual Report*, REGISTRAR-GENERAL, 1839.	248
XXXIX	COMMITTEE REPORT, *Regulation of Child Labour*, 1833.	251
XL	SELECT COMMITTEE, *The Health of Towns*, 1840.	255
XLI	D. NOBLE, *Facts and Observations Relative to the Influence of Manufactures upon Health and Life*, 1843.	260
XLII	P. STOCKS, *Occupation, Environment and Mortality*, 1938.	264
XLIII	*Supplement to the Thirty-Fifth Annual Report*, REGISTRAR-GENERAL, 1875.	271
XLIV	*Forty-Eighth Annual Report*, REGISTRAR-GENERAL, 1885.	275
XLV	*Seventy-Fifth Annual Report*, REGISTRAR-GENERAL, 1914.	278
XLVI	ROYAL COMMISSION, *Report on Population*, 1949.	283
	Indexes	289

INTRODUCTION

For a long time now scholars have recognized the existence of a reciprocal link between population change on the one hand, and the development of manufacturing industry on the other. It is, however, only in recent years that the extreme complexity of this link has become apparent. An attempt has been made in the present series of extracts to trace the evolution of ideas concerning the relationship between population and industrialization, from the oversimplified and often ill-informed assumptions of writers in the period immediately preceding the Industrial Revolution, to the more refined and soundly-based arguments of modern theorists. At the same time, we have tried to introduce the reader to a discussion of the practical contribution of the population variable to industrial growth, and of the part played by industrialization in shaping the pattern of demographic change, since the late eighteenth century. Historians and historical demographers alike have only recently begun to attempt this task, but some of their earliest, tentative suggestions can be included. Finally, in the course of these exercises, we hope to indicate the degree to which a thorough analysis depends on the availability of adequate demographic source-materials. Most of the material contained in this volume is taken from the work of British writers, and relates mainly to English society in its transition from a relatively backward, agrarian-based, to a modern, highly industrialized economy. Although this restriction of subject-matter may in some senses be regrettable, it does at least have the merit of pertaining to a population group which has passed through the various stages of economic, social, demographic and cultural 'revolution' associated with the process of industrial modernization. Much, though not all, of what can be said about the nature of the connection between population and industrialization can be discussed within these apparently limited parameters.

I

Most writers on the subject of population and economic growth during the second half of the seventeenth and first half of the eighteenth centuries, in line with predominant mercantilist values, were firmly convinced that population growth and the expansion of manufacturing industry were mutually beneficial. Their conviction rested on three assumptions: firstly, that a large and rapidly increasing population resulted in equally large and rapidly-growing increments to the size of the manufacturing labour-force, which, in turn, meant lower wages, lower costs of production, cheaper manufactured goods, and hence rapid industrial growth: secondly, that population growth automatically ensured expanding demand for manufactured products, thereby encouraging a greater division of labour and its corollaries, cheaper production, larger output and higher quality goods: thirdly, that the development of manufacturing industry itself stimulated increased rates of population growth, and thus guaranteed further industrial expansion. (Extracts I–IV). So confidently were these assumptions held that few writers troubled to examine them in any detail.[1]

From the second half of the eighteenth century, and more particularly during the early years of the nineteenth, the well-established optimistic interpretations of the relationship between population and industrial growth were subjected to increasingly heavy criticism. At first sight it is somewhat surprising that the coincidence of demographic and industrial 'take-off' in the later eighteenth century should have been paralleled by the emergence of more pessimistic doctrines. One would have expected the simultaneous upsurge of population and manufacturing industry to have lent considerable support to the view that population growth and industrialization were mutually advantageous. To a certain extent of course it did. The stimulus given by population growth to industrial development continued to be

---

[1] Among those who did question the facility with which population growth enhanced the productive power of manufacturing industry and the demand for its products see Sir W. Temple, Observations upon the United Provinces of the Netherlands, 1668; and, An essay on the Advancement of Trade in Ireland, 1673; in *The Works of Sir W. Temple*, 2 vols, London, 1740, vol. I. Sir M. Hale, *The Primitive Origination of Mankind*, London, 1677; and, *A discourse touching provision for the poor*, London, 1683. Sir W. Petty, Political Arithmetic, London, 1690, in C. H. Hull ed; *The Economic Writings of Sir William Petty*..., Cornell, 1899, Reprints of Economic Classics, 2 vols, New York, 1963, vol. I. C. D'Avenant, Discourses on the Public Revenues and on the Trade of England, 2 vols, 1698, in Sir Charles Whitworth, *The Political and Commercial Works of that celebrated writer Charles D'Avenant*..., 5 vols, London, 1771, Reprinted Farnborough, 1967, vol. II (Extract IV below). D. Defoe, *A Plan of the English Commerce*, 1728, Reprinted Oxford, 1928 (Extract V below).

stressed by numerous writers in the early nineteenth century, emphasizing its contribution to the division of labour, the size of the labour force and the efficiency with which it was organized, innovations in machinery and other improvements in the methods of production (Extracts V, VI). Similarly, it is not difficult to find examples of writers who continued to believe that the expansion of manufacturing industry stimulated population growth (Extracts XXVIII, XXIX). However, most theorists at the turn of the century were less willing to accept such arguments without substantial modification.

In part, this revision of earlier assumptions was a reflection of the same factors which made 'Malthusianism' so acceptable to influential sections of English society after the publication of the First Essay on Population in 1798.[1] In part, it was simply the result of the hold which Malthus's pessimistic thesis, that population growth was not inevitably conducive to economic and social progress, came to have in the teachings of classical economy. Both were the logical outcome of the economic and demographic changes characteristic of England since the middle of the eighteenth century.

From the mid seventeenth to the mid eighteenth centuries, the rate of population growth had been abnormally low, labour in short supply (this in an economy based on labour- rather than capital-intensive methods of production), and real wages had remained high enough to ensure the maintenance of a 'comfortable' margin between individual incomes and the costs of basic subsistence. In such circumstances, it is understandable that contemporary opinion should be more concerned with the quantity of the population (and hence of the labour force) than with its quality, and why contemporaries had little fear of the possible detrimental consequences of population growth on average income levels (and hence on the demand for industrial goods). From the middle of the eighteenth century, however, demographic conditions changed markedly. Population began to increase rapidly, and the problems of acute labour shortage were replaced by those associated with labour

---

[1] For a discussion of the historical context of Malthus's essay see H. L. Beales, *The historical context of the Essay on Population*, in D. V. Glass, ed; *Introduction to Malthus*, London, 1959, pp. 1–24. R. L. Meek, ed; *Marx and Engels on Malthus*, London, 1953, pp. 11–21.

surplus. Real wage rates stabilized, and, at least from the 1780's, may even have fallen slightly for substantial sections of the community. At the same time, the geographical distribution of the population was rapidly transformed to meet the needs of economic growth, and a steadily increasing proportion of the population was subjected to the evils of life in large manufacturing towns. The actual and potential economic, social, and political consequences of these developments provided the necessary impetus for a fresh look at the role of population in industrial growth, as well as at the effects of manufacturing industry on the rate of population increase. Low and perhaps falling real wages (apparently substantiated by rising poor law expenditures, rising food prices, and abundant evidence of economic distress), at a time of rapid population growth, led logically to misgivings about the assumption that a given increase in population automatically ensured a comparable increase in the demand for industrial products. Excess supplies of labour relative to the requirements of the economy raised doubts regarding the assumptions that a growing population would always be fully employed and that it would always guarantee expanding industrial output. Meanwhile, the role of labour in the industrializing economy was itself beginning to change. As power-driven machinery began to supersede manual labour in some of its earlier productive functions, and as the technology of industrial society became more complex, it was only to be expected that economists would switch their emphasis from the quantity of the labour-force to its quality. Finally, we should note that the growing recognition of, and concern with, the problems of urban-industrial life during the early nineteenth century, prepared the ground for those who argued that manufacturing industry could, under certain circumstances, lead to depopulation rather than to further population growth. Clearly, the pessimism with which much early nineteenth-century opinion viewed the operation of the population variable, like the optimistic view of late seventeenth- and early eighteenth-century writers, was firmly rooted in the economic and demographic conditions of their respective times.

II

Malthus was one of a growing number of writers who questioned the assumption that a given increase in population always led to a

Introduction 13

proportionate rise in the level of effective demand for manufactured products (Extracts VII)[1]. According to this view, population growth will not stimulate demand for non-agricultural goods if the resultant population is too large for available food resources. In such a situation, food prices will rise so much that the proportion of consumer incomes expendable on manufactured products may fall, and aggregate demand for all but the essentials of life may contract sharply.

Theoretically, this argument is perfectly rational. But in practice it became less and less relevant to the circumstances of English society in the nineteenth century. Any danger of a reduction in the effective demand for industrial goods was resolved by rising agricultural productivity at home and by large-scale imports of food from the New World. Together with the continued expansion of the English industrial and commercial economy, these developments ensured steadily rising real wages and a concomitant expansion of markets for manufactured products. In these circumstances, the maintenance of relatively high rates of population growth throughout the century acted as a further stimulus, not as a depressant, to the demand for industrial commodities. Consequently, nineteenth-century economists paid decreasing attention to Malthus's interpretation of the contribution made by population growth to the level of demand for non-agricultural products. Although acknowledging that an increasing population may not always imply rising demand, by and large they continued to assume that it invariably did so. Furthermore, the very success of the English economy before the First World War discouraged any deeper analysis of the relationship between population and effective demand. On the basis of their own experience, nineteenth-century writers (like those of the late seventeenth and early eighteenth centuries) felt safe in presuming that with every pair of hands God had sent a mouth.

A more refined treatment had to await the onset of economic depression in the years between the world wars. Out of the

---

[1] Recognition of the principle of effective demand long pre-dates Malthus, of course. It received increasing attention in the second half of the eighteenth century. See for example A. S. Skinner, ed; *Sir James Stewart, An inquiry into the principles of Political Economy*, 2 vols, Edinburgh 1767, Edinburgh, 1966, pp. 196–202. A. Smith, *An Inquiry into the Nature and Causes of the Wealth of Nations*, London, 1776, London, 1893, pp. 43, 130–1.

resulting re-evaluation of the standard assumptions regarding the mechanisms of economic growth came a clearer and more sophisticated appreciation of the way in which the size and growth rate of population influenced the level of demand for manufactures (Extracts VIII, IX). Thus, industrial performance depends to a large extent on the level of savings, and the use to which these are put. If a growing proportion of total savings is not invested in the production of 'material' goods or of 'services' for immediate consumption, then, even in societies in which population and real wages are both increasing, there is no reason to assume rising absolute demand for industrial products. In an unplanned, uncontrolled, market economy, decisions to save for future consumption may predominate over immediate productive investment, and result in industrial retardation and high levels of unemployment. Of course, a large and rapidly-growing population, provided it does not lead to rising costs of living (by outstripping available primary resources), does encourage productive investment at the expense of 'sterile' savings for the future via the stimulus it gives to the level of demand for industrial goods, and thus to industrial profits and profit expectations. However, particularly in societies like England which have been subject to rapid technological development and capital growth, the size and growth rate of the population alone may play only a minor role in determining the level of demand for non-food goods and services. In reality, variations in age-structure, in the number of households and families, and especially in such non-demographic variables as the level of per capita income, consumer tastes, and the propensity to consume, may result in the failure of any given change in population size to correspond exactly to changes in the level of effective consumer demand for industrial products.

At the same time as nineteenth- and twentieth-century economists were busy re-interpreting the contribution of population growth to effective demand, they were also casting a more critical eye on the facile assumption that population growth alone, by permitting a continual increase in the size of the labour force, guaranteed rising levels of industrial output and productivity.

The emphasis of nineteenth-century literature was increasingly on the quality rather than the quantity of the manufacturing work-force (Extracts X, XI). A population would be most productive only if it was well-fed, well-educated, healthy, long-lived, properly motivated by a desire to work, and efficiently organized.[1] This should not be taken to imply that nineteenth-century writers dismissed the value of a large and rapidly-expanding population as a principal agent in industrial development. On the contrary, with reservations about its quality, they continued to believe that population growth facilitated industrial development by providing regular increments to the size of the labour-force. It is true that the 'Malthusians' had some doubts about this, but these doubts were never expressed very forcibly. In practical terms, they, like everyone else, accepted the view that additions to the labour-force were rewarded by increasing returns to labour in manufacturing industry, in spite of diminishing returns in the agricultural and extractive industries (Extracts, XII, XIII, XIV).[2]

It was left to later writers to question the inherent falsity of the assumption that in 'advanced' economies further inputs of labour were invariably attended by diminishing returns in the primary sector and by increasing returns in the secondary sector. As Cannan argued, up to a certain point population growth could lead to greater returns to labour in agriculture and mining as well as in manufacturing, while beyond that point it could effect diminishing returns in all three. Theoretically, therefore, falling returns to labour are possible, albeit less likely in practice, in manufacturing industry as a

---

[1] See for instance J. R. McCulloch, *The Principles of Political Economy*, Edinburgh, 1825, pp. 115-19. Lord Brabazon, Decay of Bodily Strength in Towns, *The Nineteenth Century*, XXI, 1887, pp. 673-6. A. Marshall, *Principles of Economics*, vol. I., 3rd ed., London, 1895, pp. 274-85. For an earlier formulation see A. Fergusson, *A History of Civil Society*, 1st ed., 1767, 6th ed.; London, 1793, pp. 97-101.

[2] Indeed throughout the century, a large body of opinion clung to the belief that population growth resulted in increasing returns to labour in the agricultural as well as in the manufacturing sector of the economy, despite the forebodings of the 'Malthusians' and the teachings of classical economy. See, inter alia, S. Gray, *The Happiness of States* . . ., London, 1815, pp. 320-35. P. Ravenstone, *A few doubts as to the correctness of some opinions generally entertained on the subject of population and political economy*, London, 1821, pp. 170-5, 184-7. W. T. Comber, *An inquiry into the state of national subsistence as connected with the progress of wealth and population* . . ., 2nd ed.; London, 1822, pp. 261-82. W. Thompson, *An inquiry into the principles of the distribution of wealth most conducive to human happiness* . . ., London, 1824, Reprints of Economic Classics, New York, 1963, pp. 535-45, G. Poulett Scrope, *Principles of Political Economy* . . ., London, 1833, pp. 265-6. G. K. Rickards, *Population and Capital*, London, 1854, pp. 137-46. H. George, *Progress and Poverty*, London, 1884, pp. 106-14.

consequence of too large or too rapid an increase in the size of the labour-force (Extract XV).[1]

The modifications which have been made to earlier ideas regarding the productive function of population in industrial growth have been less dramatic than those concerning the role of population as a determinant of total demand for industrial products. In modern, industrialized, societies factors other than the size of the population unit are considered as more important influences on the level of consumer demand for manufacturers (Extract IX). On the other hand, modern theory still holds that the amount of labour available for manufacturing industry depends primarily on the sheer size of the population (Extract XVI). Of course, variations in the number of economically-active persons between population groups of the same size are recognized, and their causes (e.g. differences in age, sex, marital composition: in urban-rural residence patterns: in the levels of fertility and income: in the type and organization of production: in the relative values placed on economic and non-economic roles, and so on) are duly noted. Moreover, modern scholarship places more emphasis on the importance of the efficiency and motivation of the labour-force than was once the case. Nevertheless, the principal determinant of a large and growing labour-force in industrialized countries is still considered to be a large and growing population.

III

Although recent literature has shown a growing interest in evaluating the precise contribution of the demographic variable to English industrial development since the eighteenth century, so far the results have been slight. There are two basic difficulties inhibiting such an analysis: firstly, the absence of adequate demographic data for much of the period before the mid nineteenth century: and secondly, the quantitative problem involved in trying to isolate the specific contribution of the demographic variable from that of the many other factors which have facilitated industrial growth. If recent

---

[1] Less explicit statements of the same idea had been made earlier. See J. S. Mill *Principles of Political Economy*, London, 1848, 1936 ed., Book I, Ch. 10–13. H. Sidgwick, *Principles of Political Economy*, London, 1887, Ch. 6. Note also Edmonds's views on the optimum size of towns, T. R. Edmonds, *Practical Moral and Political Economy...*, London, 1828, pp. 92–6.

Introduction

improvements in the techniques of historical demographic analysis prove to be as fruitful as their supporters claim, the first of these problems may be overcome in the near future. But the second will continue to bedevil any accurate evaluation of the significance of population growth for industrial 'take-off'.

No one believes that the crude similarity in the timing of economic and demographic trends since the eighteenth century is entirely fortuitous. Most historians accept that population growth has played a part in shaping the pattern of English economic growth in recent generations. Where they diverge from each other is over the degree of importance attached to the population variable, and over the manner in which its influence was exerted. As an agent of production, some writers have stressed the vital contribution of a growing population to the provision of an industrial labour-force, particularly during the early days of the Industrial Revolution when labour was in short supply (Extract XVII).[1] They infer that without this demographic expansion, industrial 'take-off' would have been retarded. Others are not convinced that the correlation between the three variables involved (population growth, expanding labour supply, industrial 'take-off') is close enough to warrant such an assumption (Extract XVIII). How far population growth and an expanding labour-force continued to be an advantage to the English industrial economy in the nineteenth century also remains in doubt. At least one author has argued that, relative to American experience, the maintenance of high rates of population growth resulted in an over-abundance of labour, and that this contributed to the retardation of technological innovation and ultimately of industrial growth rates (Extract XIX).[2] Whatever the truth of this contention, and we must remember that high rates of demographic increase contributed to the emergence of an international economy upon which so much of England's prosperity was based, we obviously require a more thorough analysis of the relationship between population growth and the size of the labour-force, and between the latter and industrial growth rates, in English historical experience. In any case, as Eversley points out, the most important influence on

---

[1] And J. D. Chambers, Enclosure and labour supply in the Industrial Revolution, *Ec. H.R.* 2nd ser., V, 1952–3, pp. 319–43.
[2] For brief comments on Habakkuk's argument see A. L. Levine, *Industrial Retardation in Britain, 1880–1914*, London, 1963, pp. 76–8. P. Mathias, *The First Industrial Nation*, London, 1969, p. 426.

entrepreneurial decision-making is not the size of the labour force, but the extent of the market.[1]

To date, there have been two principal interpretations of the way in which population growth contributed to the rising demand for manufactured goods during the early years of the Industrial Revolution (Extracts XVIII, XX). According to Deane and Cole,[2] because population grew slowly (in the first half of the eighteenth century), the real incomes of the agricultural sector stayed relatively low, and (on the arguable assumption that the agricultural sector provided the largest source of demand for, and investment in, manufactured products) industrial growth was retarded. When population began to increase more rapidly (in the second half of the eighteenth century), demand for food goods rose, agricultural incomes increased, and as a result, manufacturing industry received a considerable stimulus. At the same time, the rising cost of necessities induced industrial employees to work harder and more efficiently in order to maintain their customary standards of living. In brief, via its effects on the ability of the agricultural sector to invest in and consume manufactured goods, population growth triggered off the mechanism which resulted in the series of technical and organizational innovations culminating in the Industrial Revolution.

A somewhat different interpretation of the demographic contribution to early industrial 'take-off' is given by Eversley. Relatively low rates of population growth in the 1730's and 1740's helped to produce a wider margin between total income and expenditure on basic necessities. The result was an increase in consumer purchasing power for non-agricultural goods. This vital margin remained substantial in the period 1750–80 (what happened after 1780 is left largely open to question), though it could so easily have been upset if, inter alia, population had begun to increase too rapidly. Fortunately, though population growth rates did rise, they remained closely in line with the needs of the economy, neither so small as to result in shortage of labour or demand for industrial products, nor so large as to lead to a surplus of labour, falling real wages, and the total destruction of the market for manufactures. As a consequence, the

---

[1] D. E. C. Eversley, Population, Economy and Society, in D. V. Glass and D. E. C. Eversley, eds., *Population in History*, London, 1965, p. 64.
[2] See also J. D. Chambers, The Vale of Trent, 1670–1800, *Ec. H.R. Supplement 3*, Ch. IV. H. J. Habakkuk, Essays in bibliography and criticism. The eighteenth century, *Ec. H.R.* 2nd ser., VIII, 1955–6.

Introduction

foundations for industrial 'take-off' were firmly laid in the three decades after 1750. It is to be hoped that future research will permit a thorough evaluation of these hypotheses.

Once the process of industrialization was underway, demographic trends continued to play a significant part in shaping its pace and direction through their effects on the level of consumer demand (Extracts XXI, XXII). High population growth rates throughout the nineteenth century necessitated increasing imports of foodstuffs from the New World and facilitated the development of an international trading economy from which English export industries greatly benefited. The resultant expansion of employment opportunities contributed to rising domestic demand for manufactures, and thereby encouraged further industrial investment. After the First World War however, when the rate of population growth in England and Western Europe slowed down, demand for the products of primary-producing countries also slowed and, in turn, the latter found it difficult to expand their demand for English industrial products at the old rate.[1] The delicate balance of the international economy was upset and the problems confronting English export industries were compounded. Simultaneously, reduced rates of population increase may have contributed to a fall in the rate of domestic consumer demand for certain types of industrial products. Partly as a result of all this, the rate of industrial investment declined and unemployment increased. Faced with shrinking, or at best slowly growing markets, entrepreneurs became less innovation-conscious and more inclined to continue with out-dated methods and well-tried lines of production rather than search for new techniques and new outlets. With the ageing of the population concomitant on falling birth and death-rates, the labour-force became less mobile, its qualities of initiative and 'drive' slackened, and industry as a whole became less flexible and less capable of responding successfully to the novel circumstances confronting it.

So at least runs the argument common to much of the literature, particularly that of the 1930's. Of course, no one believed that the problems facing English industry in the inter-war years were solely the result of demographic changes. But such was the widespread concern with the presumed effects of declining population growth rates that the

---

[1] For a recent comment on this argument see D. S. Landes, *The Unbound Prometheus*, Cambridge U.P., 1969, pp. 365–7.

contribution of the demographic variable to industrial performance did receive considerable stress, probably much more than it really deserved. There were a few writers who refused to accept the gloomy predictions of their contemporaries and, in doing so, cast doubt on the common assumption that a high rate of population increase was of vital importance in industrialized societies (Extract XXIII). In line with modern demographic theory, their arguments imply that the effects of population change in advanced economies have exerted much less influence on the pace and pattern of industrial development than was once believed (Extract XXIV). We must not ignore this warning.

IV

As we have already noted, most late seventeenth- and early eighteenth-century writers were convinced that the growth of manufacturing industry stimulated the rate of population increase, though they rarely troubled to analyse the demographic mechanisms through which it did so (Extracts I, IV). This view continued to have its supporters in the late eighteenth and nineteenth centuries. Young, Laing, and Gaskell are representative of those who argued that industrial growth encouraged higher rates of fertility (Extracts XXV, XXVI, XXVII). Others, like Mr. McCulloch and Kennedy, attributed demographic 'take-off' and the maintenance of high rates of population growth during the nineteenth century at least partly to the beneficial consequences of industrialization on mortality rates (Extracts XXVIII, XXIX).[1] Similar claims have been made by more recent scholars, though they have usually been more cautious in allowing for the influence on population growth of factors other than those directly associated with industrialization (Extracts XXX, XXXI). Indeed, some recent authorities have gone even further

---

[1] Other writers who associated population increase at least partly with the growth of manufacturing industry include D. Hume, Of the Populousness of Ancient Nations, in D. Hume, *Political Discourses*, Edinburgh, 1752, 1906 eds, pp. 140–2: J. Tucker, Instructions for Travellers, 1757, in R. L. Schuyler ed., *Josiah Tucker, A Selection from his Economic and Political Writings*, New York, 1931, pp. 239–47. J. Howlett, *An examination of Dr. Price's essay on the Population of England and Wales* . . ., Maidstone, 1781, pp. 8–12. W. Cooke Taylor, *Notes of a Tour in the Manufacturing Districts of Lancashire*, 2nd ed., 1842, 3rd ed., London, 1968, pp. 13–15, 54–5. K. Marx, *Capital. A critique of political economy*, 1906 ed., pp. 689–709.

towards minimizing the contribution of industrial development to the upsurge in population growth rates since the eighteenth century (Extract XXXII). In view of the fact that the 'demographic revolution' was a feature of many non-industrialized societies of western Europe, this latter approach holds particular attractions. If industrial growth has played its part in encouraging and facilitating higher rates of population growth since the Industrial Revolution it must not be accorded sole responsibility.[1]

With the germination of the idea that population growth could outrun additions to the supply of food resources, some writers in the second half of the eighteenth century began to argue that the expansion of manufacturing industry could result in population decline (Extracts XXXIII, XXXIV). Thus, Robert Wallace, one of the principal contributors to the mid-century debate on population,[2] was convinced that 'operose manufactures' had encouraged depopulation by enticing labour away from the production of foodstuffs and other basic necessities. The disproportionate pursuit of manufacturing occupations had increased the cost of living by resulting in higher food prices, and thus reduced the marriage rate and the rate of population growth. Later writers, armed with more adequate statistical data which showed population to be increasing, were perforce less pessimistic. But many continued to believe that a high rate of population growth was not a necessary corollary of the development of manufacturing industry. To Malthus, as to Wallace, the main determinant of the size and growth-rate of the population was the size and growth-rate of the 'effectual fund for the maintenance of labour', i.e. food resources. Despite the substantial growth of industry and total wealth over the previous century, population had failed to grow as rapidly, largely because the expansion of food output had been relatively slow. Although money wages had risen as a consequence of the growing demand for labour, the effect of this on living standards had been nullified by the rising cost of living associated with the pressure of population on food supplies. In fact, conditions of life among the

---

[1] See J. D. Chambers, Some aspects of E. A. Wrigley's "Population and History", *Local Population Studies*, 3, 1969, pp. 18–28.

[2] See D. V. Glass, Population controversy in eighteenth-century England. Part I. The background, *Population Studies*, VI, 1, 1952–3, pp. 69–91.

labouring classes may have worsened as they became increasingly dependent on unhealthy and uncertain industrial occupations.[1]

Basically, Malthus drew the same conclusions that Wallace had done half a century earlier, viz. firstly, that *in the long-term* the size and growth rate of the population depends not on the extent of manufacturing industry, but on the availability of food supplies: secondly, that an undue concentration of the labour-force in manufacturing industry reduces the stock of food, and hence in the *long-term* diminishes the rate at which population can increase via both the preventive and the positive checks.

Although never completely abandoning this argument, Malthus did modify it considerably in his later work (Extract XXXV). Thus, in the sixth edition of the Essay, he continued to assume that if the existing habits of society in respect to the necessities of life remained unchanged, the power of supporting children would be diminished by the inevitable pressure of population on food resources. However, he now accepted that the habits of society could be changed in such a way as to keep the rate of population increase to within the rate at which primary resources could be expanded. Among the factors responsible for this change in habits were those pertaining directly or indirectly to industrial development, viz., the growth of a 'middle-class' population of merchants, manufacturers, tradesmen, farmers, and independent labourers: and the rising demand for the conveniences and comforts of life (as opposed to the basic necessities) which followed their greater availability and the relative fall in their price in the progress of industrialization and mass production. Both factors encouraged the spread of more prudential attitudes to early marriage and large families, and ultimately, retarded the pace of demographic increase via the

---

[1] See also Skinner ed., Sir James Stuart, *op cit.*, pp. 30–3, 36–7, 38–43, 50. R. Wallace, *A dissertation on the number of mankind in ancient and modern times: in which the superior populousness of antiquity is maintained*, Edinburgh, 1753, pp. 19–31. W. Bell, *Dissertation on the following subject: What causes principally contribute to render a nation populous . . .*, Cambridge, 1756. C. Hall, *The effects of civilization on the people in European States*, 1805, London, 1850, pp, pp. 30–8. A. Bell, An enquiry into the policy and justice of the prohibition of the use of grain in the distilleries, Edinburgh, 1808, in J. R. McCulloch ed., *A select collection of scarce and valuable economical tracts*, London, 1859, Reprints of Economic Classics, New York, 1966, pp. 508–13.

Introduction

operation of the preventive check alone.¹ While the mechanisms through which industrial development affected population growth-rates may have changed, throughout his work, Malthus continued to believe that in the long-run industrialization could retard the rate of demographic expansion.²

A similar conclusion, albeit through a slightly different line of argument, was reached by Archibald Alison (Extract XXXVI). Initially, factory industry encouraged earlier marriage and higher marital fertility. Ultimately, however, the emergence of large urban populations and the substitution of manual labour by power-driven machinery would act as a brake on the fertility of the manufacturing population, and presumably on the rate of population growth. In the meantime, the level of effective fertility would be greatly restrained by the very high death-rates of urban-industrial regions. Few contemporaries were able to share Alison's opinion regarding the effects of machinery on fertility rates since most political economists believed, rightly, that the long-term result of machine and factory production would be to increase, not decrease, employment opportunities.³ However, his second contention, that urban living was somehow connected with relatively low rates of fertility, was widely accepted.⁴ Even before adequate mortality statistics became available

---

[1] For similar arguments see W. Thompson, *An inquiry into the principles of the distribution of wealth most conducive to human happiness*..., London, 1824, Reprints of Economic Classics, New York, 1963, pp. 540-1. A. H. Moreton, *Civilization, or a brief analysis of the laws that regulate the numbers and condition of mankind*, London, 1836, Chs. I, VI. N. W. Senior, *An Outline of the science of political economy*, London, 1836, pp. 30-40. W. Whewell ed., *Literary remains consisting of the lectures and tracts of the late Reverend Richard Jones*, London, 1859, pp. 245-6. Rickards, *op. cit.*, Lecture X.

[2] For an enlightening statement of the evolution of Malthus's ideas see J. J. Spengler, Malthus's total population theory: A restatement and reappraisal, *Canadian Journal of Economics and Political Science*, vol. XI, 1, 1945, pp. 83-110; and vol. XI, 2, 1945, pp. 234-64.

[3] Contrast Alison's views with those of Gaskell and Kennedy for example. (Extracts XXVII, XXIX below.)

[4] See, inter alia, J. Graunt, Natural and political observations mentioned in a following index, and made upon the Bills of Mortality, 5th ed., London, 1676, in Hull ed., *op. cit.*, pp. 372-4. D'Avenant, *op. cit.*, p. 181. D. Francklin, Observations concerning the increase of mankind..., Pennsylvania, 1751, in McCulloch ed., *op. cit.*, p. 165. J. Weyland, *Principles of population and production as they are affected by the progress of society, with a view to moral and political consequences*, London, 1816, Bk. I, Chs. 2 and 7, Bk. 3, Chs. 6 and 11. W. Bagehot, *Economic Studies*, 7th ed., London, 1908, pp. 181-93.

no one doubted his third contention, that urban-industrial populations were afflicted with relatively high death-rates.[1]

V

Where does the truth lie? What have been the consequences of industrial development for the levels of mortality and fertility, and for the growth rate of the English population since the late eighteenth century? One undeniable result has been the substantial geographic redistribution of population away from rural areas and towards large urban complexes associated with manufacturing industry (Extracts XXXI, XXXVII).[2] It is clear from later extracts that the changing pattern of residence had significant effects on the secular trends of both mortality and fertility, and hence on the overall rate of population growth. Unfortunately, largely because of the absence of reliable data on birth and death-rate fluctuations before the middle of the nineteenth century, the precise nature of the link between industrial development and the vital rates over time is partially obscured. What follows must be treated as a hypothesis.

Consider first the possible pattern of mortality since the eighteenth century. As a general rule, death-rates have been much higher in manufacturing regions than elsewhere, not as some used to believe, because of the direct effects of industrial occupations themselves (Extract XXXIX), but rather as the result of inadequate environmental standards concomitant upon the concentration of populations

---

[1] D'Avenant, *op. cit.*, pp. 178-81. R. Price, Essay containing an account of the progress from the revolution, and the present state of the population in England and Wales, in W. Morgan, *The doctrine of annuities and assurances on lives and survivorships, stated and explained*, London, 1779, pp. 303-5. Howlett, *op. cit.*, pp. 8-12. T. R. Malthus, *First essay on Population*, London, 1798, 1926 ed., pp. 125-6. P. Gaskell, *Artisans and machinery...*, London, 1836, Reprinted, 1968, pp. 196-215.

[2] On internal migration, see P. Deane and W. A. Cole, *British economic growth 1688-1959*, 2nd ed., Cambridge U. P. 1967, pp. 10-11, 106-22, 286-90. J. Saville, *Rural depopulation in England and Wales, 1851-1951*, London, 1957. M. P. Newton and J. R. Jeffrey, *Internal migration*, London, H.M.S.O., 1951. A. Redford, *Labour migration in England, 1800-1850*. 2nd ed., Manchester, 1964. A. K. Cairncross, Internal migration in Victorian England, 1841-1911, *Manchester School of Economic and Social Studies*, XVII, 1949, pp. 67-87. D. Friedlander and R. J. Roshier, A study of Internal migration in England and Wales, I, *Population Studies*, XIX, 3, 1965-1966, pp. 239-79. D. Friedlander, The spread of urbanization in England and Wales, 1851-1951, *Population Studies*, XXIV, 3, 1970; pp. 423-43.

in manufacturing towns (Extracts XXXVIII, XL, XLI, XLII).[1] This does not, however, imply that industrialization failed to contribute to the long-term decline in mortality rates over recent generations. At least from the second half of the nineteenth century it must have done so. Many of the factors to which falling death-rates were directly attributable were themselves intimately dependent on the maintenance of high rates of economic growth—rising real wages, growing outlays on public and private health facilities, expanding agricultural output, a widening range of goods and services for low income consumers, rising standards of educational attainment, and so on. Much of this would have been impossible without the rapid expansion of national income made possible by industrial development. The critical question is whether or not industrialization made a similar positive contribution to falling mortality rates during the eighteenth and first half of the nineteenth centuries. Were the advantages which ultimately accrue from industrial growth sufficiently developed during the early years of the Industrial Revolution to precipitate a decline in mortality-rates? Or were they, as yet, outweighed by the undoubted evils of life in the emerging manufacturing towns—crowded living space, bad housing, poor sanitary and public health provision, a lack of social amenities, etc.?

In the absence of reliable mortality data before the 1840's, our conclusions can only be tentative. Much depends on a personal interpretation of the mass of detailed, sometimes conflicting evidence on real wages, nutritional standards, health and environmental conditions. It does not, however, seem likely that early industrialization was conducive to falling death-rates. On the contrary, if future research shows mortality to have increased during the early nineteenth century, albeit temporarily, at least part of the explanation could be the very pace of urban-industrial development.[2] Even if death-rates did fall consistently during the years of the early

---

[1] Some writers were even more definite in their beliefs that factories did not create poor conditions for employees, see A. Ure, *The Philosophy of Manufactures...*, London, 1835, Reprinted, London, 1967.

[2] B. L. Hammond, Urban death-rates in the early nineteenth century, *Economic History*, I, 1926–9, pp. 419–28. T. H. Marshall, The population problem during the Industrial Revolution: A note on the present state of the controversy, *Economic History*, I, 1926–9, Reprinted in Glass and Eversley, eds., *op. cit.*, pp. 247–68. W. A. Armstrong, La population de l'Angleterre et du Pays de Galles (1789–1815), *Annales de demographie historique*, 1965, pp. 135–89.

Industrial Revolution, the explanation will stem not from the direct effects of industrial growth but from other factors—the introduction of new food crops like the potato; the spread of improved methods of agricultural production in response to a rapidly growing population; medical innovations such as inoculation and vaccination against smallpox; or, less tangibly, mysterious and inexplicable alterations in the virulence of epidemic diseases or in the resistance of the human host. Only from the middle of the nineteenth century, when industrialization at last began to contribute to undisputed improvements in the standards of life and when society began to take effective action to counter the insalubrity of conditions in manufacturing towns, did industrial development play a positive role in the secular decline of mortality rates.

Did industrial growth have a similar effect on the evolution of fertility rates? Did industrialization first raise, then lower the level of fertility? Once again we must work without the benefit of adequate demographic data for the period before the mid nineteenth century.

Some recent scholars have argued that English fertility rates did rise during the late eighteenth and early nineteenth centuries, and that one cause of this was industrial development.[1] Without reliable demographic data we cannot test the validity of the first part of this claim. But no one has ever seriously challenged the view that fertility rates were higher in manufacturing areas than elsewhere during the early Industrial Revolution. Indeed, according to evidence from census and registrar-generals' returns, the fertility of manufacturing populations was still relatively high in the late nineteenth and early twentieth centuries (Extracts XLIII, XLIV, XLV, XLVI). Birthrates rose with industrial expansion and fell with industrial retardation. Ages at marriage were lower amongst the industrial working classes than amongst other groups of the population.[2] The fertility-rates of unskilled industrial workers (with the notable exception of

---

[1] H. J. Habakkuk, English population in the eighteenth century, *Ec. H.R.* 2nd ser., VI, 1953-4, pp. 117-33. J. T. Krause, Changes in English fertility and mortality, 1781-1850, *Ec. H. R.* 2nd ser., XI, 1958-9, pp. 52-70. Deane and Cole. *op. cit.*, Ch. III. Chambers, Vale of Trent, *op. cit.*, pp. 50-6.

[2] Compare with similar evidence derived from an analysis of seventeenth- and eighteenth-century marriage licences in Chambers, Vale of Trent, *op. cit.*, pp. 51-2. See also, T. A. Welton, *England's recent progress* ..., London, 1911, pp. 59-83, and Cairncross, *op. cit.*, pp. 79-81, 87.

Introduction

textile workers) and miners were relatively high.[1] Considering that the estimated proportion of the total occupied labour-force involved in manufacturing, mining and other industrial occupations rose from 23·6% in 1789, to 38·4% in 1821, and to 42·9% in 1851,[2] it is at least conceivable that national average birth-rates rose during the early nineteenth century. The reality of this hypothesis becomes all the more convincing if due allowance is made for certain special features of early English industrialization.

Firstly, early industrial 'take-off' was heavily dependent on child-labour. Never before had the earning power of children been so high. Even though their earnings may have remained insufficient to cover, completely, the cost of their upbringing, the decreasing margin between the two may have been enough to encourage a temporary increase in birth-rates. After all, the decision to have children is dictated by much more than economic considerations alone. Nowadays, the majority of adults who bear children know full well the financial, social and cultural sacrifices involved. Few parents rear children for the material advantages these bring. Certainly, the economic motives underlying procreation were more significant in the past. Children could provide an important addition to family income and, in the days before effective state-controlled social welfare schemes, may have been a necessary support to parental old-age. But even so, then as now, the desire for offspring largely reflects the intangible psychological comforts which parenthood brings. Clearly, if the financial burdens imposed by children on their

---

[1] For a further discussion of socio-occupational variations in fertility during the nineteenth and twentieth centuries see J. W. Innes, *Class fertility trends in England and Wales, 1826–1934*, Princeton, U.P. 1938. T. H. C. Stevenson, The fertility of various social classes in England and Wales from the middle of the nineteenth century, *Journal of the Royal Statistical Society*, LXXXIII, 1920, pp. 401–44. A. B· Hopkin and J. Hajnal, Analysis of births in England and Wales by fathers' occupation, Part I., *Population Studies*, I, 2, 1947, pp. 187–203. N. H. Carrier, An examination of generation fertility in England and Wales, *Population Studies*, IX, 1, 1955–6, pp. 3–23. G. Rowntree and R. M. Pierce, Birth Control in Britain, Part I. Attitudes and practices among persons married since WWI, *Population Studies*, XV, 1, 1961–2, pp. 3–31. J. Matras, Social strategies of family formation. Data for British female cohorts born 1831–1906, *Population Studies*, XIX, 2, 1965–6, pp. 167–81. Compare the above with D. J. Loschky and D. F. Krier, Income and family size in three eighteenth-century Lancashire parishes: A reconstitution study, *Journal of Economic History*, XXIX, 3, 1969, pp. 429–48.

[2] The figures for 1789 and 1821 are from Armstrong, *op. cit.*, p. 150, and that for 1851 from Deane and Cole, *op. cit.*, p. 142.

parents are reduced, as they may have been during the late eighteenth and early nineteenth centuries, birth-rates may be stimulated.

Secondly, the level of technical and educational expertise required of the early factor labour-force was relatively low. Long periods of poorly paid apprenticeships were not necessary to train the growing industrial proletariat in the methods of factory production. It mattered little that this labour-force received hardly any general or technical education. As a result, young adults could earn high wages at a relatively early age, and thus achieve the financial independence which facilitated earlier marriage. Moreover, the tendency towards early marriage in manufacturing populations was reinforced by their youthful age-structures, a natural corollary of the large influx of young, able-bodied adults in search of work. Finally, we should remember that in the days before the widespread availability of reliable mechanical and chemical contraceptives, low or falling average ages at marriage were more likely to result in higher levels of fertility.

From the second half of the nineteenth century, however, the stimulus given to fertility by high industrial wages was gradually nullified by the emergence of other circumstances intimately connected with the later stages of industrialization (Extract XLVI).[1] In the first place, children became more expensive. The increasing complexity and sophistication of industrial technology necessitated higher standards of vocational and general educational attainment, and thus pressurized parents to prepare their children more thoroughly. As the quality of the work-force became more important than its quantity, society increasingly insisted on higher levels of material investment to ensure human well-being. The spread of more civilized humanitarian attitudes to life, which seem to be a feature of highly complex industrial societies, engendered increasing concern with individual welfare, particularly of children. One result of this was the gradual abolition of child-labour in manufacturing industry. At the same time, growing problems of child-cost were compounded by falling death-rates and greater possibilities of survival through the perilous years of infancy and early childhood. In

---

[1] See D. M. Heer, Economic development and fertility, *Demography*, 3, 2, 1966, pp. 423–44. D. M. Heer, Economic development and the fertility transition, *Daedalus*, 97, 1968, pp. 447–62.

part this too, as we have seen, stemmed from the beneficial effects of industrial growth on real wages and general living conditions.

Secondly, the consequences of industrialization for the structure and 'psychology' of English society had important repercussions on attitudes to fertility norms. One of the most striking characteristics of advanced, industrial populations is the relatively high degree of social mobility to which they are subject. The continuous demand for new skills and new talents, which is a natural corollary of rapid economic and technological progress, ensures the continuous emergence of new elites to challenge the dominance of the established social hierarchy. Society becomes more flexible as individual success comes to depend less on the accident of birth and rather more on one's suitability to meet the requirements of the changing economic order. Moreover, the constantly shifting needs of advancing economies make it more difficult for one social group to retain for long its pre-eminence over others, since the relative values attached to various roles alter so quickly. In rapidly advancing societies, today's skills are often soon outdated. Consequently, the effort (and expense) of maintaining one's economic and social status by acquiring the necessary physical and mental adaptability is so much greater. Inevitably, one of the results of the growing possibility of social promotion or demotion was a more intensive interest in social status, and an enhanced desire to attain higher standards for one's self or one's children. However, the difficulties of translating personal ambition into achievement remained substantial. Adequate preparation for the task was costly. Increasingly therefore, for a growing proportion of the population in the late nineteenth and early twentieth century, a choice had to be made between economic and social advancement on the one hand, and large families on the other. The acquisitive, individualistic, and more 'status-conscious' society which industrial and economic development had helped to create guaranteed that the search for material and social betterment triumphed over the natural desire for children. Simultaneously, the realization of lower fertility goals became more practicable with the greater availability of efficient and aesthetically acceptable means of contraception, themselves the results of progress in industrial science and technology.[1] By the later part of the nineteenth century,

---

[1] J. Peel, The manufacture and retailing of contraceptives in England, *Population Studies*, 1963–4, pp. 113–25

industrialization had fashioned a society committed, temporarily at least, to low birth-rate norms; and consequently, by the inter-war years, to low rates of population growth.

VI

Among the most interesting features of the debate on the relationship between population and industrialization is the marked improvement in its quality during the nineteenth century. The nature of the contributions included in this volume bear ample testimony to this. To a considerable extent, it was a reflection of the more detailed and sophisticated demographic data which became available with the inauguration of the civil registration of births, marriages and deaths in 1837, and with refinements in the methods of census-taking after 1841 and 1851.[1] Reliable information on the size and growth rate of the population, on its age, sex, and marital structures, its composition in respect of households and families, its occupational and educational characteristics, the trends in its vital rates of births, marriages and deaths, and so on, allowed economists to test long-standing assumptions and new ideas with a thoroughness hitherto undreamt of. Consequently, the welter of demographic statistics since the mid-nineteenth century has permitted a much clearer and more precise appreciation of the way in which population and industrial growth affect each other. Of course, much still remains to be done. Not enough use has yet been made of the storehouse of demographic material contained in census and registrar-general's returns. Long ago, Welton remarked that 'the figures which their publications supply are like stones in the quarry, of little use unless they are dug out, shaped and built in an intelligent manner. The official mind prepares itself to supply anticipated demands, but does not endeavour (save in one or two ways) to methodize its results, nor to expose the crudities of statistics in their first or undigested state.'[2] His comment still holds true today. A good deal more research is required both to evaluate the quality

---

[1] For a brief description of civil registration and census procedures and content see B. Benjamin, *Demographic analysis*, London, 1968, Chs. 3 and 4. P. R. Cox, *Demography*, 4th ed., Cambridge U.P., 1970, Chs. 4 and 5.

[2] Welton, *op. cit.*, p. 1.

of the available data and to prepare it for use. But the main problem confronting demographers of the nineteenth and twentieth centuries is clearly not so much the absence of reliable population data as the difficulty of quantifying the precise contribution of the demographic and industrial variable to the population-industrialization relationship.

Contrast this with the additional problem faced by seventeenth-, eighteenth- and early nineteenth-century writers, and shared by modern scholars interested in this early period. Before 1801 even crude estimates of population size and growth rates are infrequent.[1] Resort must be made to source-materials which were not originally intended for demographic purposes or which are so obviously incomplete in their coverage—taxation returns, ecclesiastical records like visitations or parish registers, bills of mortality, etc (Extracts III, XVIII, XXXI). Trends in the vital rates before 1837 depend largely on Anglican parish register returns of baptisms, marriages, and burials, notoriously deficient guides to the total number of births, marriages and deaths, particularly in the late eighteenth and early nineteenth centuries, and in the rapidly growing manufacturing towns.[2] Inadequate though early civil registration was, it was incomparably more accurate than parish registration.[3] Although data on age, sex and marital structures, on household and family size and composition are occasionally available, (Extract III) they are not sufficiently abundant to support the detailed analysis necessary for an adequate appreciation of the role of the demographic variable in industrial growth.[4] In the absence of such material, it is little

---

[1] See G. S. L. Tucker, English pre-industrial population trends, *Ec. H.R.*, 2nd ser., XVI, 2, 1963–4, pp. 205–8.

[2] On parish registers as sources of demographic data see J. T. Krause, The changing adequacy of English registration 1690–1837, in Glass and Eversley, eds., *op. cit.*, pp. 379–93. D. E. C. Eversley, Exploitation of Anglican parish registers by aggregative analysis, in E. A. Wrigley ed., *Introduction to English historical demography*, London, 1966, pp. 44–95. T. H. Hollingsworth, *Historical demography*, London, 1969, pp. 139–96.

[3] D. V. Glass, A note on the under-registration of births in Britain in the nineteenth century. *Population Studies*, V, 1, 1951–2, pp. 70–88.

[4] With the growing interest in 'listings of inhabitants', more data on the age, sex, marital structures, and on the family and household size and composition of local populations is becoming available. Ultimately this may permit a closer analysis of the relationship between population and industrialization. See P. Laslett, The study of social structure from listings of inhabitants, in Wrigley ed.,

wonder that contemporary writers failed to develop sophisticated analyses of the complex relationship between population and industrialization. Nor is it surprising that modern scholars have made only slow progress towards a more accurate understanding of the nature of the interaction between demographic and industrial change during the early stages of the Industrial Revolution.

---

op. cit., pp. 160–208. P. Laslett, Size and structure of the household in England over three centuries, *Population Studies*, XXIII, 1, 1969, pp. 87–100. Compare with W. A. Armstrong, Social structure from the early census returns. An analysis of enumerators' books for censuses after 1841, in Wrigley ed., *op. cit.*, pp. 209–37.

I

Anon, Britannia Languens, or a Discourse of Trade, London, 1680, in J. R. McCulloch ed., *Early English Tracts on Commerce*, Cambridge Economic History Society, 1952. pp. 299–302, 349–50.

The sorts of Manufacture are so various, and almost infinite, that there is no People so great or numerous but may be universally imployed by it; There are many which relate to Eating and Drinking, many more to Apparel of all sorts, Furniture of Houses, Equipage, Navigation, War, Literature and Science, unnecessary, but acceptable Toyes, to gratifie the humors and follies of Men, Women, and Children, under all which generals, there are so many species of Manufactures, that the very naming of them would make a Volume; some are of simple Materials, some of mixt.

The Labours of the People bestowed this way, must necessarily glomerate the Riches of the World, and must render any Nation a prodigy of Wealth; for whilst vast numbers of Manufacturers are thus continually improving the value of some Commodity or other, they work for the Nation where they live as well as for themselves; If 100000 Manufacturers get 6 l. per annum a piece, the Nation must gain or save 600000 l. per annum by their Labours, (supposing the Materials to be meliorated only to the value of their Wages;) If the number of the Manufacturers be greater, or if the same number gain more a piece, then is the National gain still greater and greater in proportion: All which is too evident in the present instance of France, and the contrary of that of Spain, which although supplied with the Wealth of the Indies, is, for want of home Manufactures, the poorest and weakest of all Nations, and the most dispeopled.

For by Manufactures, a Nation may support many hundred thousands of Families, besides the meer Tillers of Lands and Keepers of Cattel, which increase of people shall live well, without being a clog and vexation to the Landholders, and shall be highly beneficial to the rest of the Natives in times of Peace, as otherwise they will not be; and as the People increase, so may the kinds and quantities of Manufacture; the very Women and Children may ordinarily get good Livelihoods in Manufacture.

Hence must follow a sweet Harmony in a Nation which hath property, when every one's Hand and Head is employed, and when there comes a reciprocation of advantage to the Landholders, and all others, as necessarily there must; And as Manufacture seems a kind of debt to the laborious part of the people, who by nature are intitled to live; so it is the highest of all Charities; as it is most substantial and universal; What signifies the distribution of a little broken meat amongst a few Wretches, in Comparison of the support of hundreds of thousands of Families? And lastly, it is attended with the promised Rewards of Charity, viz. Plenty, Glory, and Prosperity to a whole Nation.

This, and what hath been said in the last Section, may administer occasion to consider what sorts of Trades, Imployments, and Professions do add to the Riches of a Nation, and what not.

It is evident that all sorts of home Manufactures must advance or save the National Wealth, the like may be said of those who are imployed in the Fishing-Trade, so may the Trade and Profession of a Merchant add to the National Riches.

There are another sort of home-Traders, who live meerly by buying cheaper and selling dearer at home, such are Retailers of all sorts in the City and Country, whom we call Shopkeepers; of which a convenient number are necessary in every Nation to keep open Marts and Markets for the vending of Commodities; These may advance their private Stocks and Estates by buying cheaper and selling dearer, but cannot (meerly by this way of Trade) add a peny to the National Riches, so that it may truly be said of one poor Manufacturer, that he adds more in a year to the Wealth of the Nation than all such Retailers and Shop-keepers in England.

And if these Shop-keepers deal over-much in Consumptive Forreign Wares, they may assist in the beggary of the Nation; so may the Trade of a Merchant export and exhaust the National Riches, if he trade over-much in meer Consumptive Importations.

And therefore though the gain of the persons imployed be one main end and design of all Trades and Imployments, and in that respect they are all alike; Yet they differ in this; That in some of them the persons imployed do immediately or ultimately gain money from Forreigners; But in the other, they gain from the people, and from one another.

Of the last sort, are all Imployments relating to the Law and Physick, so are Offices of all kinds (which I do not say to insinuate any of these Imployments to be useless in a Nation, or to diminish from that due respect which ought to be given to Men of Place). There is no question but they are highly necessary for the Regulation of the Body-Politick, and the Body-Natural; so are the Clergy for the Information of Mens Consciences; and therefore in every Nation convenient numbers of the people ought to be set apart for these purposes; But as far as they are Imployments, and intended for private gain, 'tis plain they add no Treasure to the Nation, but only enable the persons so imployed to share and heap up the Treasures already Imported; The like may be said of all other ways of living by meer Literature and the Pen, and some inferior In-land Imployments mentioned before; It must therefore be of dangerous Consequence if the Trade of a Nation run into over-much Shop-keeping, or if too many of the people withdrawing themselves from Manufactures, and the beneficial parts of Trade, should throng themselves into the Clergy, Law, Physick, Literature, and such other Professions as bring no increase of National Riches; And the rather, because these Imployments and Professions are narrow, and can support but a few Families in a Nation with convenience; so that it may endanger Depopulation, and by their numbers will prejudice one another; Whereas Manufacture and a great Forreign Trade, will admit of and oblige an increase of people even to infinity: And the more the Manufacturers increase, they will the more enrich one another, and the rest of the people....

The odds in Populacy must also produce the like odds in Manufacture; plenty of people must also cause cheapnesse of wages: which will cause the cheapnesse of the Manufacture; in a scarcity of people wages must be dearer, which must cause the dearnesse of the Manufacture; But this populacy I speak of, must not be understood of those people which the Extent of Territory makes necessary for the meer tilling of the ground, keeping of Cattle, &c. for in this sense there is no doubt but the grand Seigniors or Spanish Dominions are more populous than Holland; The populacy I intend and which only can be serviceable to Manufacture, are those exuberant numbers which cannot find Imployment in husbandry, nor otherwise but in Trade; in which sense France and the United Provinces are most populous; their

Trade and people have grown up together, having nourished one another; the like may be said of some parts of Germany and Italy.

But on the other side England never was so populous as it might have been, and undenyably must now be far lesse populous than ever, having so lately peopled our vast American Plantations and Ireland; the decay of our Manufactures hath much depopulated our Inland Corporations of the Villages Adjacent; the decay of our Fishing Trade our Sea-Towns; I know this want of people is hardly credible with so many who see no farther than their own ease and gain; they will tell us, we have so many people already that we know not what to do with them; which is true, and so they have in Spain, where their Villages are in a manner foresaken, and many of their great Cities and Towns lie half empty; most of their ordinary people having no employment at home, are gone to America, those that remain chiefly consisting in Gentlemen, Lawyers, Officers and Shopkeepers, with their necessary men of husbandry and servants: I must not omit Priests and beggars, since to the honour and comfort of Spain they make about a fourth or fifth part of the whole; there little or no support for other ranks of men: how near this we are in England let any man judge, or how soon we shall come to it through the decay of our Manufactures;

II

Josiah Tucker, The elements of commerce and the theory of taxes, 1755, in R. L. Schuyler, *Josiah Tucker, A selection from his economic and political writings*, New York, 1931, pp. 63–7, 89.

I. Where a Country is thinly peopled, it is impossible to promote a brisk and general Circulation of Industry and Labour, by reason of the Distance and Dispersion of the People from each other, and the Consequence of that, their Want of Rivalship and Emulation:— So that the greater Part of those few Inhabitants must lead a sauntering, lazy, and savage life, thereby making near Approaches to the State of mere Animals, the most wretched of all others for an human Creature to be in. This Observation is confirmed by Experience; For in every Country, extremely thin of Inhabitants, the People are proportionably poor and miserable, and lead such Lives as are but a few Removes from the brute Savages of the Woods and Mountains. Suppose only Ten Thousand Inhabitants left in Great Britain, and what would be the Consequence? —These few Inhabitants would soon degenerate into British Savages, correspondent to the Clans of the Highlands of Scotland, or the Indians of America. Suppose the Country better peopled, and then the Evil would lessen in Proportion. It is moreover observable, That in Country Places, where there is a scarcity of Inhabitants, one Trade will not be sufficient for a Man's Subsistence, but several distinct Occupations must be joined together in order to obtain a bare and wretched Support:—By which means it comes to pass, that there cannot be that Quantity of Work performed, as where every one exercises and improves himself in one particular Calling: And as to the Quality, or Workmanship itself, that must necessarily be clumsy, rude and imperfect.

II. Where a Country is thinly peopled, the very Activity, or in other Words, the exciting Cause of that Activity, viz. the Self-Love of the Inhabitants, will take a wrong Turn. For in such a Situation, the Figure that Commerce can make, must be very mean and contemptible: So that Country Gentlemen, who at the best do not entertain a very kind Opinion of the Advantages of Commerce, are confirmed in their Prejudices against it, and choose rather to vie with each other in the Dangers of the Chace, or the Pretensions of Birth and Family, and the Length of their Pedigrees, than in giving Incouragement to the Increase of low-born Tradesmen and Mechanics.

III. Where a Country is thinly peopled, the Property of Lands will be the more easily ingrossed, and intailed in a few Families; by which means the Land-holders become more absolute and despotic over their Vassals. In this Case, Numbers are kept in Poverty and Wretchedness to raise the comparative Grandeur of one Family, and flatter the Pride of their petty Tyrant:—I say, the Pride only; for as to the Comforts of Life, he will not be on a Level with a common Tradesman in a populous and industrious Country; because he cannot have the Convenience of Markets, the Supplies of Foreign Trade, the Variety of useful Manufactures, or even the Pleasures of Society: And all that he has to put in the Scale against these real Disadvantages, is the imaginary and ungenerous Satisfaction derived from the greater Misery of his wretched Dependents. Whereas Commerce, as it is calculated to extend Industry, Happiness, and Plenty, equalizes Mankind more than any other Way of Life; and at the same time that it connects them together in Bonds of mutual Interest, it renders them FREE. Trade and Vassalage, Commerce and Slavery are, in their Natures, repugnant to each other.

IV. A Country thinly peopled, has neither the Strength, nor Riches it would have, were it better inhabited; so that it cannot make that Figure in Peace, or War, it ought to do. For Numbers of People are the Strength, as Industry is the Riches of a Country. Nay, this very Depopulation, unless preventive Remedies are used, and a proper Polity introduced, must occasion a farther Diminution of Inhabitants; because several Persons will be obliged to seek for Work in other Countries, as not having sufficient Imployment, or a proper Consumption of the Produce of the Lands, or the Labour of the Manufacturer among themselves. The Lands must lie waste, where there are no Markets: and the Artificers cannot be employed without Customers.

Now when a Country, blessed with the Advantages of Liberty and Peace, commodiously situated, and happy likewise in a mild and healthy Climate, with a Soil productive of great Quantities of good

Materials both for foreign and domestic Commerce;—When such a Country increases very slowly in the Number of its Inhabitants, which might have increased very fast, we must conclude, that some Canker in Polity, or lurking Disorder, is preying upon the Vitals of that Commonwealth; which, if not timely prevented, may bring on the most fatal Consequences.

Now though Great Britain enjoys many signal Advantages, yet she will be found to labour under sore Difficulties at present, through a bad System of Polity, and the mistaken Notions of public Welfare, and National Commerce, in the following Respects;

I. Because the Marriage State is loaded with many Taxes and Expences, from which a Single Life is free. For this Burden has the same effect in its Operations, as if the Legislature had actually passed a Law to discourage Marriage, and incourage Celibacy. For the Father of a numerous Family, in paying the several Duties and Excises laid on those Commodities which his Family consumes, is fined as it were in those respective Sums, from which a Batchelor is exempt: And yet the Batchelor is not put under any Discouragements of another Nature, whereby the Scale might be brought even, or rather inclined to favour the Matrimonial Side. Nay, as Places of Diversion are continually multiplying, a Single Person with 200 l. a Year, can make a more modish Appearance, and partake of a greater Variety of Pleasures, and consequently appear in a Condition more desirable to the Generality of Mankind, than a Married Man with twice that Sum.

II. Such an Inducement to Celibacy must be greatly prejudicial to good Morals; because an Increase of Temptation will always cause an Increase of Vice. And again, a general Corruption of Morals is fatal to the Populousness of a Country in various Ways. Thus the Evil operates back upon itself, spreading and increasing as it goes on. Nay, as the Sexes will naturally associate together in the single State, and form Parties of Pleasure, the very least bad Consequence that can happen, is a giddy, thoughtless Turn of Mind, and an utter Indisposition for the Discharge of those domestic Duties, on which the Good and Happiness of Society greatly depend.

III. The Country grows thinner of Inhabitants in those Parts of the Kingdom where the Practice of destroying Cottages prevails, and joining several small Farms together to make one great Farm: For every Cottage or Farm-House thus destroyed, occasions the Loss of so many laborious, working Families to the Country. The same bad Effects are also produced by the unlimited Power of ingrossing Landed Estates; by the Power of intailing them upon the Male Heir; the Power of settling them all upon the Eldest Son at the Marriage-Contract; and lastly, by the Common Law of the Land, which gives all the Landed Estates of intestate Persons to the First-born Son, without shewing the least Regard to the rest of the Children. These Monopolies of Land must occasion, according as they prevail, a great Diminution of People.—Besides, it is always observable, that in Proportion the Ground is better manured, cultivated and improved: And a great number of Farms, and middling Landed Estates, thick set together, not only occasion a very great Number of Inhabitants, but also render it necessary that many of the Children of such Inhabitants should be brought up to Trades and Manufactures. And I will venture to add, that Manufacturers of this Class are the most useful, and the least subject to Corruption of Morals.—But more of this hereafter.

IV. The Nobility and Gentry of England are deterred from entering into the married State during the Prime of Life, because they can have little or no Command over their Children, when they advance towards Years of Maturity. And a Father is by no Means desirous of being treated disrespectfully by his Son, merely because he is not likely to make a Vacancy as soon as the young Heir could wish him. Yet this Consequence, bad as it is, too frequently happens to a middle-aged Man, as his Son draws towards the Years of twenty one. For at that Period of Life (such is our wrong Polity) the Parental Authority is almost at an End, and the Son can shew an undutiful Behaviour with Impunity.

Therefore to avoid this disagreeable Circumstance, the Father sends his hopeful Heir to travel into Foreign Parts, at the Age of Sixteen or Eighteen, a Season of all others, in which it is most improbable he should make any real Improvement; an Age in which he is too old for a School-boy, and too young to be able to make any useful Observations on Men or Things, being destitute of a proper Stock of Knowledge to form Comparisons between his own and foreign Countries, and without knowing the Difference between his own and foreign Countries, and without knowing the Difference between the Religion or Laws, the Polity or Government, the Commerce or Taxes of one Country from another. In short, he is strictly and literally a Traveller, that is, a Passenger through various Countries, and the greatest Stranger to his own. However, as he stays Abroad for several Years, this is some Comfort and Relief to his Father.

But in general, as I said before, Men of Fashion do not marry in the Prime of Life. And it is observable, that they stay later in England, than in any other Country in Europe,—as if it were on purpose to be ready to move off the Stage, when their Successors come on. But alas! if they continue single during the Prime of their Years, in what manner do they spend their Time?—Generally in all the Excesses of Riot and Debauchery: so that those of higher Rank, who ought to set the Example, seldom think of raising a Family, till they are fitter for an Hospital than the Bridal Bed. What an Offspring! what Members of Society, or Defenders of their Country, are we to expect from such Parents!

V. The very Liberty which the English enjoy above other Nations, becomes in the Event, as Matters are now circumstanced, a means of dispeopling the Country. For it corrupts their Morals, hurries them into Vice and evil Courses, shortens their Days, and destroys the natural Fertility of the Sexes. In one Word, If the regular Course of Providence hath taken off its Thousands by natural Death, the Gallows and Electioneering, Spirituous Liquors and Debauchery have destroyed their Millions.

VI. Our numerous Colonies, extensive and distant Navigation, perilous and unwholesome Trades, are great and continual Drains upon us.—Add to all this, That Holland, France, and Spain keep great Numbers of British Troops in their Pay. Moreover, almost all the States of Europe draw off as many as they can of the Artificers, Sailors and Manufacturers of these Kingdoms, into their own; whilst we are so far from retaliating the like upon them, that we are for discouraging those few Foreigners who would voluntarily come over.

The way to supply these Losses, and to put a Stop to many of the Evils here complained of, is to establish such a Polity as shall give Incouragement for increasing the Numbers of People both by Matrimony, and by the Introduction of industrious Foreigners. . . .

Though the Polities for promoting Marriage, and inviting Foreigners are the more immediate Ways of increasing the Number of People, yet all other Polities which tend to imploy Mankind in useful Labour, and to preserve and improve their Morals, are greatly subservient to the same good End.

A Set of Polities, for Example, which promote Industry and discourage Vice, hath the same (nay indeed a much better) Effect in its Operations, as a Sum of Money given by way of Portion to incourage Marriage. For it puts Mankind into a Capacity of increasing their Species, without bringing Misery on themselves, or intailing it on their Posterity; and by opening new Sources of Wealth and Prosperity, it incourages them to ingage in the Marriage State with a good Prospect of supporting their Families with Credit and Comfort.

When Idleness is removed, Poverty is removed likewise; and when Industry is properly and generally excited, Numbers of Hands will of Course be wanted; so that a Stock of Children may be so far from being a Burden in certain Circumstances, that they may very literally and truly become the Wealth and Riches of the Parents.

III

C. D'Avenant, Discourses on the Public Revenues and on the Trade of England, 2 vols, 1698, in Sir Charles Whitworth, *The Political and Commercial Works of that celebrated writer Charles D'Avenant*..., London, 5 vols., 1771, reprinted, Farnborough, 1967, vol. II. pp. 175, 179–82, 183, 184–5, 191–2, 192–3, 202–5.

The writer of these papers has seen the before-mentioned Mr. King's natural and political observations and conclusions upon the state and condition of England in manuscript.[1] The calculations therein contained are very accurate, and more perhaps to be relied upon than any thing that has been ever done of the like kind. This skilful and laborious gentleman has taken the right course to form his several schemes about the numbers of the people; for besides many different ways of working, he has very carefully inspected the poll books,[2] and the distinctions made by those acts, and the produce in money of the respective polls going every where by reasonable and discreet mediums; besides which pains, he has made observations of the very facts in particular towns and places, from which he has been able to judge and conclude more safely of others; so that he seems to have looked further into this mystery than any other person. . . .

Mr. King further observes, that by the assessments on marriages, births and burials, and the collector's returns thereupon,[3] and by the parish registers, it appears, that the proportions of marriages, births and burials, are according to the following scheme: . . .

Whence it may be observed, that in 10,000 co-existing persons,

There are 71 or 72 marriages in the country, producing 343 children.

---

[1] G. King, *Natural and political observations and conclusions upon the state and condition of England*, 1696.—Ed.

[2] 1692 Poll Tax Returns.—Ed.

[3] 1694 Act, imposing taxes to help the war effort against France. For discussion of King's analyses see D. V. Glass, Two Papers on Gregory King, in D. V. Glass and D. E. C. Eversley eds., *Population in History*, London 1965.—Ed.

People		Annual Marriages		
530,000	London and bills or mortality—	1 in 106	In all, 5,000.	Producing 4 Children each
870,000	The cities and market towns—	1 in 128	In all, 6,800.	Producing 4·5 Children each
4,100,000	The villages and hamlets—	1 in 141	In all, 29,200.	Producing 4·8 Children each
5,500,000		1 in 134	41,000	4·64

		Annual Births		Annual Burials	
	London and bills of mortality—	1 in 26½	In all, 20,000.	1 in 24·1	In all, 22,000
	The cities and market towns—	1 in 28½	In all, 30,600.	1 in 30·4	In all, 28,600
	The villages and hamlets—	1 in 29·4	In all, 139,400.	1 in 34·4	In all, 119,400
		1 in 28·95	190,000	1 in 32·35	170,000

Discourses on the Public Revenues

94 Marriages in London, producing 376 children.

Whereby it follows,

1st, That though each marriage in London produces fewer people than in the country, yet London in general having a greater proportion of breeders, is more prolific than the other great towns, and the great towns are more prolific than the country.

2dly, That if the people of London of all ages were as long lived as those in the country, London would encrease in people much faster pro rata than the country.

3dly, That the reasons why each marriage in London produces fewer children than the country marriages, seem to be,

1st, From the more frequent fornications and adulteries.

2dly, From a greater luxury and intemperance.

3dly, From a greater intenseness on business.

4thly, From the unhealthfulness of the coal smoke.

5thly, From a greater inequality of age between the husbands and wives.

6thly, From the husbands and wives not living so long as in the country.

He farther observes, accounting the people to be 5,500,000, that the said five millions and a half (including the transitory people and vagrants) appear by the assessments on marriages, births and burials, to bear the following proportion in relation to males and females, and other distinctions of the people, viz. . . .

	Males	Females	Males	Females	Both
In London and bills of mortality,	10 to 13		230,000	300,000	530,000
In the other cities and market towns,	8 to 9		410,000	460,000	870,000
In the villages and hamlets,	100 to 99		2,060,000	2,040,000	4,100,000
	27 to 28		2,700,000	2,800,000	5,500,000

Upon these schemes of Mr. King, we shall make several remarks, though the text deserves much a better comment.

The people being the first matter of power and wealth, by whose labour and industry a nation must be gainers in the Balance, their encrease or decrease must be carefully observed by any government

	London and bills of mortality	Souls	The other cities and great towns	Souls	The villages and hamlets	Souls
Husbands and wives,	37 per cent	196,100	36 per cent	313,200	34 per cent	1,394,000
Widowers,	2 per cent	10,600	2 per cent	17,400	1½ per cent	61,500
Widows,	7 per cent	37,100	6 per cent	52,200	4½ per cent	184,500
Children,	33 per cent	174,900	40 per cent	348,000	47 per cent	1,927,000
Servants,	13 per cent	68,900	11 per cent	95,700	10 per cent	410,000
Sojourners,	8 per cent	42,400	5 per cent	43,500	3 per cent	123,000
	100	530,000	100	870,000	100	4,100,000

that designs to thrive; that is, their encrease must be promoted by good conduct and wholesome laws, and if they have been decreased by war, or any other accident, the breach is to be made up as soon as possible, for it is a maim in the body politic affecting all its parts. . . .

In order to have hands to carry on labour and manufactures, which must make us gainers in the Balance of Trade, we ought not to deter, but rather invite men to marry, which is to be done by privileges and exemptions for such a number of children, and by denying certain offices of trust and dignities to all unmarried persons; and where it is once made a fashion among those of the better sort, it will quickly obtain with the lower degree.

Mr. King, in the foregoing scheme, (see p. 180) (for which he has as authentic grounds as perhaps the matter is capable of) lays down, that the annual marriages of England are about 41,000 which is one marriage out of every 134 persons: Upon which we observe, that this is not a due proportion, considering how few of our adult males (in comparison with other countries) perish by war or any other accident; from whence may be inferred, that our polity is some way or other defective, or the marriages would bear a nearer proportion with the gross number of our people; for which defect, if a remedy can be found, there will be so much more strength added to the kingdom.

From the books of assessment on births, marriages, &c. by the nearest view he can make, he divides the 5,500,000 people into 2,700,000 males, and 2,800,000 females; from whence (considering the females exceed the males in number, and considering that the men marry later than women, and that many of the males are of necessity absent in the wars, at sea, and upon other business) it follows, that a large proportion of the females remain unmarried, though at an adult age, which is a dead loss to the nation, every birth being so much certain treasure; upon which account, such laws must be for the public good, as induce all men to marry whose circumstances permit it. . . .

A country that makes provision to encrease in inhabitants, whose situation is good, and whose people have a genius adapted to Trade, will never fail to be gainers in the Balance, provided the labour and industry of their people be well managed and carefully directed.

The more any man contemplates these matters, the more he will come to be of opinion, that England is capable of being rendered one of the strongest nations, and the richest spot of ground in Europe.

It is not extent of territory that makes a country powerful, but numbers of men well employed, convenient ports, a good navy, and a soil producing all sort of commodities. The materials for all this we have, and so improveable, that if we did but second the gifts of nature with our own industry, we should soon arrive to a pitch of greatness that would put us at least upon an equal foot with any of our neighbours.

If we had the compliment of men our land can maintain and nourish; if we had as much trade as our stock and knowledge in sea-affairs is capable of embracing; if we had such a naval strength as a trade so extended would easily produce; and if we had those stores and that wealth which is the certain result of a large and well-governed traffic, what human strength could hurt or invade us? On the contrary, should we not be in a posture not only to resist, but to give the law to others?

The bodies of men are without doubt the most valuable treasure of a country; and in their sphere, the ordinary people are as serviceable to the commonwealth as the rich, if they are employed in honest labour and useful arts: And such being more in number, do more contribute to encrease the nation's wealth, than the higher rank.

But a country may be populous and yet poor, (as were the ancient Gauls and Scythians) so that numbers, unless they are well employed, make the body politic big, but unwieldy; strong but unactive; as to any uses of good government.

Theirs is a wrong opinion, who think all mouths profit a country that consume its product: And it may be more truly affirmed, that he who does not some way serve the commonwealth, either by being employed, or by employing others, is not only a useless, but hurtful member to it.

As it is charity, and what we indeed owe to human kind, to make provision for the aged, the lame, the sick, blind and impotent; so it is a justice we owe to the commonwealth, not to suffer such as have health, and who might maintain themselves, to be drones, and live upon the labour of others.

The bulk of such as are a burthen to the public, consists in the cottagers and paupers, beggars in great cities and towns, and vagrants.

Upon a survey of the hearth books, made in Michaelmas 1685, it was found, that of the 1,300,000 houses in the whole kingdom, those of one chimney amounted to 554,631; but some of these having land about them, in all our calculations, we have computed the cottagers but at 500,000 families. But of these a large number may get their own livelihood, and are no charge to the parish, for which reason Mr. King very judiciously computes his 'cottagers and paupers decreasing the wealth of the nation but at 400,000 families;' in which account he includes the poor houses in cities, towns, and villages, besides which he reckons 30,000 vagrants; and all these together, to make up 1,330,000 heads.

This is a very great proportion of the people to be a burthen upon the other part, and is a weight upon the land interest; of which the landed gentlemen must certainly be very sensible.

If this vast body of men, instead of being expensive, could be rendered beneficial to the commonwealth, it were a work no doubt highly to be promoted by all who love their country.

It seems evident to such as have considered these matters, and who have observed how they are ordered in nations under a good polity, that the number of such who, through age or impotence, stand in real need of relief, is but small, and might be maintained for very little; and that the poor rates are swelled to the extravagant degree we now see them at, by two sorts of people, one of which, by reason of our slack administration, is suffered to remain in sloth; and the other, through a defect in our constitution, continue in wretched poverty for want of employment, though willing enough to undertake it.

All this seems capable of a remedy; the laws may be armed against voluntary idleness, so as to prevent it; and a way may probably be found out to set those to work who are desirous to support themselves by their own labour: And if this could be brought about, it would not only put a stop to the course of that vice which is the consequence of an idle life, but it would greatly tend to enrich the commonwealth; for if the industry of not half the people maintains in some degree the other part; and besides, in times of peace, did add every year near 2,500,000 to the general stock of England, to what pitch of wealth and greatness might we not be brought, if one limb were not suffered to draw away the nourishment of the other; and if all the members of the body politic were rendered useful to it?

Nature in her contrivances has made every part of a living creature either for ornament or use, the same should be in a politic institution rightly governed.

It may be laid down for an undeniable truth, that where all work, nobody will want; and to promote this would be a greater charity and more meritorious, than to build hospitals, which very often are but so many monuments of ill-gotten riches attended with late repentance.

To make as many as possible of these 1,330,000 persons (whereof not above 330,000 are children too young to work) who now live chiefly upon others, get themselves a large share of their maintenance, would be the opening a new vein of treasure of some millions sterling per ann. it would be a present ease to every particular man of substance, and a lasting benefit to the whole body of the kingdom; for it would not only nourish but encrease the numbers of the people, of which many thousand perish every year, by those diseases contracted under a slothful poverty.

IV

D. Defoe, *A Plan of the English Commerce*, 1728. Reprinted. Oxford 1928. pp. 13–15, 63–9.

Trade encourages Manufacture, prompts Invention, employs People, increases Labour, and pays Wages: As the People are employ'd, they are paid, and by that Pay are fed, cloathed, kept in Heart, and kept together; that is, kept at Home, kept from wandering into Foreign Countries to seek Business, for where the Employment is, the People will be.

This keeping the People together, is indeed the Sum of the whole Matter, for as they are kept together, they multiply together; and the Numbers, which by the Way is the Wealth and Strength of the Nation, increase.

As the Numbers of People increase, the Consumption of Provisions increases; as the Consumption increases, the Rate or Value will rise at Market; and as the Rate of Provisions rises, the Rents of Land rise: So the Gentlemen are with the first to feel the Benefit of Trade, by the Addition to their Estates.

And here it would not have been improper to have made a Transition to our English History, and to have enquir'd how punctually the Course of Things have obey'd the Laws of Nature in this very particular; how as Trade has increased; so by equal Advances, Provisions have been consum'd, Lands cultivated, Rents raised, and the Estates of the Gentry and Nobility been improv'd: I mean as to Periods of Time, as well as to the Proportion of Value; which Enquiry would have been an unanswerable Proof of the Fact; but I am confin'd here to Generals, and must only lay it down as a Proposition.

As the Consumption of Provisions increase, more Lands are cultivated; waste Grounds are inclosed, Woods are grubb'd up, Forests and common Lands are till'd, and improv'd; by this more Farmers are brought together, more farm-houses and Cottages are built, and more Trades are called upon to supply the necessary Demands of Husbandry: In a Word, as Land is employ'd, the

People increase of Course, and thus Trade sets all the Wheels of Improvement in Motion;—for from the Original of Business to this Day it appears, that the Prosperity of a Nation rises and falls, just as Trade is supported or decay'd.

As trade prospers, Manufactures increase; as the Demand is greater or smaller, so also is the Quantity made; and so the Wages of the Poor, the Rate of Provisions, and the Rents and value of the Lands rise or fall, as I said before.

AND here the very Power and Strength of the Nation is concern'd also, for as the Value of the Lands rises or falls, the Taxes rise and fall in Proportion; all our Taxes upon Land are a Kind of Pound Rate; and bring in more or less, as the stated Rents of the Land are more or less in Value; and let any one calculate, by the Rate of Lands in England, as they went in the Times of Edward IV or even in King Henry VII Time, when Trade began, as it were, just to live in England; and tell us how much they think a Land Tax would then have brought in: For example,

If a Tax of Four Shillings in the Pound now brings in above Two Millions, I suppose it would have been thought very well then, if it had brought in Three hundred thousand Pound, all the rest is an Increase occasion'd by Trade, and by nothing else; Trade has increas'd the People, and People have increas'd Trade; for Multitudes of People, if they can be put in a Condition to maintain themselves, must increase Trade; they must have Food, that employs Land; they must have Clothes, that employs the manufacture; they must have Houses, that employs Handicrafts; they must have Household Stuff, that employs a long Variety of Trades; so that in a Word Trade employs People, and People employ Trade. . . .

BUT to return to the Populous Towns rais'd by these Manufactures, let the curious examine the great Towns of

Manchester,	Leeds,	Froom,
Warrington,	Wakefield,	Taunton,
Macclesfield,	Sheffield,	Tiverton,
Hallifax,	Birmingham,	

and many others.

Some of these are meer Villages; the highest Magistrate in them is a Constable, and few or no Families of Gentry among them; yet they are full of Wealth, and full of People, and daily encreasing in both; all which is occasion'd by the meer Strength of Trade, and the growing Manufactures establish'd in them; and of every one of them it may be said, they have severally more People in them, than the City of York; besides that, (as I have said above) they are all visibly and daily encreasing, which York is not.

FROM these which are all Inland Towns, let the same curious Enquirer cast his Eye upon some of our Seaport Towns, where Trade flourishes, as well foreign Trade, as home Trade, and where Navigation, Manufacturing, and Merchandize seem to assist one another, and go Hand in Hand to encrease both the Wealth and the People: Few Cities in England, London and Bristol excepted, can equal them; and in Time, some of them bid fair to be superior to even Bristol itself; such as

Yarmouth,	Hull,	Plymouth,
Liverpool,	New-castle,	Whitehaven,
Colchester,	Lyn,	Biddeford,
Deal		

and several others.

How are all these Towns raised by Trade, and the Numbers of their Inhabitants drawn to them by the Employment, and consequently the Money which Trade spreads and diffuses so liberally among the people.

BUT this is not all; let the curious Enquirer travel a little farther, and look into the Countries adjacent to these Towns, and there they will see a manifest Difference in the very Face of Things, where the Manufacturers are settled and carry'd on; they shall see the Villages stand thick, the Market Towns not only more in Number, but larger, and fuller of Inhabitants; and in short, the whole Country full of little End-ships or Hamlets, and scattered Houses, that it looks all like a planted Colony, every where full of People, the People everywhere full of Business.

LET them view the County of Devon, and for 20 Miles every Way round the City of Excester, where the Trade of Serges is carry'd on.

The county of Norfolk, and for as many Miles every Way about the City of Norwich, where the Stuff-weaving is carry'd on.

The County of Essex, for near 40 Miles every way, where the Bay-making Trade is carry'd on.

The County of Wilts, thro' that whole flourishing Vale, from Warminster South, to Malmsbury North inclusive, and all the great Towns of Bradford, Troubridge, Westbury, Tedbury, Froom, and the Devizes, &c. where the Manufacture of fine Spanish, and Medley-Clothing, and Drugget-making is carry'd on.

The Counties of Gloucester and Worcester, from Cirencester and Stroudwater, to the City of Worcester, where the White-Clothing Trade, for the Turkey Merchants is carry'd on.

The Counties of Warwick and Stafford, every Way round the Town of Birmingham, where the Hard-Ware Manufacture and Cutlery Trade is carry'd on; as also about Coventry.

The Counties of Yorkshire and Lancashire, round about, and every Way adjacent to the great Manufacturing Towns of Manchester, Sheffield, Leeds and Hallifax, where the known Manufactures of Cotton-ware, Iron-ware, Yorkshire-Cloths, Kersies, &c. are carry'd on.

In all these, and many others which might be mention'd, how infinitely populous is the Country? not to say how rich; how thick the Towns, how full the Markets, how stor'd with People are the Villages, and even the open Country! in so much, that in the Parish or Vicaridge of Hallifax alone, they reckon up sixteen Chapels of Ease, and an hundred thousand Communicants, besides fourteen or fifteen Meeting-houses, the People of all which live at large, scatter'd and spread over Hill and Dale, (for 'tis a mountainous Country) as the Convenience of Water, Coal, and other Things proper to their Manufacture obliges them; so that the whole Parish, which is a Circle of twelve Miles diameter, is, as before, like a planted Garden, or a Colony where every Family lives as it were within it self, and by it self, for the propagating their Business; and where, tho' the whole Country is infinitely populous, yet, if you pass in the middle of the Day thro' the Villages, and by the straggling Houses on the Road, you shall hardly see any Body to ask the Way of: But if you go in the Evening, after working Hours, you are surpriz'd at the Multitude of the People every where to be seen.

Having taken a View of these Countries, let the same Person take a Tour through those few Counties in England, where Trade has the least Concern, and where the Inhabitants consist chiefly of Landlord and Tenant, the Gentry and Husbandmen; and tho' there you see no want of needful People to cultivate the Ground, or to dispatch the necessary Labours of the Place; yet the Face of Things differs extremely, and the following Particulars discover it.

1. The Market Towns are few and small, compar'd with such as I

A Plan of the English Commerce

have named, and compar'd with the general Bulk of the smaller Towns, not fit to rank with those great ones nam'd; nay, the Villages in those manufacturing Countries, are equal to the Market Towns in these.

2. The Villages are distant and remote, small and thinly inhabited; and as for the open Country, you see here and there a Farm-house, and a Cottage indeed, but nothing like the numerous Dwellings which spread the enclosed Counties mention'd above, and where the Roads as you travel are like one continued Street, for sometimes twenty or thirty Miles together, and full of Inhabitants.

3. In these unemployed Counties, you see the Women and Children idle, and out of Business; these sitting at their Doors, and those playing in the Streets; even in the Market Towns, and the most populous Villages, where they might be supposed to be employ'd, the Poor by the Rich, yet there 'tis the same, much more in the single scattering Villages, where they have no Business but their own.

Whereas, in the manufacturing Counties, you see the Wheel going almost at every Door, the Wool and the Yarn hanging up at every Window; the Looms, the Winders, the Combers, the Carders, the Dyers, the Dressers, all busy; and the very Children, as well as Women, constantly employ'd.

4. As is the Labour, so is the Living; for where the Poor are full of Work, they are never empty of Wages; they eat while the others starve; and have a tolerable Plenty; while in the unemploy'd Counties it goes very hard with them: And whence is all this? Look to the Lands, and consequently to the Estates of the Gentry, the manufacturing Counties are calculated for Business, the unemploy'd Counties for Pleasure; the first are throng'd with Villages and great Towns, the last with Parks and great Forrests; the first are stored with People, the last with Game; the first are rich and fertil, the last waste and barren; the diligent Part of the People are fled to the first, the idler Part are left at the last; in a Word, the rich and thriving Tradesmen live in the first, the decaying wasting Gentry in the last.

The Product of the first, tho' improv'd by Diligence and Application, is all consumed among themselves; the Product of the last, tho' not half what it might be, is carried away for want of

Money to the Markets of the first; the first eat the Fat and the Kernel of all, and enjoy the Soft, being by their Diligence made able to buy it; and the last eat the Husk, the course, and the hard; pinch, and live miserable, being without Employment, except meer Drudging, and consequently without Money.

The Reason of the Thing answers for it self; a poor labouring Man that goes abroad to his Day Work, and Husbandry, Hedging, Ditching, Threshing, Carting, &c. and brings home his Week's Wages, suppose at eight Pence to twelve Pence a Day, or in some Counties less; if he has a Wife and three or four Children to feed, and who get little or nothing for themselves, must fare hard, and live poorly; 'tis easy to suppose it must be so.

But if this Man's Wife and Children can at the same Time get Employment, if at next Door, or at the next Village there lives a Clothier, or a Bay Maker, or a Stuff or Drugget Weaver; the Manufacturer sends the poor Woman comb'd Wool, or carded Wool every Week to spin, and she gets eight Pence or nine Pence a Day at home: the Weaver sends for her two little Children, and they by the Loom, winding, filling Quills, &c. and the two bigger Girls spin at home with their Mother, and these earn three Pence or four Pence a Day each: So that put it together, the Family at Home gets as much as the Father gets Abroad, and generally more.

This alters the Case extremely, the Family feels it, they all feed better, are cloth'd warmer, and do not so easily nor so often fall into Misery and Distress; the Father gets them Food, and the Mother gets them Clothes; and as they grow, they do not run away to be Footmen and Soldiers, Thieves and Beggars, or sell themselves to the Plantations, to avoid the Goal [sic] and the Gallows, but have a Trade at their Hands, and every one can get their Bread.

V

S. Gray, *The Happiness of States: or, an inquiry concerning population, the modes of subsisting and employing it, and the effects of all on human happiness*, London, 1815, pp. 91–8, 102–4.

There is a well-known general effect produced on the different species of labour, by an increase of population, of such importance as to require particular notice. This increase has a natural tendency to divide, or, if I may use the expression, to elementize labour, that is, to employ individuals more and more in one sort of it.

If we attend to the progress of a hamlet to a village, a town, a city, we shall easily discover how this is effected. Let us imagine the hamlet to contain ten families. These ten families, supposing them unconnected with populous districts, from the smallness of their number, and the poverty consequent on this, are individually obliged to do everything as much as they can within themselves. They are all more or less employed in cultivating the ground for subsistence; for if one family were to give up its time entirely to making shoes, for example, they could scarcely get employment for the one-fifth part of their time. If we suppose the whole to amount to 50, and to require, at an average, a pair of shoes a year; and two individuals of any of the given families to be capable of making shoes, while the rest of the family assisted in spinning the hemp, and getting victuals ready, these two persons, with all their bunglingness, could make these 50 pair of shoes in 40 days at the most: and supposing 20 days employed in mending, we have 60 days in a year employed, out of 300, excluding the odd 65 for Sundays and holidays: which is only the one-fifth. This family, therefore, could not support itself solely by shoemaking. It must consequently, like its neighbours, apply to some other branches of labour.

The same thing would be true of bakers, butchers, tailors, and others engaged in the more necessary employments. All the families are, therefore, obliged to apply themselves to various sorts of works. They usually employ the greatest part of their time in the business of agriculture, which is always the most necessary. The other parts of labour, to adopt an expression used by people in some parts of our island, in the very circumstances of this supposed hamlet, they do within themselves. They all bake, brew, make and mend clothes, and so forth, each of them for itself.

Some, however, from having a liking to one species of labour, put themselves more in the way of getting jobs of the sort from their neighbours. Thus even in this hamlet the division or elementization of labour begins to appear. One or two are bakers, shoemakers, tailors more than others, though not completely so, from their not being able to find sufficient employment in the particular line. As the hamlet grows a village, the elementizing influence of an increase of population gradually displays itself more and more. The total of the demand in most lines keeps increasing, and besides, as individual circulators, in consequence, gradually give up combining different occupations, more of the demand in each line is left for those who make choice of it. The persons disposed to follow certain particular modes of labour, therefore, find more constant employment in these. When the hamlet has grown a village, consisting, suppose, of a hundred families, not only is the demand for certain sorts of articles increased in proportion to the additional number of inhabitants, but, agreeably to the principles already explained, the average annual demand from these is more than proportionally greater than before, from the increasing ratio of consumption. The higher price of things and accumulation of capital, which necessarily arise from an increase of population, and its tendency to augment and quicken circulation, equally incite and enable the inhabitants to use a greater variety of the articles of subsistence, as well as of dress. Thus the baker, butcher, shoemaker, tailor and others, find an increased demand for their articles among a given number of customers, as well as from the greater number of these in the increased population.

The same process keeps going on, in proportion as the village becomes a little town, a large town, a city, and a great city. Not only does the town contain a greater number of persons than the village, to increase the demand in every line; but each of these persons, speaking of an average, from increasing circuland, consume more than the average quantity of each individual of the village population per annum. The demand thus keeps increasing with the population in a two-fold manner, both from mere number, and the increasing average consumption of this number. The average consumption of the articles of subsistence and dress is consequently greater in towns than in villages, and in cities than in towns. And as the elementizing power depends on the demand, its influence is more minute and complete, in proportion to the populousness of the town or city.

The population of small towns, which consist of from 1500 to 3000 inhabitants, is sufficient to elementize the more common species of labour, such as baking, making shoes and clothes, building and the like. Thus in such towns we find bakers, shoemakers, tailors, carpenters and masons very distinct. This arises from the constant and universal demand for the articles of these circulators among all classes, however poor. But in the articles of the superfluous or luxurious sort, the consumption of which depends chiefly on the richer classes, the elementization is not so complete. In towns of this description we find the shopkeeper, for example, a linen and woollen draper, a haberdasher, a grocer, a druggist, a patent medicine vender, a cheesemonger, a hat-seller, a hosier, a tallow-chandler, a watch-dealer, a hardwareman, a stationer, a bookseller and a farmer frequently in one. The doctor as they call him is an apothecary, man-midwife, surgeon, physician, farrier, and patent medicine seller. The lawyer is a pleader, a conveyancer, a steward, a gatherer of rents, a banker's agent, and so forth. As towns increase, and rise to 5000 and more, this mixture decreases; and the various classes of mechanics and dealers in a population of from 10,000 to 20,000 become, with some exceptions, pretty pure. In large cities containing 50,000 and upwards, the elementizing power is so strong, as to subdivide the portions of the same sort of labour. In sum, it uniformly holds, from the lowest to the highest amount, that the greater the number of inhabitants in a place, the more minute is the subdivision and the more complete the elementization of employment. In the immense population of London the shoemaking class, for instance, is divided into makers of men's shoes, makers of women's shoes, makers of children's shoes, boot-cutters, boot-closers, boot-makers: women's shoe-sellers, men's shoe-sellers, boot-sellers. Some tailors make coats only, others waistcoats, a great many breeches, and some gaiters: some confine themselves to jobbing or mending: and others make chiefly dress clothes. Among shopkeepers we find distinct subdivisions: grocers, cheesemongers, druggists, linen-drapers, woollen-drapers, haberdashers, hatters, hosiers, and so forth.

All this minute subdivision arises from the elementizing causes mentioned already. On the one hand, an increased demand for every article from an increased population renders a given article sufficient to employ the supplier; and on the other, the supplier, besides perhaps having a greater liking to dealing in a particular article, finds it necessary, from the demand as well as his own convenience, to confine himself to it.

Populousness, and an increase of population tend also, by means of increasing the wealth of the great body, to introduce the use of many articles of comfort and luxury, which are unknown in thinly-peopled districts or small villages, and which few members of these can afford to purchase when they are known. Among articles of this description may be noticed expensive pieces of furniture, jewellery, services of plate, high-priced engravings and pictures. It is true, however, that large provincial towns are apt to borrow in these cases from the metropolis; smaller towns from these again, and villages from small towns, and sometimes all directly from the metropolis. Thinly-peopled states are apt to imitate more populous and rich ones in these cases also. Thus the use of articles of luxury, or of cheaper imitations of them, spreads with considerable rapidity through all classes, and even into districts thinly-peopled, or poor. But it is in large metropolises and the more populous countries, that articles of luxury are first introduced, because it is in these only that there is a demand for such articles to stimulate the suppliers of luxuries. Now from the nature of many of these, and the period of population and society, at which they are all introduced, which is when the elementizing principle is in full energy, as well as from the place of their introduction, their elementization is, in general, nearly complete from the beginning.

This division, or elementization of labour, which is the natural effect of the increase of population, tends to excellence in the work. By concentrating the attention of the workman on one species of work, it renders him more skilful in it, and by keeping him constantly employed on this, it gives him not only superior manual adroitness, but greater rapidity. When a manufacturer does the same thing over again every day, he acquires a mechanical neatness and cleverness without any particular effort of the mind.

The excellence thus produced, it is true, is for the most part rather in the appearance than the substance. What the all-work artificer makes, with all its clumsiness and coarseness, generally possesses substantiality, while the one-work artisan frequently sacrifices strength to show. Yet though this must be admitted with respect to many articles, in others the latter combines superior excellence of fabric with a more finished style of execution.

This elementization of labour, and the excellence produced by it, were observed by the ancients; and, indeed, how could what is so obvious be overlooked? From it is derived, as will be hereafter more particularly noticed, the eminence of certain towns and districts for certain species of manufactures. It is even favourable to cheapness in production. Much higher wages, it is true, are commonly paid to those who work at certain branches only; but this confining of their attention and exertions to one thing, gives them such a rapidity added to masterliness in execution, that they produce a much greater quantity of it, and that well-finished, in a given time than the bungling all-work artificers; and, therefore, their employers are enabled to sell a better, or, at least, a more pleasing, article at a lower price.

Excellence, both in the worker and the work, is much promoted by the regular and systematic application of the grand directing principle of Intention. This principle seems so obvious, that we should be apt to expect to find it regularly resorted to as the uniform practical rule in every species of work or art from the beginning. What is the intention of the instrument or machine which I am going to make, or of the article which I am preparing to fabricate; and how shall I most effectually, and yet, at the same time, with the greatest ease to myself, as well as at the cheapest rate, execute that intention? Nothing appears more natural than for a workman to ask himself this question. It seems level to the capacity even of the savage. Yet how seldom is it ever regularly asked in the early and less populous stages of society. It is only in a high state of population, and chiefly amid the crowded masses of great towns, that it is asked expressly at all. The truth is, one generation of workmen quietly succeed another, and as quietly adopt the instruments and machines, and imitate the manners of the former, without giving themselves the trouble to inquire whether these be the best, or most suited to the purpose: indeed, perhaps, without ever bestowing a thought on the matter. It requires some eminent artist or some leading genius in a certain line, assisted by the stimulating influence of a crowded population, to make the workers in that line think of consulting what the intention dictates. Even in Britain, high as it has reached in populousness and the effects of populousness, with respect to how many things has the question, What is the intention?

never yet been regularly asked. Of this we are furnished with abundance of proofs wherever we cast our eyes. The clumsy inefficient instruments and machines which are used by most classes of workmen, and the unsuitedness of so many works of every kind to the purposes for which they are intended, show us, that the artificers either never considered what was the intention of the instruments which they used, or of the works at which they laboured, or had very indistinct ideas on the subject.

These effects spring out of the old inveterate habits produced in less populous periods. As population increases and approaches nearer to its complement, they gradually disappear. The increasing capital and demand, with the higher cultivation of mind, which are the products of this increase and movement, make the question of the intention be more generally asked in the execution of all kinds of work. Mutual emulation, and, indeed, necessity compel artisans of every class seriously to put it to themselves, in order to get beyond, or even to keep pace with their neighbours, and thus acquire, or retain, a share of the public favours. The natural effects of this are progressive improvements in the various instruments and machines that are retained, the rejection of those that are inadequate, the introduction of more effective ones, and a greater simplicity, and suitedness, as well as a superior masterliness of execution, in every work that is attempted. . . .

In the early periods of mankind, only the more necessary and simple machines were thought of, as being felt wanting. In proportion as men advance in population, and, consequently, civilization, their wants become more numerous, their works more various and on a grander scale, their ingenuity more acute, or at least more employed, and their capital, or circulandary ability to execute their ideas, more extensive. The advantage of machines is then distinctly seen, and the opportunities of inventing increase yearly. In the works of peace, as well as of war (and, perhaps, in the case of the latter, to the disgrace of mankind, their ingenuity has been more keen, and their attention more alive), the various mechanical powers were gradually adopted, and combined in various ways. The progress in machinery, after the more necessary was invented, seems to have been very slow; and during the dark ages, perhaps, it was rather retrograde. But among the many great and advantageous effects, which the reformation, assisted by that wonderful machine, the press, produced by rousing the human mind out of its torpid state through the means of free inquiry, we may reckon the vast progress made since the time of Luther in the grand art of shortening labour by machines. This has been particularly conspicuous during the last 150 years. Perhaps, in this period, more has been done to shorten labour and execute various useful purposes by machinery, than had been achieved before it, since the commencement of the human race. And this noble art, far from being neglected, is still more eagerly pursued than ever: scarcely a month elapses, but some machine or other is introduced. Indeed this age may be justly characterized as the age of machines. And no country has stood more eminently forward here, as usual, than Great Britain.

It is in populous and well-employed, and, of course, rich countries, that machines principally originate: at least, those of the less necessary sort. Countries, however, connected with these, though but thinly peopled, and not so fully employed, may borrow, and use them prematurely, or before the period of society, in which their natural circumstances would have urged them to invent similar ones themselves. The United States of North America afford an example of this. From the British habits and character of the great mass of people throughout those states, as well as their connexion with this island, they have adopted many things before the natural time. And they have all the predilection of the present race of Britons for machines, without having such a real need of them. Travellers among them inform us, that they frequently meet with very extensive machinery, which the circumstances do not require. The apparatus is vast; but the result is trifling.

VI

G. K. Rickards, *Population and Capital. Being a course of lectures delivered before the University of Oxford in 1853-4*, London, 1854, pp. 155-6, 162-3, 166-9.

I observed in my opening remarks upon Mr. Malthus' work, that the main defect of this theory is that it is entirely one-sided. He has considered the increase of numbers in a community solely with reference to the increase of consumption which it involves disregarding the natural effect of the same cause upon production. An increase of population is indeed as he says an effect of natural prosperity; but it is a cause also. It is the consequence no doubt but it is at the same time the prolific source of the wealth of nations. Its operation in the latter point of view Mr. Malthus has almost wholly overlooked. The tendency of the density of population to make industry more productive is a chapter omitted in his essay. Writing under the influence of a panic fear not altogether unwarranted by the then circumstances of this country sinking deeply as it appeared to be into a gulf of pauperism he depicted the principle of human fecundity as a gigantic power encroaching continually with rapid strides upon the limited fund of human subsistence. But he omitted to display the reverse side of the picture which represents the prolificness of mankind as the great motive power of society—the prime stimulant to industry and enterprise—the incentive of art and commerce of invention and improvement—the means by which the burthen of toil is lightened and its reward increased—by which the earth is replenished with inhabitants and the powers of nature are made subservient to human necessities and enjoyment. . . . .

Now to apply these statements to the subject of population — labour being the instrument of all wealth of every nation increasing in direct proportion to the effectiveness or in other words the economy of its labour this economy is incompatible with a scanty population and is naturally promoted and facilitated by a large and dense one. I have pointed out the three principal modes by which the smallest amount of labour is made to conduce to the largest result of profit. I shall proceed to show how each of these three pregnant sources of wealth requires an ample population, in order to its due development. That powerful lever of industry, the division of employments, is limited, as Adam Smith has clearly explained, by the extent of the market. It depends simply on the measure of the demand whether it will answer or not to carry on the business of production or trade upon that system of separation of employments, which is always, wherever it is practicable, the best economy. It is obvious that what can be done with great advantage in a large town is impracticable in a small village. Consequently, in the former the division, in the latter the concentration, of occupations, is observed to take place. In the crowded and wealthy city you find a great variety and subdivision of trades. Many businesses of a cognate kind, such as those of the haberdasher and the linendraper, the watchmaker and the silversmith, the baker and the confectioner, the bookseller and the stationer, are carried on in separate establishments. In a rural village, on the other hand, a single emporium, familiarly known as the shop, supplies all the wants of the little community.

Wearing apparel and household utensils, tea and tobacco, bread and shoes, stationery and drugs, with numberless other articles of the most multifarious kind, form the promiscuous assortment of the village shopkeeper. While his returns from the miscellaneous collection of wares are far less than those of the wealthy town tradesmen, whose dealings are confined to one sort of commodities, his customers nevertheless pay at a higher rate than in the larger market, and usually get an inferior article for their money. In a like manner, as Adam Smith remarks "a country carpenter deals in every sort of work that is made of wood: a country smith in every sort of work that is made of iron. The former is not only a carpenter, but a joiner, a cabinet-maker, and even a carver in wood, as well as a wheelwright, a ploughwright, a cart and waggon maker". Again, "there are some sorts of industry", as the same writer observes, "even of the lowest kind, which can be carried on nowhere but in a great town. A porter, for example, can find employment and subsistence in no other place. A village is by much too narrow a sphere for him; even an ordinary market-town is scarce large enough to afford him constant occupation"....

It is therefore evidently, as Adam Smith says, the extent of the market which limits the division of labour. A large consuming power is an essential element in the economy of production. The larger the population, coeteris paribus, the more complete the organisation of industry will be. As the market expands, occupations will become more and more subdivided; if, on the contrary, the demand contracts, they will relapse into their pristine state of concentration.

2. Of the combination of labour as an advantage depending on the condition of a populous community I need say little. The fact speaks for itself. The great operations and improvements by which the wealth of nations is rapidly increased—the construction of railways, canals, piers, breakwaters, and harbours—the drainage and redemption of extensive tracts of land—the intersection or removal of natural obstacles to communication—can only be accomplished in the maturity of rich and well-peopled societies; because such works require the combined labour of large masses of men on a given point, which, in a small community, it is impossible to procure. For the execution of great works there must be a well-supplied labour-market: it is not only the command of a large capital, but the power at any moment to bring together and set in motion a small army of workmen, that enables the great contractors in this country at the present time to undertake, and rapidly to execute, those prodigious operations, which no natural impediments, or "engineering difficulties", as they are called, are now capable of arresting. On the other hand, in the Australian colonies, previously to the late gold discoveries, population was so thin, and labour consequently so dear, that one of the first requisites of civilisation and chief sources of wealth—the formation of roads and bridges—had long been obstructed and postponed for no other cause than the want of hands to make them.

Consider, also, the numerous forms of association, the natural growth of a populous society, but impossible in a small one, which conduce to the enjoyment of life, to intellectual improvement, to habits of economy and prudence, to the advancement of science; and, by these various means, more or less directly to the increase of national wealth; such as colleges, museums, libraries, clubs, benefit societies, savings banks, insurance companies, and the like. It is by the power of numbers that these institutions subsist; it is on the principle that "many a little makes a mickle", that their benefits are founded.

Lastly, let us see how the increase of population bears upon the production of wealth by means of commercial exchange. To recapitulate briefly what I before stated, the benefit of exchange is in effect this—that it enables every man to get whatever he wants best and cheapest in return for that which he does best and cheapest himself. The American gives the Englishman that which, for local reasons, has cost America little labour, but which would cost England much; and the Englishman gives in return that which has cost him little labour, but in America could not be had without a great deal. Thus, each gets the advantage of the other's facilities of production, minus only the cost of conveyance. Now what, if we go to the root of the matter, is the object and effect of all those improvements in the means of communication by which we are incessantly striving to abridge distance, and to bring countries and provinces of each other? It is simply this—to produce an artificial condensation of population. It is a good thing, no doubt, to find customers for our cottons, woollens, and hardware, and dealers in corn and breadstuffs, on the opposite side of the Atlantic. It has become a greater advantage since we have virtually brought the United States within less than half their former distance by means of steam-navigation. It would be better still if we could further reduce, by one-third or one-half, the time and cost of the voyage; but it would be best of all,—I mean, of course, in a commercial point of view,—if such things were possible, to get rid of the marine impediment altogether. The distance which now separates us from our customers is evidently a mercantile loss; and, under that conviction, we are striving to diminish it more and more every year by mechanical improvements. Suppose, now, we add, in the course of a century, to our domestic population a number of persons equal in consuming power to that of the American market at present; such an addition will be equivalent, in point of national gain, to the accomplishment of the desideratum we are now straining after, viz., to make England and America, commercially, one continent. In this hypothesis I am, of course, assuming that wealth increases in England pari passu with the increase of population. You will observe, that I have all along been speaking of the effect of increased populousness on a country, coeteris paribus; my argument being that, per se, populousness is a cause of wealth. Compare a country having ten millions of people with another having twenty millions on an equal surface, the relation of the numbers to the capital and to the means of subsistence in each case being, at a given time, the same. I say that, starting from this point, with equal advantages in other respects, the more populous country must outstrip the less populous in the accumulation of wealth, because, for the reasons pointed out, the concentration of numbers necessarily makes labour more productive; and, as the larger community affords twice as good a market for the productions of industry, the benefit derived from exchange (in other words, the profits of its trade) will be, in a more than twofold proportion, greater than in the other case. In fact, all the gain which the smaller country might derive from trading with a foreign neighbour equally wealthy and populous with itself, is reaped by its more populous rival, minus the deduction of freight, risk, insurance, customs' duties and other expenses of transport.

VII

T. R. Malthus, *Principles of Political Economy*, 2nd ed., London 1836, Reprinted, Frank Cass & Co., London 1951. pp. 311-14.

Section II—Of the Increase of Population considered as a Stimulus to the continued Increase of Wealth

Many writers have been of opinion that an increase of population is the sole stimulus necessary to the increase of wealth, because population, being the great source of consumption, must in their opinion necessarily keep up the demand for an increase of produce, which will naturally be followed by a continued increase of supply.

That a continued increase of population is a powerful and necessary element of increasing demand, will be most readily allowed; but that the increase of population alone, or more properly speaking the pressure of the population hard against the limits of subsistence, does not furnish an effective stimulus to the continued increase of wealth is not only evident in theory but is confirmed by universal experience. If want alone or the desire of the labouring classes to possess the necessaries and conveniences of life, were a sufficient stimulus to production, there is no state in Europe, or in the world, which would have found any other practical limit to its wealth than its power to produce; and the earth would probably before this period have contained at the very least, ten times as many inhabitants as are supported on its surface at present.

But those who are acquainted with the nature of effectual demand, will be fully aware that, where the right of private property is established, and the wants of society are supplied by industry and barter, the desire of any individual to possess the necessaries, conveniences and luxuries of life, however intense, will avail nothing towards their production, if there be no where a reciprocal demand for something which he possesses. A man whose only possession is his labour has, or has not, an effective demand for produce according as his labour is, or is not, in demand by those who have the disposal of produce. And no productive labour can ever be in demand with a view to profit unless the produce when obtained is of greater value than the labour which obtained it. No fresh hands can be employed in any sort of industry merely in consequence of the demand for its produce occasioned by the persons employed. No farmer will take the trouble of superintending the labour of ten additional men merely because his whole produce will then sell in the market at an advanced price just equal to what he had paid his additional labourers. There must be something in the previous state of the demand and supply of the commodity in question, or in its price, antecedent to and independent of the demand occasioned by the new labourers, in order to warrant the employment of an additional number of people in its production.

It will be said perhaps that the increase of population will lower wages, and, by thus diminishing the costs of production, will increase the profits of the capitalists and the encouragement to produce. Some temporary effect of this kind may no doubt take place, but it is evidently very strictly limited. The fall of real wages cannot go on beyond a certain point without not only stopping the progress of the population but making it even retrograde; and before this point is reached, the increase of produce occasioned by the labour of the additional number of persons will have so lowered its value, and reduced profits, as to determine the capitalist to employ less labour. Though the producers of necessaries might certainly be able in this case to obtain the funds required for the support of a greater number of labourers; yet if the effectual demand for necessaries were fully supplied, and an adequate taste for unproductive consumption, or personal services had not been established, no motive of interest could induce the producers to make an effectual demand for this greater number of labourers.

It is obvious then in theory that an increase of population, when an additional quantity of labour is not required, will soon be checked by want of employment and the scanty support of those employed, and will not furnish the required stimulus to an increase of wealth proportioned to the power of production.

But, if any doubts should remain with respect to the theory on the subject, they will surely be dissipated by a reference to experience. It is scarcely possible to cast our eyes on any nation of the world without seeing a striking confirmation of what has been advanced. Almost universally, the actual wealth of all the states with which we are acquainted is very far short of their powers of production; and among those states, the slowest progress in wealth is often made where the stimulus arising from population alone is the greatest, that is, where the population presses the hardest against the actual limits of subsistence. It is quite evident that the only fair way, indeed the only way, by which we can judge of the practical effect of population alone as a stimulus to wealth, is to refer to those countries where, from the excess of population above the funds applied to the maintenance of labour, the stimulus of want is the greatest. And if in these countries, which still have great powers of production, the progress of wealth is very slow, we have certainly all the evidence which experience can possibly give us, that population alone cannot create an effective demand for wealth.

To suppose a great and continued increase of population is to beg the question. We may as well suppose at once an increase of wealth; because such an increase of population cannot take place without a proportionate or nearly proportionate increase of wealth. The question really is, whether encouragements to population, or even the natural tendency of population to increase beyond the funds destined for its maintenance, will, or will not, alone furnish an adequate stimulus to the increase of wealth. And this question, Spain, Portugal, Poland, Hungary, Turkey and many other countries in Europe, together with nearly the whole of Asia and Africa, and the greatest part of America, distinctly answer in the negative.

VIII

W. H. Beveridge, *Full employment in a free society*, London, 1944, pp. 93–4.

The Keynesian Analysis of 1936

120. A new era of economic theorizing about employment and unemployment was inaugurated by the publication in 1936 of The General Theory of Employment, Interest and Money by J. M. Keynes, now Lord Keynes. No account, however brief, of all the changes of economic thought and language induced by this epoch-making work can be attempted here. The gist of the new approach to the problem of employment that has resulted from it can be put shortly. Employment depends on spending, which is of two kinds—for consumption and for investment; what people spend on consumption gives employment. What they save, i.e. do not spend on consumption, gives employment only if it is invested, which means not the buying of bonds or shares but expenditure in adding to capital equipment, such as factories, machinery, or ships, or in increasing stocks of raw material. There is not in the unplanned market economy anything that automatically keeps the total of spending of both kinds at the point of full employment, that is to say, high enough to employ all the available labour. Adequate total demand for labour in an unplanned market economy cannot be taken for granted.

121. According to the Keynesian analysis, the possibility of prolonged mass unemployment lies in the fact that decisions to save and decisions to invest are made by different sets of people at different times and for different reasons and may thus get out of step. The amount which any community will try to save is governed, not primarily by the outlets for saving, i.e. the opportunities for investment, but by the total income of the community and its distribution; broadly speaking, if incomes are evenly distributed, less will be saved out of the total than if they are unevenly distributed.

The amount which any community will seek to invest is governed, not primarily by the amount of savings available for investment, but by expectation of profits. Savings and investment do not start with any initial tendency to march in step and there is no automatic painless way of keeping them in step or bringing them together if they fall out.

IX

United Nations, *The determinants and consequences of population trends*, New York, 1953, pp. 210-11, 211, 212-13, 213, 214, 215, 217, 219.

5. If consumption varied in direct proportion to the number of people, the question of the influence of population changes on the composition and upon the aggregate volume of consumption could be easily determined. Any population increase or decrease would be accompanied by a corresponding change in the amount of each type of goods and services required; the aggregate volume of consumption would also follow closely the changes in total population. In reality, the relationships between population changes and consumption are more complex. Changes in the size of the population are accompanied by changes in its age structure and by disproportionate changes in the number of families, so that both the per capita needs for particular kinds of goods and services and total per capita consumption are altered. Furthermore, the level of per capita income may rise or fall, the tastes of consumers may change, the propensity to consume may be altered; wherever such changes occur a given population change may not be accompanied by a corresponding change in consumption.

6. At a given time the consumption pattern in a given society is fixed by knowledge, tradition, habit and custom as well as by the disposable resources and techniques of production. There are differences in the manner of living among various groups in the population, although these are differences of degree only. The specific content of consumption varies in quantity and quality with age, economic level and geographic location, but not in substance. When there are changes in the size and composition of the population, the demand for goods and services tends to change in a definite manner as dictated by the existing pattern of consumption. If other circumstances permit, population changes—i.e. an increase in the absolute size of the population, migration from rural to urban communities, a decrease in the size of households, an increase in the average

age—result in a greater aggregate demand and in substantial shifts in the relative importance of specific goods and services. Rising real income within any population group leads almost automatically to a higher level of consumption. . . .

8. Consumption patterns are apparently very rigid, as national food habits illustrate. Yet the history of mass migrations shows that in the course of time circumstances may alter radically the content of consumption. Populations that survived in greatly changed environments have learned to use the foods and other goods that could be economically produced in their new locations and have altered their modes of living accordingly. The successes and disasters in the chronicles of pioneers have revealed their apparent universal tendency to resist change in their consumption habits, but ultimately to adapt them to the surroundings. Likewise, changing conditions within a country may force the people to alter their habits of consumption. Such changes may occur where there is an increase of population, but where the capacity to produce does not keep pace with the expanding capacity to consume.

9. The state may take action to encourage changes in consumption for the purpose either of providing for the needs of a growing population or conserving resources in order that a larger share can be devoted to productive investments. In some situations the investment in capital goods may be accomplished by restraining consumption increases within the customary consumption pattern or by introducing more economical items into current use through some effective means of consumer education. The investment may, in other situations, be assured by first fostering the increases in consumption that lead to improvements in the health and productivity of the people. . . .

12. An increase or decrease in the size of the population, regardless of its structure, affects the composition of consumption in various ways depending on associated changes in the level of per capita income. Findings summarized in the following chapters of this report indicate that some authors attach great importance to the possible unfavourable effect of population growth on income levels, and, hence, on consumption levels, in the densely populated

under-developed countries. In highly industrialized countries, this relationship is generally considered to be less important.

13. In countries where the population is large in relation to the available amounts of agricultural land and other developed resources, and where the people live on a low level, an economical pattern of consumption is a necessity. An increase of population under such conditions may force the adoption of a still more economical pattern, in order to avoid disastrous shortages of food and other necessities. ...

17. If population increases are accompanied by a rising level of per capita real income, and if the higher incomes accrue to all elements of the population, there is likely to be an increase in the ratio of consumption of "superior" to "inferior" goods. Those goods which the consumers regard as "superior" (that is, goods which will be purchased in greater quantities as their economic condition improves) differ from country to country, according to cultural differences and variations in the level of income.

18. Population changes may possibly affect consumption in other indirect ways. For example, should the price of labour rise or fall due to changes in the size of the labour force relative to the supplies of other productive agents, consumers would in some measure substitute goods requiring much labour in their production for goods requiring little labour, or vice versa. Or, should population growth affect the degree of inequality of income distribution, as it might possibly do in some circumstances, the ratio of consumption to savings would be altered as well as the composition of consumption.

19. When the influence of non-demographic factors, such as the development of technology, the formation of capital, and the shifts in consumers' preference, is compared with the influence of population changes, it becomes evident that the latter are, in many circumstances, only minor factors affecting the consumption of particular goods and services. The relative importance of population growth is greater in countries where economic progress is relatively slow than in those countries where technology is progressing and capital is growing more rapidly. Its importance is also greater in the case of goods and services which are consumed by most individuals

at rates near the level of satiation, than in those cases where goods and services are consumed at rates far below that level. For example, the influence of population growth on the demand for most food products is more important than its influence on the demand for most manufactured goods.

20. The impact of population growth on consumption depends partly on the concomitant changes in the age structure. . . .

21. People at different ages do not have the same needs; therefore, with a changing age structure the need for certain categories of goods and services will increase (or decrease) more than for certain other categories. . . .

22. There is reason to believe that a relatively young population, whether it is growing rapidly or not, will spend a larger share of its income on food than an older population with the same per capita income . . . . The aging of the population in industrialized countries has probably accentuated the tendency of a rising per capita income to reduce the proportion of total food expenditures. . . . .

25. The relation between the age structure of the population and the composition of consumption is not the same in communities where a large part of economic activity consists of the work of household members producing for home consumption as in communities where most goods and services are marketed. In all countries, including those where the market economy has been most fully developed, a substantial part of total consumption is produced in households, but of such consumption only the home-produced food that is consumed on farms is usually included in the statistical measures used for economic analysis. In certain types of communities, the consumption of home-produced goods and services is extremely important; practically all food production, the fabrication of clothing and furnishings, and even the education of children are performed by household members within the home. The greater the relative importance of such consumption, the slower is likely to be the effect of a changing age structure upon that part of consumption which appears in national accounts and which affects the functioning of the market economy.

26. The proportion of total consumption represented by home-produced goods and services is subject to important changes with the passing of time and with the social and economic changes occurring within the community; and population trends are among the factors involved in such changes. Before the widespread employment of women outside the home in Western countries, women performed many services and produced many goods that are now within the province of the market. Urbanization, industrialization, and increasing employment outside the home tend to increase total consumption and to alter the composition of consumers' expenditures for goods and services in the market in ways that do not correspond to real changes in the volume or composition of consumption.

27. The number of families in relation to the size of the population has an important bearing on the volume and the composition of consumption, for many goods and services are consumed by households as units rather than by individuals. Examples are dwellings and household furnishings. . . .

30. The trend in the number of families in any area does not exactly parallel the trend in the size of the population. For example, if the birth rate continues to decline until the population becomes stationary or begins to decline, the rate of growth in the number of families also eventually declines. However, this takes place only after the elapse of time with the result that the number of families may go on increasing for a few decades after the population has ceased to grow. The ratio is also subject to considerable short-term variation, such as that which occurs with the fluctuation of the business cycles. During the recovery and boom phases of business cycles the marriage rate tends to rise, and the number of families increases faster than the population. Conversely, during the depression phase young people tend to delay marriages, and the rate of growth in the number of families decreases. The proportion of widowed and single adults who occupy separate quarters, and thus are counted as "families" or "households", may change with changing habits of life, and tends to increase when the level of income rises . . .

33. The composition of families also has an important bearing on housing needs and other items of consumers' demand. The numbers

of families of different sizes, the numbers with children of various ages, the proportions of families headed by widows or widowers and of single-person families, the numbers of three-generation families, etc., are all relevant in this connexion. These characteristics of families are related in complex ways to the trends of marriage rates, birth rates, death rates, and population growth. . . .

42. Changes in the per capita quantities of various goods and services consumed, due to changes in the rate of population growth or to shifts in population structure, may have a bearing on the total per capita consumption of all goods and services, and thus on the amount of saving. If population changes have such effects, they may play an important part in economic development and in the trend of per capita income. . . .

56. Population changes are intricately related to economic, political and social developments. Consumption continuously links population changes to economic changes which, in turn, through consumption, influence population changes. For a better understanding of this dynamic process the existing historical and statistical information on the relations between consumption and the demographic and economic characteristics of population in many countries needs to be summarized and integrated. The analysis of existing empirical material needs to be supplemented by new studies on subjects which have not received adequate attention in the past. The role of the household in producing for its own members, a subject of considerable importance in international comparisons of income levels, needs much more attention in empirical studies. The actual long-run changes in consumption that follow migration have not been studied extensively enough to permit valid generalization. The potential efficacy of various techniques of education and communication in changing consumption patterns, as may be necessary in situations where it is desirable simultaneously to improve the health and efficiency of the population and to divert some part of the national product to investment, needs much more study. The whole question of priority of investment, in human capacity or in material capacity, is still a matter mainly of subjective opinion and requires serious attention from students of population trends, economists and sociologists.

X

Thirty-Ninth Annual Report of the Registrar-General of Births, Deaths and Marriages in England (Abstracts of 1876), London, H.M.S.O., 1878, pp. v–x.

Various attempts have been made to estimate the amount, and the increase of the capital of the United Kingdom. The most recent attempt of the kind has been made by the chief of the statistical department of the Board of Trade. The value of the most important part of the capital of the United Kingdom and its increase have yet be determined; I mean the economic value of the population itself. To that I propose to call attention briefly.

As lands, houses, railways, and the other categories in the income tax schedules are of value, because they yield annual returns; so for the same reason, and on the same principle the income of the population derived from pay of every kind for professional or other services, and wages can be capitalized; not precisely, it is true, unless the income of every person living were returned at least as nearly as the incomes subject to income tax; but sufficiently near to the true value to show that the value of the population itself is the most important factor in the wealth of the country.

It will be sufficient to state here that the capitalization of personal incomes always proceeds upon the determination of the present value at any age of the future annual earnings at that and all future ages; hence the Value of future wages rises from the date of birth, when it is a notable quantity; is highest in the labouring classes at the age of 25; and declines as age advances, until in extreme age when no wages are earned, it disappears. The living by the Life Table are most numerous in childhood, and gradually fall off till they are all extinct; and so in the population enumerated at the Census the numbers decline from the first year to the ultimate year of age. While the rates of wages rise rapidly from birth to the age of manhood, and afterwards decline, the numbers living constantly decline. Taking a series of observations on the wages of agricultural labourers some years ago at different ages; determining their value by a Life Table at five per cent. rate of interest for each age; and multiplying the numbers living by these values, it is found that the mean gross value at all ages is £349. But the mean value of the subsistence of the labourer as child and man, determined by the same method, is about £199; and deducting this sum from £349, there remain £150 as the mean net value of the male population, estimated by this standard of the agricultural labourer. To extend the value to the whole population, including females the standard might be lowered from £150 to £110 a head.

Then multiplying the population of the United Kingdom by 110 we have as the aggregate value £3,640 million, this including only as much of the income as approximates in annual amount to the wages of agricultural labourers. Only a small part of it is subject to assessment under the income tax schedules. The gross assessment under the income tax affords the means of estimating the value of incomes exceeding £100 a year under schedules D and E; excluding companies, mines, and works, these profits and salaries amount to £214 million a year, to which about £92 million a year may be added for incomes above £30 and below £100 a year; thus making the aggregate of such incomes £306 million a year; which when the assessments of B (farmers') are added becomes £373 million a year. Deduct the half of this revenue as due to external capital, and as required for the necessary sustenance of farmers, tradesmen, and professional men and there remain £186½ million a year as pure profit; which cannot be capitalized as a perpetuity inasmuch as the interest is limited by the lives of the producers, but taking life contingencies into account may be capitalized at ten years' purchase. This makes the value of these incomes £1,865 million. Allowing £255 million for the part of the incomes of about a million people paying the income tax previously valued in the £3,640 million, and for other deductions, £1,610 million remain, which, added to the £3,640 million already obtained, make £5,250 million.

Thus by capitalizing the earnings, fees, salaries, wages of the professional, mercantile, trading, and working classes, £5,250 million are obtained as an approximation to the value which is inherent in the people, and may be fairly added to the capital in land, houses, cattle or stock, and other investments. The amount would be increased by taking into account the rise of wages, and the income omitted in the returns of Schedule D. With an industrial census an accurate estimate can be made of this most important part of the capital of the country.

The minimum value of the population of the United Kingdom,

men, women, and children, is £159 a head; that is the value inherent in them as a productive, money-earning race. The incomes chiefly under schedules D, E and B, raise the mean value from £110 to £159 (see above).

Against it must be borne in mind that the value under Schedule A is dependent upon the population; where there is little population land itself is of little value. The increase of the value of house property is directly due to the increased numbers and earnings of the inhabitants. The railways yield no profit where there is no population. The profits of quarries, mines, ironworks (Schedule D) and other concerns are mainly due to the skill and industry of the masters and men who work them. Upon the other hand the products of human industry are multiplied a hundredfold by the tools, machinery, steam power, and all the appliances which capital commands and represents. Should the population of a country decay, the value of its capital might sink to the vanishing point.

What I wish further to point out is that during the $39\frac{1}{2}$ years this office has existed there have been added to the population of the United Kingdom 7,619,759 people, who valued as land is valued by the annual yield of net profit, constitute an addition of £1,212 million to the wealth of the nation.

The value of labour—that is of working men—varies, and is greatest where there is the greatest facility for profitable use, and where it is in greatest demand. Thus a large stream of the population of England flows to the Metropolis; and England is to the United Kingdom what the Metropolis is to England. So the populations of Ireland and Scotland flow into England, where they find more profitable employment, and are of more value than they are at home.

For the same and other reasons large armies of the population of the United Kingdom passed into the colonies and the United States; during the thirty-nine and a half years (1837-76) the excess of births over deaths was nearly 16 millions, of which nearly 8 millions augmented the ranks of the population at home, and more than 8 millions settled in other lands; chiefly in the midst of the old English stock of the United States and in the Colonies extending from Canada in America, to Africa and to Australasia.

Of the 8,013,267 people who must have left the country, only about 6,580,000 are accounted for by the Emigration Commissioners, whose returns were imperfect in two ways; they neither included the whole of the emigrants nor recognised emigrants returning recently in large numbers.

The emigrants are chiefly adults married and unmarried; the men greatly exceeding the women in number. A few infants accompany their parents. Valuing the emigrants as the agricultural labourers have been valued at home—taking age and service into account—the value of emigrants in 1876 was £175 per head.

If we may venture to apply this standard to the whole period it will follow that the money value of the 8,000,000 people that left England, Scotland, and Ireland in the years 1837–76, was £1,400 million, or on an average about £35,000,000 a year. In round numbers taking into account their aptitude to earn wages in future years at the home rates the annual industrial army that went out was worth at starting £35,000,000. Many of the emigrants are skilled artisans, and considerable numbers are returned as farmers, gentlemen, professional men, and merchants; some of whom no doubt carried away a certain amount of capital which is not here brought into account.

The policy of the people of this country has thus been a policy of progress; instead of resting as they were in 1837, they have added since that year on an average 192,873 souls annually to the population at home, and sent 202,868 sons and daughters to seek their fortune abroad in other fields of labour. The women, instead of to 644,214 children, who would just replace the population removed by deaths, have given birth to 1,039,987 annually, at a certain loss of their own lives with intermingled sorrows and joys such as befall mothers in rearing children: while the men instead of expending the whole of their gains on themselves have devoted a large share to their wives and families; besides that as we have seen the external wealth of the country has increased as the nation has without conquering territory or levying heavy contributions on its European neighbours.

The value of men varies with their earnings, which differ considerably in the colonies from the earnings of agricultural labourers at home; and on the whole before the civil war the emigrants to the United States got higher wages, and at the same time gave a higher value to the territory.

It may be contended that emigration is a loss to the mother country. It seems so. It is like the export of precious goods for which there is no return. But experience proves that simultaneously with this emigration there has been a prodigious increase of the capital of the country, especially in recent years. Wages have risen, and the value of the labourer has risen in proportion. In Norfolk where wages are intermediate between the rates in the north and south the rise has apparently been about 20 per cent.; so a fifth may be added to the estimated value of the workman. When the man leaves the village where he was born and bred, he leaves the market open to his fellows; he removes to a field where his work is in demand, and carries his fortune with him. It is the same when he emigrates to the colonies. His parents in rearing him have expended their gains in the way most agreeable to themselves. They have on an average five children, instead of two or three, or none. Taking a wider view, the emigrants create articles of primary use with which in exchange they supply the mother country; they have sent to England in the 39 years wheat, cotton, wool, gold to the value of hundreds of millions. What is of still more vital importance, they grow into new nations; they multiply discoveries; by confederation they will be to the Anglo-Saxon race outposts of strength across the Atlantic, in the Pacific, in South Africa, and in Australasia on the flank of India. And, moreover, to all it is an advantage to speak a wide spread language, and thus to be in social, literary, and scientific communion with millions of the same race. The increasing numbers enable them, advanced as they are in the arts, in the sciences, and in civil government, to do more for the good of kindred races; and to endow them with advantages which could not be attained in other ways for centuries. They govern India.

The economic value of a population depends very much on their command over the powers of nature; which they acquire by education. Put barbarians in possession of the land, the mines, the manufactures, the machines, the ships, the triumphant position of these islands on the sea between two continents, and what would be the result? Another Asia Minor, Egypt, or Syria? The better educated the English people become, the more skilful they will become, and the more valuable in an economic sense they will be. The clever artisan is worth more than the rude labourer. Now the art of reading and writing their own language is by no means proof of complete education, or of any technical training, but it is a proof that men in possession of it are preparing to enter on the heritage of thought, and knowledge, and sentiment, which men of all ages have bequeathed to mankind, and which is enshrined in the writings of an admirable language. In 1837 not more than 58 in 100 men and women possessed this art; but there has been progress, and I have year by year assiduously noted the increase of their numbers in the 39 years, so that I am now able to report, that instead of 58, eighty-one in a hundred write their names in the marriage registers.

It is evident that there are other elements on which the economic value of the working population depends; and foremost among them stand health and long life. The longer men live, and the stronger they are, the more work they can do. Epidemic diseases in rendering life, render wages, insecure. These diseases are most fatal in cities whither the population—to secure all the advantages of the division of labour—have been congregating every year in increased numbers: villages have become populous or have grown into towns; so the population has been growing denser. And that by a definite law, other things being equal, tends to increase weakness, sickness, and mortality. There have been counteracting agencies in operation in the thirty-nine years. Asiatic cholera was epidemic in England in 1831-2; influenza followed at intervals in 1833, 1837, and 1847; and laid thousands of the population low; in 1848-9 the cholera epidemic in England and Wales alone was fatal to fifty-three thousand people; its ravages in every corner of the kingdom were described; the conditions of its diffusion and fatality were brought to light, and the further investigations of the slighter epidemics of 1854 and 1866 prove that this plague is under the control of science. Other epidemics have since been fatal especially to children, and fever has struck at princes and peers as well as peasants; but upon the whole the great zymotic diseases have been quelled. Plague in its various forms has been kept at bay by a series of defences based upon minute precautions. In some epidemics I found it necessary to publish daily particulars respecting deaths in the Metropolis. By pursuing such inquiries, year after year, not only many of the causes that induce sickness and destroy life have been discovered, but observations of the same kind have shown that their removal has been followed by health and longer, more vigorous life. The economic value of the population of several towns has been increased by sanitary measures. The truths established, the facts ascertained, the remedies discovered in the thirty-nine years past await their full administrative applications in the years to follow; and the savings of time wasted in sickness, as well as of precious lives prematurely lost in youth and manhood, will enhance the value of the population to an incalculable extent. The famines so fatal in Ireland are not likely to recur; part of the population has emigrated to England or to America, and the intelligent landowners of Ireland through the extension of the Poor Law now insure their countrymen against death by starvation. The same beneficent law has in the thirty-nine years been extended to the Highlands of Scotland. Every improvement in health recorded makes it clearer and clearer that the gloom of sickness and premature death flies away before sanitary measures; and when the qualified health officers whom the Universities are offering to examine, are in suitable positions under enlightened local authorities all over the country they will no doubt prove as efficient in preventing as their medical brethren are in treating sickness. The result on human happiness cannot be calculated; but a future Industrial Census will show in a very definite shape its effect in raising the economic value of the population. The mean lifetime by the English Life Table is 40·86 years; by the Healthy Life Table it is 49·0 years, which is attainable in every well organized State. It is fair to assume that if a fifth part be added to the mean lifetime, at least a fifth part will be added to the worth of a living and labouring population. Upon this estimate £1,050 million will be added to the economic value of the population of the kingdom. Its value will increase with its numbers, and so will the value of its emigrating thousands.

XI

H. Sidgwick, *Principles of Political Economy*, London 1883, pp. 98–9, 100, 101–2, 103–4, 104–5, 107, 108, 109, 110–13.

On this view we may distinguish four different ways in which the labour of one community may be less than the labour of another, in proportion to the whole number of the population, for (1) the workers may bear a smaller ratio to the non-workers, or (2) the number of years during which they work may bear a smaller ratio to the whole period of life, or (3) they may work for fewer days in the year, or (4) for fewer hours in the day. It may however be urged that we ought to regard labour as having intensive as well as extensive quantity; and no doubt we commonly speak of men as doing more or less work in the same time, meaning not merely that they produce more or less result, but that they make more or less effort. But since I cannot find any satisfactory measure of the amount of such effort, applicable to all kinds of labour alike, it seems best to include this source of variation under the third head of 'efficiency' of labour. The question is not of great practical importance; because the variations in quantity and quality of labour respectively are on any view largely due to the same causes.

3. Let us begin, then, by analysing briefly the differences in the productiveness of labour that are due to external conditions. In the first place the "spontaneous bounties of nature" (as they are called) are very unequally distributed....

Secondly, as we pass from one part of the earth's surface to another, we find similar variations in the conditions unfavourable to production or to the preservation of what has been produced: either periodic conditions of inorganic nature such as extreme dampness or extreme heat; or occasional disturbances as floods, storms, earthquakes, &c; or plants or insects noxious in various ways. Here also we may notice the direct physical effect of climate on the labourer's energy, as well as its effects in varying the period during which labour can be usefully employed in agriculture: though these might equally be brought under the other heads.

In short, the external world upon which man operates requires in its original state very different degrees of adaptation to bring it to the same degree of aptitude for human uses. We have now to observe that, in the regions of the earth which have been for some time in the possession of civilized man, each succeeding generation receives its portion of the earth's surface in a somewhat different condition from the preceding generation. For the most part it finds its inheritance in a state more favourable to labour; the benefits of its predecessor's work being inextricably mingled with the "spontaneous bounties" of nature.

On the other hand, we have to notice certain respects in which the earlier generations are liable to render the land they live in worse adapted for the requirements of their successors. They tend to exhaust the useful minerals that are most conveniently situated for extraction—and also certain useful organic products accumulated in previous ages, such as Peruvian guano. They may exhaust the fertility of certain soils by frequent crops, so that these soils will afterwards require more labour to render them as fertile as they were originally. They tend to diminish the number of useful wild animals and drive them into places where they are more difficult to catch; and to carry the clearing of forests beyond the point at which the tree is less useful than the ground on which it stands. But these and other similar deteriorations, so far as we have yet had experience of them, cannot be said to weigh heavily in the balance against the improvements before mentioned.

There is however one specially important way in which a generation may find itself with a material environment less adapted to its needs, through the action of its predecessors. It may find that, through the increase in its numbers, the country it inhabits has become too small for the most effective application of the aggregate of its labour: that is, the increase in the advantages of Division of employments (to be presently noticed) may be more than neutralized by the diminution in the proportional amount of agricultural produce that can be annually extracted from the land, in return for the extra labour applied to it. . . .

Passing from these conditions, which are in the main unalterable, we may notice variations in the quantity and personal efficiency of labourers which depend on such physical and social circumstances of the labourers' lives as admit of being at any time modified by the action either of individuals or of the society to which they belong. In the first place, it is obvious that the proportion of effective workers to the rest of the community will be less, other things being equal, where the population is increasing rapidly, owing to the larger number of children that have to be supported; it will be less, again, the greater the number of children that die in infancy, owing to want of care or want of proper food, clothing, &c. Again, unsanitary conditions of life tend in another way to reduce the quantity of labour performed by a given population; by diminishing, through premature death or early and prolonged decrepitude, the average proportion which the working period of life bears to the whole; and again, by diminishing the number of working days in the year, through increased frequency of incapacitating disease.

Similarly, bad air and water, uncleanliness, over-indulgence in alcohol, and other unhealthy habits may lower the physical tone of the labourer and thus impair the quality of his work without causing positive illness; on the other hand the strength and energy of the labourer may be largely increased by an ampler supply of the necessities of life.

Even more important than the differences in the physical strength and vigour of labourers are the variations that we find in their skill and intelligence, their foresight, quickness, vigilance, and resource in availing themselves of advantages that further production and avoiding or removing all that impairs it. Superiorities in these respects are partly, as I have said, congenital and transmitted through physical heredity: but to a great extent they are handed down from generation to generation by conscious training and learning; primarily by technical training and learning of special arts and processes, though the effect of general education in developing industrial intelligence must not be overlooked. We must also bear in mind the extent to which industrial efficiency is transmitted by association and unconscious imitation....

5. Still, in explaining differences in the degree of energy of individual labourers or groups of labourers, as well as differences in the (extensive) quantity of the labour performed by a given population, a chief place must be given to differences in

the strength of the motives for work presented to their minds.

Among these varying motives the most powerful is undoubtedly that "desire for wealth" which economists have often treated as the sole possible spring of industrial activity. . . .

But the stimulus given to labour by the desire for wealth does not vary simply according to the strength of this resultant impulse; it is modified at least equally by the extent to which the labourer is impressed with the belief (1) that additional wealth may be obtained and kept by additional labour, and (2) that there is no other more easy and agreeable way of obtaining it. Here it is to be observed, in the first place, that the range of opportunities of obtaining wealth has been largely extended and restricted by the action of government. . . .

Supposing the species of industry determined, the strength of the labourer's motive to exertion and care depends, of course, partly on the amount of his earnings; but it should be observed that the relation between the two is not one of simple proportion, as is implied in the statements of some economists; since if a man's earnings are already sufficient to satisfy all his keenly felt needs, the power of earning more by the same amount of labour may operate as an inducement to work less. It is more important to observe that the connexion between earnings and efforts depends greatly on the mode in which industry is organized. The connexion is most simply effective when a labourer works independently and owns the whole produce of his labour. So far as this simple arrangement is precluded by its incompatibility with the full advantages of co-operation, the labourer's interest in production will correspond to the precision with which, in dividing the produce of the combined labour, reward is proportioned to work. . . .

The foregoing analysis has led us more than once to consider differences in the moral qualities of labourers, as causes of variations in production. The economic importance of these may be briefly summed up thus; so far as it is made each labourer's interest to work his utmost, the more prudence and self-control he has, the more he will increase the wealth of the community; while again, the more he is actuated by sense of duty and wide public spirit, the more productive his labour will be under circumstances in which the coincidence between his own interest and that of society is wanting or obscure. The dishonest workman who scamps piece-work and is slothful if paid by the day, the dishonest manufacturer who employs labour and capital in producing the illusory semblance of utility, the tradesman who spoils his wares by adulterating them, all diminish produce. But besides self-interest on the one hand, and the influence exercised by common morality and regard for the general good on the other, we have to take special note of the narrower esprit de corps fostered by combinations of persons with similar interests; especially among the labourers in particular industries by such organizations as Trades-unions. So far as the rules of such associations, and the general opinion and sentiment which they produce or intensify, are directed towards the maintenance of a high standard of workmanship, their beneficial effect on production is obvious. In some cases, however, the rules and practices of Trades-unions have acted in an opposite direction, by resisting measures designed to economize labour; it being considered to be the interest of labourers in any particular industry that the field of employment should be as large as possible. . . .

6. In examining variations in the personal efficiency of individual labourers, we have been led to treat of the indirect effects of co-operation and association of workers, in developing skill and energy and esprit de corps. Let us now pass to consider the more obvious and important gains in productiveness of labour, due directly to the same association and co-operation.

We may notice first the more elementary advantages obtained by co-operation in its simplest form. There are many things which one man alone cannot do, but which are readily accomplished by the simultaneous action of several men. The raising of a given weight, for example, requires a certain force, which is obtained when the power of two men is simultaneously applied, but could not be obtained by any amount of successive effort on the part of a single man. But further, it is soon found that frequently little or no more labour is required to render a given service to several persons than is required to render it to one. "The fire and the water and the care requisite to prepare the food of one person will equally prepare the food of three or four. Consequently when two men have to do two different things, if in place of each performing his two several acts, they can with the same or nearly the same effort perform for their joint benefit each one act sufficient for the two, there is a clear saving of half their labour". Thus as simple co-operation increases power, Division of Employments, or as it has been called by economists since Adam Smith, "Division of Labour", economizes its use; and in this way division of employments would in many cases cause a most important gain, independently of any consequent increase of aptitude in the labourers whose functions are thus divided. Postal communication affords a striking example of this. There is not much room for increase of dexterity in the simple process of delivering a letter; the economic advantage of making letter-carrying a separate employment depends almost entirely on the great diminution of labour that each separate delivery requires, when one man delivers all the letters in the same street. In many cases, again, there is a great advantage in saving the time lost in passing from one set of actions to another; especially when the subdivision of employments is carried—as it is in many modern manufactures—so far that each worker has only to perform one very short series of actions, repeated as often as possible. Still by far the most striking advantage of the division of employments is the increased dexterity of the workmen; the vastly greater ease, rapidity, and accuracy which repetition gives to the performance of any act or set of acts. This I need hardly illustrate; since probably no paragraph in Adam Smith's works is so widely known as that in which he contrasts the number of pins that a man could make by himself with the number that he can make in combination with others he confines himself to a single part of the process,[1] and no point has been more abundantly exemplified by succeeding economists. And certainly the degree of additional efficiency that a worker can acquire, in work of a tolerably simple and uniform kind, under a highly developed system of divided employment, is greater than anyone without specific experience would have imagined. There is a further economic advantage in the fact that the training required to bring each labourer up to full efficiency tends to become shorter and less expensive as the work he has to do becomes limited and simplified. A more important gain than this last consists in the economy of aptitudes that becomes possible, through the continually increasing variety of employments; there is thus greater opportunity of setting different individuals to do what they can do best; especially all new gifts and talents become indefinitely more profitable to society when their possessor can be set free from all work except that for which he is specially gifted. We may notice as an instance of this that

---

[1] A. Smith, *An inquiry into the nature and causes of the Wealth of Nations*, London, 1893, p.4.—Ed.

the chief part of the knowledge, foresight, and power of complicated calculation, that are indispensable to the successful conduct of many industries, need only be possessed by the comparatively small number of persons required for the function of management. Finally, the division of employments enables mankind to utilise to the utmost not only the special qualities of human beings, but similarly the superior natural provision of the materials or instruments of production in different countries and districts. Through this division each article consumed by any one may be produced in the place where the labour of producing it is most effective, due allowance being made for the labour and time lost in carrying it to the consumer; and also for certain other disadvantages and risks which I shall presently notice.

The division of employment has different economic effects according as the co-operating workers are organized under one management, or under several different managements. So far as the simultaneous, or nearly simultaneous, combination of a number of different acts is required for the accomplishment of a single result, it is necessary that the labourers should be in one place, and obviously expedient that their work should be under the direction of one mind. And even when the operations to be performed on the same material, before it becomes a finished product, are merely successive, there is still a considerable economic advantage in uniting the labourers under one management, and, so far as is possible, either in one building or buildings nearly adjacent. For in the first place the most difficult and valuable kind of labour, that of management, is thus both economized and made more efficient in important respects; e.g. it is easier to adapt the product to the changing needs and tastes of society when all the required changes in production can be carried out under one direction; again, a more exact adjustment is possible of the supply of each kind of labour required, so that every class of producers can be kept in full work; and further, there is less loss of labour and time in carrying the product in different stages from one set of producers to another, and taking care of it till it is wanted.

For similar reasons, an economy of labour, especially the labour of management, as well as of the utility of buildings and other instruments, tends to be realized, generally speaking, by any considerable (if well adjusted) increase in the scale on which a business is organized. A large business, too, can afford various kinds of expenditure on the whole profitable, which are too costly or too uncertain for smaller concerns: such as the employment of elaborate machinery, or highly skilled and specialised labour, outlay for experiments, for obtaining information, &c. The extent of these advantages, however, varies greatly with the nature of the industry; and in estimating it with a view to practical conclusions, we have to compare it with the drawbacks that attend industry on a large scale, especially if the terms of co-operation are adjusted in the manner that is at present most common.

XII

R. Torrens, *An essay on the production of wealth*, London, 1821, Reprints of Economic Classics, New York, 1965, pp. 110-11, 120-3, 128, 133, 144-6.

In the last chapter we perceived, that there are no natural limits set to the effective powers of manufacturing industry; but that, on the contrary, an increase in the quantity of labour and capital applied, leads to the use of improved machinery, and to a more perfect subdivision of employment, and thus enables a given number of workmen to produce a greater quantity of goods. Now it is important to remark, that the reverse of this takes place with respect to agricultural industry; and that upon every increased quantity of labour and capital applied to the soil, we obtain a less proportional return. . . .

The principles, that each successive portion of capital which is employed either to bring in inferior soils, or to ameliorate those of a better quality, effects a less proportional addition to the produce than that which was effected by the capital previously applied; and that, in the progress of improvement we are constantly approaching the ultimate limits, beyond which cultivation can be neither extended nor heightened, lead to some of the most important conclusions in the science of political economy. We have already seen how intimately and inseparably one branch of industry is connected with another. In manufactures, each additional portion of labour and capital which is employed, produces not merely an equal, but a greater proportional effect than that which was previously applied; and where one hundred workmen can fabricate one thousand yards of cloth, there two hundred workmen, from being able to establish among themselves more perfect subdivisions of employment, will be able to fabricate, not merely two thousand yards, but some greater quantity; say two thousand five hundred yards. But though manufacturing industry has not in itself any natural limits, yet it is affected by those which nature has assigned to agriculture; and its advancement must necessarily be arrested when cultivation can be pushed no farther. Though additional portions of capital might still be capable of producing a higher proportional effect than those previously applied; yet, as the productive powers of agriculture became stationary, it would be impossible that such additional portions should be attained. Manufacturing capital consists of subsistence, materials, and instruments for abridging labour; and as these implements were formed by labour employed upon other materials, and supported by other subsistence, into subsistence and material all manufacturing capital ultimately resolves itself. Now, in a country that has advanced beyond the hunting or savage state, the greater part of material, and almost the whole of subsistence, is extracted from the soil. Hence, when no additional capital can be applied to the soil, no additional capital can be obtained for manufactures; and where the progress of agricultural industry is arrested, there the progress of manufacturing industry must be arrested also.

From the principles above stated, respecting the application of capital to land, it necessarily follows, that every improvement in agricultural science removes to a great distance the point at which the spread of tillage and the amelioration of the soil must cease. Everything which can with propriety be termed an improvement in agriculture, enables a given quantity of labour to raise a greater quantity of produce; or, what comes to the same thing, allows a given quantity of produce to be obtained by a less quantity of labour. . . .

Improvements in agricultural science, as throwing to a greater distance the point beyond which cultivation can be neither heightened nor extended, necessarily remove to a greater distance the point beyond which manufacturing capital can be no farther accumulated. . . .

I have before remarked that in the work of production, the different kinds of industry unite, and reciprocally augment each other's effective powers. As improvements in agriculture increase the quantity of capital which can be employed in manufactures; so improvements in manufactures remove to a greater distance the ultimate limits of agricultural prosperity, and admit of additional applications of capital to the soil. . . .

As population increases, and it becomes necessary to take in new soils, or to cultivate the old in a more expensive manner, it constantly requires an augmenting quantity of capital to raise the same quantity of produce; while, on the contrary, the advance of a country in wealth and population, by giving occasion to improvements in machinery, and to more perfect divisions of employment, enables the same number of hands, and consequently the same expenditure for food, to work up a greater quantity of material. From the conjoint operation of these causes, the value of raw produce is, in the progress of society, perpetually increasing with respect to manufactured goods; or to express the same thing in a different form, the value of manufactured goods is perpetually diminishing with respect to raw produce. But notwithstanding the operation of this two-fold cause, it is impossible that the period should ever arrive, when the manufacturer shall be unable to do more than add to the raw material the value of the subsistence which he consumes while at work. From the law of competition, the products of equal capital will be of equal value. If an agricultural capital equal to food for one hundred can raise a produce equal to food for one hundred and one, then a manufacturing capital equal to food for fifty, with material equivalent to food for fifty, will produce wrought goods which will be equal in value to food for one hundred and one; or, in other words, which will exceed in value the value of the food added to that of the material. While agricultural capital does more than replace itself, manufacturing capital will give products of more value than itself. But it is evident, that cultivation can never be permanently pushed so far that agricultural capital will be unable to replace itself; and that therefore the period never can arrive when manufacturing industry shall not be able to add to the raw material a value greater than that of the subsistence consumed in carrying it on. Thus again we find that the distinguishing tenet of the French Economists, namely, that manufacturing industry is unproductive of wealth, because the manufacturer does no more than add to the material the value of the subsistence consumed while at work, turns upon a gratuitous assumption which is not only unsupported by evidence, but which never had, and from the nature of things, never can have, any foundation in fact.

XIII

J. S. Mill, *Principles of Political Economy*, 7th ed., 1871, New Impression, Sir W. J. Ashley ed., London, 1920, pp. 183–6, 188, 189, 190–3.

I do not assert that the cost of production, and consequently the price, of agricultural produce, always and necessarily rises as population increases. It tends to do so; but the tendency may be, and sometimes is, even during long periods, held in check. The effect does not depend on a single principle, but on two antagonizing principles. There is another agency, in habitual antagonism to the law of diminishing return from land; and to the consideration of this we shall now proceed. It is no other than the progress of civilization. I use this general and somewhat vague expression, because the things to be included are so various, that hardly any term of a more restricted signification would comprehend them all.

Of these, the most obvious is the progress of agricultural knowledge, skill, and invention. Improved processes of agriculture are of two kinds: some enable the land to yield a greater absolute produce, without an equivalent increase of labour; others have not the power of increasing the produce, but have that of diminishing the labour and expense by which it is obtained. Among the first are to be reckoned the disuse of fallows, by means of the rotation of crops; and the introduction of new articles of cultivation capable of entering advantageously into the rotation. The change made in British agriculture towards the close of the last century, by the introduction of turnip husbandry, is spoken of as amounting to a revolution. These improvements operate not only by enabling the land to produce a crop every year, instead of remaining idle one year in every two or three to renovate its powers, but also by direct increase of its productiveness; since the great addition made to the number of cattle, by the increase of their food, affords more abundant manure to fertilize the corn lands. Next in order comes the introduction of new articles of food, containing a greater amount of sustenance, like the potato, or more productive species or varieties of the same plant, such as the Swedish turnip. In the same class of improvements must be placed a better knowledge of the properties of manures, and of the most effectual modes of applying them; the introduction of new and more powerful fertilizing agents, such as guano, and the conversion to the same purpose of substances previously wasted; inventions like subsoil-ploughing or tile draining; improvements in the breed or feeding of labouring cattle; augmented stock of the animals which consume and convert into human food what would otherwise be wasted; and the like. The other sort of improvements, those which diminish labour, but without increasing the capacity of the land to produce, are such as the improved construction of tools; the introduction of new instruments which spare manual labour, as the winnowing and threshing machines; a more skilful and economical application of muscular exertion, such as the introduction, so slowly accomplished in England, of Scotch ploughing, with two horses abreast of one man, instead of three or four horses in a team and two men, &c. These improvements do not add to the productiveness of the land, but they are equally calculated with the former to counteract the tendency in the cost of production of agricultural produce to rise with the progress of population and demand.

Analogous in effect to this second class of agricultural improvements, are improved means of communication. Good roads are equivalent to good tools. It is of no consequence whether the economy of labour takes place in extracting the produce from the soil, or in conveying it to the place where it is to be consumed. Not to say in addition, that the labour of cultivation itself is diminished by whatever lessens the cost of bringing manure from a distance, or facilitates the many operations of transport from place to place which occur within the bounds of the farm. Railways and canals are virtually a diminution of the cost of production of all things sent to market by them; and literally so of all those, the appliances and aids for producing which, they serve to transmit. By their means land can be cultivated, which could not otherwise have remunerated the cultivators without a rise of price. Improvements in navigation have, with respect to food or materials brought from beyond sea, a corresponding effect.

From similar considerations, it appears that many purely mechanical improvements, which have, apparently at least, no peculiar connexion with agriculture, nevertheless enable a given amount of food to be obtained with a smaller expenditure of labour. A great improvement in the process of smelting iron would tend to cheapen agricultural implements, diminish the cost of railroads, of waggons and carts, ships, and perhaps buildings, and many other things to which iron is not at present applied, because it is too costly; and would thence diminish the cost of production of food. The same effect would follow from an improvement in those processes of what may be termed manufacture to which the material of food is subjected after it is separated from the ground. The first application of wind or water power to grind corn tended to cheapen bread as much as a very important discovery in agriculture would have done; and any great improvement in the construction of corn-mills would have, in proportion, a similar influence. The effects of cheapening locomotion have been already considered. There are also engineering inventions which facilitate all great operations on the earth's surface. An improvement in the art of taking levels is of importance to draining, not to mention canal and railway making. The fens of Holland, and of some parts of England, are drained by pumps worked by the wind or by steam. Where canals of irrigation, or where tanks or embankments are necessary, mechanical skill is a great resource for cheapening production.

Those manufacturing improvements which cannot be made instrumental to facilitate, in any of its stages, the actual production of food, and therefore do not help to counteract or retard the diminution of the proportional return to labour from the soil, have, however, another effect, which is practically equivalent. What they do not prevent, they yet, in some degree, compensate for. The materials of manufacture being all drawn from the land, and many of them from agriculture, which supplies in particular the entire material of clothing; the general law of production from the land, the law of diminishing return, must in the last resort be applicable to manufacturing as well as to agricultural history. As population increases, and the power of the land to yield increased produce is strained harder and harder, any additional supply of material as well as of food, must be obtained by a more than proportionally increasing expenditure of labour. But the cost of the material forming generally a very small portion of the entire cost of the manufacture, the agricultural labour concerned in the production of manufactured goods is but a small fraction of the whole labour worked up in the community. All the rest of the labour tends constantly and strongly towards diminution, as the amount of production increases. Manufactures are vastly more susceptible than agriculture of mechanical improvements, and contrivances for saving labour; and it has already been seen how greatly the division of labour; and its skilful and economical distribution, depend on the extent of the market, and on the possibility of production in large masses. In manufactures, accordingly, the causes tending to increase the productiveness of industry, preponderate greatly over the one cause which tends to diminish it: and the increase of production, called forth by the progress of society, takes place, not at an increasing, but at a continually diminishing proportional cost. This fact has manifested itself in the progressive fall of the prices and values of almost every kind of manufactured goods during two centuries past; a fall accelerated by the mechanical inventions of the last seventy or eighty years, and susceptible of being prolonged and extended beyond any limit which it would be safe to specify.

Now it is quite conceivable that the efficiency of agricultural labour might be undergoing, with the increase of produce, a gradual diminution; that the price of food, in consequence, might be progressively rising, and an ever growing proportion of the population might be needed to raise food for the whole; while yet the productive power of labour in all other branches of industry might be so rapidly augmenting, that the required amount of labour could be spared from manufactures, and nevertheless a greater produce be obtained, and the aggregate wants of the community be on the whole better supplied, than before. The benefit might even extend to the poorest class. The increased cheapness of clothing and lodging might make up to them for the augmented cost of their food.

There is, thus, no possible improvement in the arts of production which does not in one or another mode exercise an antagonist influence to the law of diminishing return to agricultural labour. Nor is it only industrial improvements which have this effect. Improvements in government, and almost every kind of moral and social advancement, operate in the same manner. . . .

Before pointing out the principal inferences to be drawn from the nature of the two antagonist forces by which the productiveness of agricultural industry is determined, we must observe that what we have said of agriculture is true, with little variation, of the other occupations which it represents; of all the arts which extract materials from the globe. Mining industry, for example, usually yields an increase of produce at a more than proportional increase of expense. It does worse, for even its customary annual produce requires to be extracted by a greater and greater expenditure of labour and capital.

As a mine does not reproduce the coal or ore taken from it, not only are all mines at last exhausted, but even when they as yet show no signs of exhaustion, they must be worked at a continually increasing cost; shafts must be sunk deeper, galleries driven farther, greater power applied to keep them clear of water; the produce must be lifted from a greater depth, or conveyed a greater distance. The law of diminishing return applied therefore to mining, in a still more unqualified sense than to agriculture: but the antagonizing agency, that of improvements in production, also applies in a still greater degree. Mining operations are more susceptible of mechanical improvements than agricultural: the first great application of the steam-engine was to mining; and there are unlimited possibilities of improvements in the chemical processes by which the metals are extracted. There is another contingency, of no unfrequent occurrence, which avails to counter-balance the progress of all existing mines towards exhaustion: this is, the discovery of new ones, equal or superior in richness.

To resume; all natural agents which are limited in quantity, are not only limited in their ultimate productive power, but, long before that power is stretched to the utmost, they yield to any additional demands on progressively harder terms. This law may however be suspended, or temporarily controlled, by whatever adds to the general power of mankind over nature; and especially by any extension of their knowledge, and their consequent command, of the properties and powers of natural agents. . . .

From the preceding exposition it appears that the limit to the increase of production is two-fold; from deficiency of capital, or of land. Production comes to a pause, either because the effective desire of accumulation is not sufficient to give rise to any further increase of capital, or because, however disposed the possessors of surplus income may be to save a portion of it, the limited land at the disposal of the community does not permit additional capital to be employed with such a return as would be an equivalent to them for their abstinence. . . .

But there are other countries, and England is at the head of them, in which neither the spirit of industry nor the effective desire of accumulation need any encouragement; where the people will toil hard for a small remuneration, and save much for a small profit; where, though the general thriftiness of the labouring class is much below what is desirable, the spirit of accumulation in the more prosperous part of the community requires abatement rather than increase. In these countries there would never be any deficiency of capital, if its increase were never checked or brought to a stand by too great a diminution of its returns, It is the tendency of the returns to a progressive diminution, which causes the increase of production to be often attended with a deterioration in the condition of the producers; and this tendency, which would in time put an end to increase of production altogether, is a result of the necessary and inherent conditions of production from the land.

In all countries which have passed beyond a rather early stage in the progress of agriculture, every increase in the demand for food, occasioned by increased population, will always, unless there is a simultaneous improvement in production, diminish the share which on a fair division would fall to each individual. An increased production, in default of unoccupied tracts of fertile land, or of fresh improvements tending to cheapen commodities, can never be obtained but by increasing the labour in more than the same proportion. The population must either work harder, or eat less, or obtain their usual food by sacrificing a part of their other customary comforts. Whenever this necessity is postponed, notwithstanding an increase of population, it is because the improvements which facilitate production continue progressive; because the contrivances of mankind for making their labour more effective keep up an equal struggle with nature, and extort fresh resources from her reluctant powers as fast as human necessities occupy and engross the old.

From this, results the important corollary that the necessity of restraining population is not, as many persons believe, peculiar to a condition of great inequality of property. A greater number of people cannot, in any given state of civilization, be collectively so well provided for as a smaller. The niggardliness of nature, not the injustice of society, is the cause of the penalty attached to over-population. An unjust distribution of wealth does not even aggravate the evil, but, at most causes it to be somewhat earlier felt. It is in vain to say, that all mouths which the increase of mankind calls into existence, bring with them hands. The new mouths require as much food as the old ones, and the hands do not produce as much. If all instruments of production were held in joint property by the whole people, and the produce divided with perfect equality among them, and if, in a society thus constituted, industry were as energetic and the produce as ample as at present, there would be enough to make all the existing population extremely comfortable; but when that population had doubled itself, as, with the existing habits of the people, under such an encouragement, it undoubtedly would in little more than twenty years, what would then be their condition? Unless the arts of production were in the same time improved in an almost unexampled degree, the inferior soils which must be resorted to, and the more laborious and scantily remunerative cultivation which must be employed on the superior soils, to procure food for so much larger a population, would, by an insuperable necessity, render every individual in the community poorer than before. If the population continued to increase at the same rate, a time would soon arrive when no one would have more than mere necessaries, and, soon after, a time when no one would have a sufficiency of those, and the further increase of population would be arrested by death.

Whether, at the present or any other time, the produce of industry proportionally to the labour employed, is increasing or diminishing, and the average condition of the people improving or deteriorating, depends upon whether population is advancing faster than improvement, or improvement than population. After a degree of density has been attained, sufficient to allow the principal benefits of combination of labour, all further increase tends in itself to mischief, so far as regards the average condition of the people; but the progress of improvement has a counteracting operation, and allows of increased numbers without any deterioration, and even consistently with a higher average of comfort. Improvement must here be understood in a wide sense, including not only new industrial inventions, or an extended use of those already known, but improvements in institutions, education, opinions, and human affairs generally, provided they tend, as almost all improvements do, to give new motives or new facilities to production. If the productive powers of the country increase as rapidly as advancing numbers call for an augmentation of produce, it is not necessary to obtain that augmentation by the cultivation of soils more sterile than the worst already under culture, or by applying additional labour to the old soils at a diminished advantage; or at all events this loss of power is compensated by the increased efficiency with which, in the progress of improvement, labour is employed in manufactures. In one way or the other, the increased population is provided for, and all are as well off as before. But if the growth of human power over nature is suspended or slackened, and population does not slacken its increase; if, with only the existing command over natural agencies, those agencies are called upon for an increased produce; this greater produce will not be afforded to the increased population, without either demanding on the average a greater effort from each, or on the average reducing each to a smaller ration out of the aggregate produce.

As a matter of fact, at some periods the progress of population has been the more rapid of the two, at others that of improvement. In England during a long interval preceding the French Revolution, population increased slowly; but the progress of improvement, at least in agriculture, would seem to have been still slower, since though nothing occurred to lower the value of the precious metals, the price of corn rose considerably, and England, from an exporting, became an importing country. This evidence, however, is short of conclusive, inasmuch as the extraordinary number of abundant seasons during the first half of the century, not continuing during the last, was a cause of increased price in the later period, extrinsic to the ordinary progress of society. Whether during the same period improvements in manufactures, or diminished cost of imported commodities, made amends for the diminished productiveness of labour on the land, is uncertain. But ever since the great mechanical inventions of Watt, Arkwright, and their contemporaries, the return to labour has probably increased as fast as the population; and would have outstripped it, if that very augmentation of return had not called forth an additional portion of the inherent power of multiplication in the human species. During the twenty or thirty years last elapsed (1857), so rapid has been the extension of improved processes of agriculture, that even the land yields a greater produce in proportion to the labour employed; the average price of corn had become decidedly lower, even before the repeal of the corn laws had so materially lightened, for the time being, the pressure of population upon production. But though improvement may during a certain space of time keep up with, or even surpass, the actual increase of population, it assuredly never comes up to the rate of increase of which population is capable; and nothing could have prevented a general deterioration in the condition of the human race, were it not that population has in fact been restrained. Had it been restrained still more, and the same improvements taken place, there would have been a larger dividend than there now is, for the nation or the species at large. The new ground wrung from nature by the improvements would not have been all used up in the support of mere numbers. Though the gross produce would not have been so great, there would have been a greater produce per head of the population.

XIV

A. Marshall, *Principles of Economics*, vol. I, 3rd ed., London, 1895, pp. 397–400.

In other words, we say broadly that while the part which Nature plays in production conforms to the law of diminishing return, the part which man plays conforms to the Law of Increasing Return, which may be stated thus:—An increase of capital and labour leads generally to an improved organization; and therefore in those industries which are not engaged in raising raw produce it generally gives a return increased more than in proportion; and further this improved organization tends to diminish or even override any increased resistance which Nature may offer to raising increased amounts of raw produce. If the actions of the laws of increasing and diminishing return are balanced we have the Law of Constant Return, and an increased produce is obtained by labour and sacrifice increased just in proportion.

For the two tendencies towards increasing and diminishing return press constantly against one another. In the production of wheat and wool, for instance, the latter tendency has almost exclusive sway in an old country, which cannot import freely. In turning the wheat into flour, or the wool into blankets, an increase in the aggregate volume of production brings some new economies, but not many; for the trades of grinding wheat and making blankets are already on so great a scale that any new economies that they may attain are more likely to be the result of new inventions than of improved organization. In a country however in which the blanket trade is but slightly developed, these latter may be important; and then it may happen that an increase in the aggregate production of blankets diminishes the proportionate difficulty of manufacturing by just as much as it increases that of raising the raw material. In that case the actions of the laws of diminishing and of increasing return would just neutralize one another; and blankets would conform to the law of constant return. But in most of the more delicate branches of manufacturing, where the cost of raw material counts for little, and in most of the modern transport industries the law of increasing return acts almost unopposed.

We shall long be occupied with the details and the limitations of the broad truths which have just been sketched out: but before closing the present Book we may stay a little to consider their bearing on the problem of the pressure of population on the means of subsistence. We are not yet in a position to deal with it thoroughly, but there is some advantage in taking a rapid survey of it at this early stage.

Our discussion of the character and organization of industry taken as a whole tends to show that an increase in the volume of labour causes in general, other things being equal, a more than proportionate increase in the total efficiency of labour. But we must not forget that other things may not be equal. The increase of numbers may be accompanied by more or less general adoption of unhealthy and enervating habits of life in overcrowded towns. Or it may have started badly, outrunning the material resources of the people, causing them with imperfect appliances to make excessive demands on the soil; and so to call forth the stern action of the law of diminishing return as regards raw produce, without having the power of minimizing its effects: having thus begun with poverty, an increase in numbers may go on to its too frequent consequences in that weakness of character which unfits a people for developing a highly organized industry.

All this and more may be granted, and yet it remains true that the collective efficiency of a people with a given average of individual strength and energy may increase more than in proportion to their numbers. If they can for a time escape from the pressure of the law of diminishing return by importing food and other raw produce on easy terms; if their wealth is not consumed in great wars, and increases at least as fast as their numbers; and if they avoid habits of life that would enfeeble them; then every increase in their numbers is likely for the time to be accompanied by a more than proportionate increase in their power of obtaining material goods.

For it enables them to secure the many various economies of specialized skill and specialized machinery, of localized industries and production on a large scale: it enables them to have increased facilities of communication of all kinds; while the very closeness of their neighbourhood diminishes the expense of time and effort involved in every sort of traffic between them, and gives them new opportunities of getting social enjoyments and the comforts and luxuries of culture in every form. It is true that against this must be set the growing difficulty of finding solitude and quiet and even fresh air. This deduction is a weighty one; but there may still remain a balance of good.

Taking account of the fact that an increasing density of population generally brings with it access to new social enjoyments we may give a rather broader scope to this statement and say:—An increase of population accompanied by an equal increase in the material sources of enjoyment and aids to production is likely to lead to a more than proportionate increase in the aggregate of enjoyment of all kinds; provided firstly, an adequate supply of raw produce can be obtained without great difficulty, and secondly there is no such overcrowding as causes physical and moral vigour to be impaired by the want of fresh air and light and of healthy and joyous recreation for the young.

The accumulated wealth of civilized countries is at present growing faster than the population: and though it may be true that the wealth per head would increase somewhat faster if the population did not increase quite so fast; yet as a matter of fact an increase of population is likely to continue to be accompanied by a more than proportionate increase of the material aids to production: and in England at the present time, with easy access to abundant foreign supplies of raw material, an increase of population is accompanied by a more than proportionate increase of the means of satisfying human wants other than the need for light, fresh air, &c. Much of this increase is however attributable not to the increase of industrial efficiency but to the increase of wealth by which it is accompanied: and therefore it does not necessarily benefit those who have no share in that wealth. And further, England's foreign supplies of raw produce may at any time be checked by changes in the trade regulations of other countries, and may be almost cut off by a great war, while the naval and military expenditure which would be necessary to make the country fairly secure against this last risk, would appreciably diminish the benefits that she derives from the action of the law of increasing return.

XV

E. Cannan, *Wealth, a brief explanation of the causes of economic welfare*, 3rd ed., London, 1928, pp. 56–62

At any given time (or if the reader prefers, circumstances remaining unchanged) increase of labour up to a certain point is attended by increasing proportionate returns (called for short increasing returns) and beyond that point further increase of labour is attended by diminishing proportionate returns (called for short diminishing returns). Mankind cannot produce an unlimited amount of calico more than an unlimited amount of wheat. It would be impossible to produce more than a certain amount however many persons were engaged upon the production: and long before that amount was reached, the amount of additional labour would begin to diminish. At any given time, or which comes to the same thing, knowledge and circumstances remaining the same, there is what may be called a point of maximum return, when the amount of labour is such that both an increase and a decrease in it would diminish proportionate returns. It is a crude and barbarous idea of agriculture which represents it as almost entirely dependent upon original fertility of soil and foot-pounds of human muscular energy, and as scarcely affected at all by the world-wide co-operation of mankind which provides it with appropriate tools and suitable seed, and combines the products of different regions so as to make them wholesome or palatable to the consumer.

The most we can say in contrasting agriculture and manufacture is that the advantages of producing a large aggregate quantity and therefore the advantages of a large population to produce and consume the large quantity are more obvious in manufacture than in agriculture. If we measure returns from the starting-point of nil suggested by the historical progress of population and assumed by Malthus, West, and Ricardo in 1814, we can say that in both agriculture and manufacture returns increase up to a certain point and beyond that point they decrease. If we can start from what I have called the point of maximum return, we can say of manufacture as well as of agriculture that returns diminish as we move in either direction from that point.

If we suppose all difficulties about the measurement of the returns to all industries taken together to be somehow overcome, we can see that at any given time, knowledge and circumstances remaining the same, just as there is a point of maximum return in each industry, so there must be in all industries taken together. If population is not large enough to bring all industry up to this point, returns will be less than they might be; if, on the other hand, population is so great that the point has been passed, returns are again less than they might be.

The course which the development of theory on this subject has taken has led to the use of a great deal of very unsatisfactory phraseology which ought to be discarded. Writers have said that "the law of diminishing returns had not come into operation", when they only meant that returns had not begun to diminish, and they have spoken of the law "undergoing a temporary supersession" when they meant only that returns had left off diminishing for a time. They have talked of "commodities which obey the law of diminishing returns" when they meant commodities the supply of which could not at the moment be increased without a diminution of returns, and of "commodities which obey the law of increasing returns" when they meant commodities of which some increase of supply would be at the moment accompanied by increased returns. They have even imagined an intermediate class "obeying the law of constant returns". All these expressions involve misuse of the term "law". A scientific law should be true at all times and places, and should not be liable to "temporary supersessions" or failures to come into operation, nor capable of being suddenly replaced by a contrary law. No one says that the law of gravity had not come into operation in Newton's garden until the apple broke from its stalk, nor that the law would have undergone temporary supersession if Newton had caught the apple as it fell. Nor do we say that a falling balloon is "subject to another law, that of rising bodies", while a balloon which remains at the same level is "subject to the law of constant height".

If we want to preserve the phrase "diminishing returns" we must take the point of maximum return as the starting-point, and say that returns diminish in either direction, all commodities or industries being always and everywhere subject to this "law of diminishing returns".

The Optimum, or best possible Population

Great caution must be exercised in applying the idea of a point of maximum return to the question what is the most desirable population. In the first place, it is very important not to fall into the error of supposing that the point of maximum return remains permanently fixed, either for particular industries or for industry taken as a whole. The position of the point is perpetually being altered by the progress of knowledge and other changes. The discovery of the principle of rotation of crops and the invention of steam locomotion on rails, coupled with the provision of the requisite appliances, not only made increase of population possible without diminution of returns and consequent deterioration of wealth, but also made or tended to make that increase desirable. These changes shifted the point of maximum return, pushing it farther along in the direction favourable to large population. Hence it is quite possible that the world was over-populated in some past age when there was not a tithe of the present number of people on the globe, and that all the same it is not over-populated now. In the meantime the point of maximum return may have been shifted.

Secondly, we must remember that population is not so agile in its movements as to be able to follow every shifting of the point of maximum return immediately. We can easily imagine some change in knowledge shifting the point rather suddenly, while it is obvious that the number of living mankind cannot be altered except slowly by an alteration in the balance of births and deaths, and that an increase of workers will only follow from an increase of births after an interval of more than a decade, while deaths cannot be accelerated or retarded except in so far as the moral or religious principle that human life must be preserved as long as possible is not maintained in practice.

Consequently it is useless to condemn the population of any one point of time as too great or too small simply because if it were smaller or larger the returns to industry would be greater at that time. The population of any moment is dependent for its magnitude on the population of the past, and will in its turn affect the population of the future. We have no right to isolate it and pick it out in preference to others. Very probably it could not be different from what it is without causing the past or future population to diverge so much more from the optimum or best possible that the result on all the periods taken together would be worse than the actual state of things.

So what we have to look for is not the best population at any particular moment without reference to what has gone before and what is to follow after, but the best at all the moments taken together. In other words, we have to treat the ideal or optimum in regard to population as being the right movement (i.e. increase or decrease) of population rather than define it in reference to one particular point of time. The right movement is that which will give the largest returns to industry in the long run, the interests of the people of all the generations being taken into the account.

Thirdly, the general population theory should not be rashly applied to national or other local or tribal subdivisions of mankind. Of course it could be applied without any modification at all to a subdivision which was entirely isolated from all the others, but in so far as movement of men and goods is possible between a subdivision and the outside world, it must take its share in the effects of the general movement. The smaller it is and the greater the mobility between it and the others, the more its position approximates to that of the individual family, which is unable to make returns to industry appreciably higher or lower by more or less rapid propagation.

XVI

United Nations, *The determinants and consequences of population trends*, New York, 1953, pp. 194, 194–5, 200, 201, 202, 202–3, 203, 203–4, 206, 207, 208, 209.

1. The amount of labour available for the production of economic goods in a society is determined by the variety of demographic, economic and social factors, the most important of which are those associated with the size and structure of the population. Long-term trends in fertility, mortality and migratory movements determine the size of the population and its composition with respect to sex and age, and establish the maximum limits of the number of persons who can participate in economic activity. Other demographic factors, such as the urban-rural composition of the population and the proportions of women who are married and have responsibility for the care of children also play an important part in determining the proportions of the population which will be represented in certain age groups in the labour force. A large variety of economic and social factors, among them the type and organization of production, level of income, and the relative values placed on competing economic and non-economic roles, are also believed to be influential in deciding how many of the total number of persons at a given age contribute to the labour supply.

2. The size of the economically active population alone is not a complete measure of the labour supply, since it takes no account of the efficiency of workers or the differing amounts of time workers are willing to contribute to economic activities. The amount of working time offered per member of the economically active population is influenced by demographic factors, since women, young people who may still be attending school, and older workers are, on the average, less likely than other workers to work full-time. Likewise, the sex and age composition of the work force may affect its efficiency. The number of workers available

for employment is, however, the principal element in the labour supply. . . .

5. As noted above, the size of the economically, active population, which is the principal element in labour supply, depends to a large extent on the size of the total population. Where the population is growing at a rapid rate, this growth is the most important factor affecting change in the supply of labour. This relationship is so obvious that economists have sometimes ignored the possibility of changes in the ratio of the economically active to the total population, and have treated population changes as if they were identical with changes in labour supply. For more precise analyses, however, account must be taken of other factors, among them the age and sex structure of the population, which have an important bearing on the size of the economically active population. . . .

33. The size of the total population and its composition with respect to age and sex are not the only determinants of the size of the economically active population. This is evidenced by the fact that within specific age-sex groups the ratios of active persons to the total number of persons in the group change with time, and vary among different countries and different regions of the same country. The proportion of men in the age groups from approximately 25 to 60 years who participate in economic activities remains fairly constant, since men of these ages by tradition pursue gainful occupations, and the size of the male labour force is determined to a great extent directly by the number of men in this age class. Among women, young people and older workers, however, the proportions in the labour force are influenced by many social and economic factors.

34. Characteristic trends in the percentages of economically active persons among women, young people at the ages of transition from school to employment, and men at the ages of retirement have been observed in many parts of the world. So far as the levels of the percentages for different countries are concerned, the statistics are not comparable, being greatly affected by differences in coverage, for example, with respect to persons working without pay in a family farm or business and persons engaging both in gainful work and in non-gainful activities such as home housework or attendance at school. Even within a country, the trends shown over periods of time

must be interpreted with caution because of changes in concepts or census procedures which might affect the results.

35. In many industrialized countries the percentage of women engaged in economic activities has been increasing. . . .

36. This tendency towards increasing representation of women in the labour force is not universal, even in industrialized countries. . . .

39. Long term declines in the percentage of young people under 20 years of age who engage in economic activities reflect a tendency for young people to remain in school longer before entering the labour market. . . .

40. The tendency to enter gainful employment at a later age has been accompanied, in industrial countries, by a progressive lowering of the age at which men cease working, with the result that the span of their working life has been shortened at both ends. . . .

41. Urbanization has been shown to influence the trend of employment among women, the age at which young people begin work, and the age at retirement. In agricultural communities where farming is done in family enterprises, women and children commonly share, at least to some extent, with men the work of producing goods for home consumption or for the market. There is also a tendency for men to work to a more advanced age in agricultural areas. This participation of family members in the work of breadwinners is also characteristic, in a lesser degree, of communities where handicrafts and small-scale manufacturing are carried on within or near the home. On the other hand, in highly urbanized communities where production is centred in large-scale establishments, the locus of economic activities is usually outside the home. Gainful employment for city women, therefore, tends to conflict with their long-established role as home-makers and mothers. Where emphasis is placed on the fulfilment of this traditional role, few women, and particularly few married women, in the cities may be found in the economically active population. Thus urbanization may, under some conditions, tend to reduce the female labour force. It appears likely that it did so in many

Western countries during the nineteenth century, and that it may still be having that effect at present in some parts of the world where women contribute a large share of the labour supply in agriculture but a relatively small share in urban occupations.

42. On the other hand, urbanization may have the opposite effect in countries where the idea of women leaving the home is widely accepted and where there is an increasing demand for their services in a broad occupational field. . . .

44. Children in rural areas customarily work on the family farm even during the years when they are attending school, and they may often put in substantial amounts of work during the peak agricultural seasons. In the cities, however, part-time or seasonal work for children of school age is generally difficult to find and their employment for wages is generally restricted by law. Their economic activities are therefore likely to be narrowly limited until they reach the age at which it is legal and customary for them to become full-time members of the labour force.

45. A number of factors associated with urbanization tend to reduce the age at which persons withdraw from the labour force. "In agriculture, the handicrafts, and the keeping of small shops the process of retiring can be gradual and adjusted to the weakening faculties of the individual. As the economy has become more complete with larger and less flexible units and more narrowly specialized occupations, individuals tend to be employed fully or not at all. It becomes difficult to find a place for the person who fails to keep the general pace. Moreover, rigid prescriptions that ignore the capacities of the individual tend to lower the age of retirement." The decline in the proportion of independent entrepreneurs which results both from the declining relative importance of agriculture as a field of employment and from changes in the average size of urban enterprises, tends to limit men's chance of continuing work when they grow old.

46. Another demographic factor which has a bearing on the extent to which women participate in economic activities is the level of fertility. Responsibility for the care of children tends to interfere with the gainful employment of women, particularly in urban areas

where women must typically leave home if they wish to work at gainful occupations. . . .

47. The decline in birth rates has been closely associated with the process of urbanization and industrialization and with increasing employment of women outside the home. Most working wives in urbanized countries have few children and many have none. . . .

49. A number of explanations have been advanced for the fact that declining birth rates have coincided with rising employment rates among women. Married women may seek employment outside the home because they have no responsibility or only a light responsibility for child care; they may refrain from bearing children in order to be free to work; or their employment and low birth rate may be regarded as means whereby they seek to improve their economic position. To the extent that the first explanation applies, a falling birth rate in an urbanized country has a tendency to increase the number of economically active women.

50. It has been pointed out that it is chiefly the presence of any young children rather than the number of such children which is an obstacle to the mother's taking a job. In the United States it has been shown that the proportion of married women having no children has not increased to the same extent that the birth rate has fallen; in fact, the reduction in fertility has taken place mainly through a decline in the average number of children borne by women. The conclusion reached is that declining fertility has played a significant but not a major role in raising the percentages of economically active women.

51. The relationship between the size of the economically active and the size of the total population is determined by many variables in the social and economic setting, in addition to the demographic variables discussed up to this point The relevant social and economic factors are too many to list; among the most important are: (*a*) the standards of behaviour which are accepted by the community, with reference to the status of women as home-makers or potential breadwinners, the age at which young people should leave school and go to work, and the age at which workers should retire; (*b*) the levels of income and employment; (*c*) the health of the population,

in so far as it affects the proportion of persons who are physically able to work at various ages; (*d*) the technology and structure of the economy, in so far as they affect the relative demand for the types of labour which can be supplied by children and by men and women of various ages; (*e*) those aspects of the mores and of the institutional structure of society which affect the weight of home-makers' domestic duties and the amount of time which they have available for outside activities. . . .

64. The same demographic economic and social factors which determine the size of the economically active population also affect its composition with respect to age and sex. It has been shown, for example, that trends in the age composition of the active population usually parallel trends in the age composition of the population, though they do not necessarily conform exactly. The sex ratio of the economically active population is, on the other hand, mainly determined by factors other than the proportion of women in the population of working age. . . .

71. As indicated at the beginning of this chapter, changes in the size of the economically active population are not equivalent to variations in the supply of labour, since the latter is affected also by the efficiency of the workers and by the amount of time they offer to spend at work, in terms of hours per day or week and days or weeks per year. Both working efficiency and the amount of time offered per member of the active population are influenced to some extent by demographic factors.

72. The average number of hours per day or week and the average number of days or weeks per year that members of the economically active population are willing to work differ among men and women in different age groups. Many of the women, youths and aged persons who engage in economic activities are available only for part-time or seasonal work. Thus a reduction in the number of children or aged persons in the economically active population makes a less than proportionate reduction in the supply of labour. Likewise, an increase in the number of working women means a less than proportionate increment to the labour supply. . . .

73. The amount of working time offered by members of the active

population may also be affected by the state of health of the population. The health of the working population bears a relation to its age composition, since sickness rates are generally higher among older persons. . . .

74. The distributions of the economically active population by age and sex and by occupation and industry of workers are believed to have effects on the efficiency of the workers, but the available statistical analyses are inadequate to clearly establish the nature of the relationship. . . .

80. Education is of great importance as a means of improving efficiency in many lines of work. Advances in the average educational level which young people attain before going to work are facilitated by the aging of the population, which implies a reduction in the relative number of young people to be educated. Health also has an important relation to efficiency; in areas where large proportions of the people are afflicted by debilitating diseases, improvement in the health status of the population may be the most rapid means of increasing the efficiency of labour. . . .

84. Numerous studies available for most of the highly industrial countries provide a basis for understanding the effects of population trends on the size and demographic characteristics of the economically active population. Such studies have been made possible by the availability of census data on the economically active population, classified by important demographic characteristics such as age and sex, and covering a sufficient period of time to establish a pattern of long-term trends. However, not all of the relevant relationships have been fully explored even where statistics are available, and certain types of analyses have been handicapped by the lack of comparable data for different census years, owing either to changes in concepts or to improvements in the coverage of certain groups. Labour force projections have been calculated for a few countries on the basis of future population estimates by age and sex, and past trends in the proportions of economically active persons within these particular age-sex groups.

85. The existing studies of the relationship between various non-demographic factors and the size of the economically active popu-

lation are not adequate, even for the highly developed countries. In many cases the types of statistical data required to evaluate the influence of these other factors are lacking, while in other cases the available data for such analyses have not been fully exploited. The association between urbanization and the size and composition of the labour force has not been clearly demonstrated. Further investigations of the relationships between fertility and the proportions of economically active women in various countries is also needed. Existing studies show a correlation between declining birth rates and rising employment rates among women, but this relationship has not been fully explained. The long-run effect of rising per capita income on the labour supply has not yet been established. The available analyses of the short-run effect of income changes on the labour supply are likewise not conclusive. In particular, the behaviour of the labour force during periods of economic boom and economic depression requires additional study. Other important fields which have received little attention to date are the long-time effects of improvements in public health and education upon the size and composition of the labour supply. . . .

87. Adequate statistical evidence of the influence of demographic factors on aspects of the labour supply other than the size of the economically active population is lacking. Little is known of the amount of working time offered by workers, though this factor, as well as the number of workers, has an important bearing on the total quantity of labour supply.

88. There is as yet little statistical basis for the theories advanced by various writers regarding the ways in which the efficiency of workers is related to their demographic characteristics. Measures of the capacities and performances of persons in different age groups are generally lacking, and it is difficult to obtain the data for these analyses even in statistically advanced countries. The relationship of demographic changes to other factors affecting the efficiency of the labour force—notably health and education—also needs more study.

XVII

J. D. Chambers, *The Vale of Trent 1670–1800*, Economic History Review, Supplement 3, 1957, pp. 2–5.

The progress of England in the eighteenth century towards an industrial society is a subject of more than academic interest. Now that economists are trying to persuade so-called 'backward economies' to take the same road, they sometimes look to England to see how it was done in the home of industrialism two hundred years ago. It is the less easy to understand today, for it was achieved not through planners—or policemen—but rather in spite of them. It was the outcome of free choice within a context of law and custom of long historical growth, and can be described as an industrial revolution by consent—a phenomenon which grows more significant as it recedes in time.

As Professor Ashton has recently shown, England was a nation of individualists busily pursuing their own interests in their own way, and thereby unconsciously foreshadowing the ideal prescription for the advancement of the wealth of nations. They had, he says, one characteristic in common: a refusal to conform;[1] but enough of them accepted the unspoken assumptions of an essentially economic society to enable them to overcome the inertia which, both then and now, has always provided one of the most stubborn obstacles to economic change. Their activities, however, were circumscribed by physical limitation of transport; and until the last quarter of the eighteenth century, when roads and canals had established a national market even for such an intractable commodity as coal, it is possible to distinguish regional areas with a recognizable economic life of their own.

Such a region was the Vale of Trent, with its resources of agricultural and mineral products forming a basis of exchange between east and west, and its central waterway, the Trent with its

---

[1] T. S. Ashton, *An Economic History of England, the Eighteenth Century* (1955) p. 17.

tributaries, providing a medium for this exchange and for the entrepot traffic with the outside world. By virtue of its varied resources, topography and geographical position, it reflected most of the contemporary currents of economic change, and it presents the same kinds of questions with which the student of the national economy is confronted, but in a less complex form and in a simpler setting.

This approach to a common set of problems has advantages and disadvantages. The regional historian is closer to the field of action; he can see, and may know intimately, the places where the events of the story took place; through the proxy of his own not-so-distant ancestors, he may even have participated in them; and since the volume of evidence is on a regional and not a national scale, he can examine, or at least sample, all that is physically accessible. Here lie both the strength and the weakness of the regional approach. Such evidence does not include the data of the movement of trade, or of the money market or of industrial production: on the other hand it is most abundant exactly where the resources of national economic history are most deficient, on the demographic side. The parish registers provide an almost unbroken series of baptisms, burials and marriages for the whole area for the whole period; there are, in addition, collections of marriage certificates and allegations in which brides usually gave their ages and sometimes their occupations, and bridegrooms gave both. Evidence on this scale and of this quality cannot be ignored, but owing to its inherent imperfections it can only give approximate results. For this reason the present enquiry has been mainly confined to the discovery of tendencies rather than to the calculation of quantities. Little light has been thrown, for instance, on the vexed question of the changes in the birth and death rates and the relation between them. The procedure of applying a uniform ratio of correction by which baptisms and burials could be turned into births and deaths was rejected in view of the diverse characteristics of the agricultural, industrial and urban centres studied, the unreliability of the population estimates, and the fluctuating influence of migration and non-conformity to which they were subject. The records of non-conformity have been consulted as far as they exist; and with this correction, the figures of the registers and transcripts have been used to present comparable burial, baptism and marriage rates on the basis of estimates of population made by contemporaries at different points of the period. They re-emphasize the familiar phenomenon of a very high birth rate being maintained alongside a falling death rate, but they leave the question of the change in the age structure unanswered. It may be inferred that the fall of the death rate of children was beginning to take place from the middle of the century, but to verify this statistically would have involved a laborious search beyond the scope of this enquiry. The chief purpose served by the use of parish records in this particular study has been to show the general trend of population movement by reference to the changing relation between baptisms and burials in what are believed to be representative groups of agricultural, industrial and urban parishes.

The main result of the enquiry is to suggest that economic and demographic growth within the region was subject to a recognizable ebb and flow falling into three main phases: the first a period of expansion in both from about 1690 to 1720: the second a period of deceleration on the economic side and, for certain years, of actual retreat on the demographic side until perhaps the 1740's: and the third, a period of activity in all directions on such a scale and with such sustained strength that it presages the birth of a new age.

In an economy in which labour was a vitally important factor of production, and (in spite of under-employment and mass poverty) in which 'there was generated a pressure tending to push up wages', it is difficult to believe that the correspondence which has been noted between the movements of economic and demographic change is altogether fortuitous. A sustained improvement in labour supply may, for instance, have contributed to the success of the framework knitting industry in its struggle with hand knitting of cheap worsted hose at the end of the seventeenth century. At any rate, cheap labour was certainly among the attractions which drew capital from London and helped to establish the industry in the Midlands at this time; and it is not without significance that it took root most firmly in the villages to the west of the country where an abundance of waste land had already attracted unusually large village populations. A thickening of population seems to have been a factor in establishing a labour-saving device at the expense of a home industry for a product that was in general demand, a not unreasonable inference in view of the expanding nature of the economy at that time. Another notable advance of the period, the famous silk mill at Derby, the prototype of all subsequent power textile units, depended upon the availability of 300 workers from the immediate neighbourhood as well as the £30,000 of merchant capital from London; and the navigation of the Derwent, the opening of the first stretch of the Great North Road turnpike and the transference of land tax from landlord to tenant are consistent with the demographic advance of which the records give more than a hint.

The decade 1720–30 started with a check to population growth and ended with a retreat; the epidemic of 1727–30 is an event of great importance, and recovery was retarded in the areas under review by the visitations of 1736, 1741–2, 1747–8 which, as far as the town population was concerned, were even more destructive especially of the lives of children. A succession of good harvests glutted a market already depleted by disease, and induced what has recently been described as the agricultural depression 1730–50. It was a period of advance for labour in terms of living standards, and, if the complaints of contemporaries are to be believed, of a preference for leisure, but not surprisingly it seems to have been a period of pause for capital; investment in enclosures, turnpikes and industrial enterprise has left little for the historian to record.

From the middle of the century, the pace of population growth quickened again; the upward movement of marriages and baptisms in the 1750's probably reflected the spurt in both which followed the onslaught of 1727–30: but the five-yearly 'distemperature' which the local historian, Deering, took for granted in the 1730's failed to materialize in the 1750's; between 1747 and 1766 there was no high epidemic peak in the villages and in Nottingham the period from 1755 to 1764 was one of continuous natural increase. From this time, in spite of the setbacks in the town between 1764 and 1773, the menace of epidemics in the region receded and there seems no doubt that as far as Nottinghamshire is concerned the turn of its demographic tide took place about the mid-point of the century.

The 1750's also marked a return of prosperity to agriculture, and by the end of this decade a new phase of investment had opened which, in the measurable terms of enclosures and turnpikes, was on an entirely unprecedented scale. The next decade saw the first canals and important new industrial enterprises; and the continuous though uneven industrial growth that now took place was sustained by an expanding labour force which was stimulated both on the side of supply, through increased competition and the pressure of larger families, and of demand through the habit which, according to

Arthur Young, had grown upon the poor during the long period of low prices, of consuming a 'greater quantity of superfluities',[1] and an immensely vigorous and prosperous agriculture which reflected in its progress a uniquely favourable combination of factors deriving as much from institutional as from economic sources.

---

[1] A. Young, *Political Arithmetic*, London, 1774, p. 76—Ed.

XVIII

P. Deane and W. A. Cole, *British Economic Growth, 1688–1959*, 2nd ed., Cambridge University Press, 1967, pp. 5, 6, 89–90, 92–7.

One of the most striking manifestations of the expansion of the United Kingdom economy in the modern period was an unprecedented growth of population. The origins of this movement are somewhat obscure. There was no full census of population in Great Britain before 1801 or in Ireland before 1821 and no attempt was made to collect age data at the censuses until 1821. Hence the population figures for the eighteenth century are imprecise. Although there are enough data available to provide reasonable estimates of the broad trends involved, the specific turning-points cannot be located and the character and causes of the initial changes are still a matter of controversy.

For England and Wales estimates are generally based on the returns of baptisms, burials and marriages, at decade intervals, which Rickman collected from the keepers of the parish records. These were published in the Parish Register Abstracts of the 1801 census and amended in the 1811 census and have given rise to several series of plausible estimates of total population, the differences between the series being a consequence of each author's assumptions concerning the completeness of the data and the appropriate conversion coefficients....

The estimates for England and Wales suggest that the population stagnated for the first four decades of the century although there may have been short sub-periods of more or less sharp increase or decrease within this period. Taking the century as a whole it appears that there were two periods in the eighteenth century in which the rate of population growth tended to accelerate, one from 1740 to 1760 and the other from 1780 onwards. The former upsurge is interesting in that it marked the beginning of an entirely new trend in population—a sustained increase. The latter was stronger and continued at an increasing rate into the nineteenth century. Between 1781 and 1811 the increase for England and Wales was of the order of 38 per cent, and over the sixty years between 1771 and 1831 the population practically doubled. . . .

As we have already observed, it is impossible not to be struck by the close connection between the pattern of growth at home and the course of population change, and it is natural to inquire how far the two were causally related. Recent research has done much to emphasise the part played by population increase in easing the labour scarcity which seems to have been an outstanding feature of the British economy in the late seventeenth and early eighteenth centuries, and in providing the labour force on which the industrial system rested. But at first sight the correlation seems too close to fit this explanation. For an increase in population might be expected to have a significant effect on the supply of labour only after an interval of sixteen or eighteen years; even when all allowances have been made for the uncertainty of the statistics and the possible influence of child labour, it does not seem possible for the acceleration in the rate of economic growth in the 1740's and again in the 1780's to have been directly due to an increase in the size of the labour force, at any rate as a result of population increase. Nor is it obvious that an increase in population would have promoted an acceleration in the rate of economic growth through its effect on demand. For although an increase in the number of mouths to be fed and bodies to be clothed may enlarge wants, will it necessarily increase effective demand? Clearly, therefore, if we are to understand the significance of the population changes, we must consider some of the other factors in the situation.

A good deal of recent discussion has been devoted to the effects of variations in harvests on agricultural prices and the distribution of incomes. In an economy still so largely dominated by agriculture, it is, of course, natural to ascribe a major role to changes in the fortunes of the farming community, and the debate on the consequences of high and low agricultural prices is probably as old as the English Corn Laws. Professor Ashton, following Adam Smith, has suggested that in the eighteenth century good harvests meant, not only an increased return to human effort in the agricultural sector, but also an increased demand for labour to gather the harvest, higher real wages, and hence an increase in the demand for the products of industry.[1] As an explanation of short-run fluc-

---

[1] T. S. Ashton, *An economic history of England. The Eighteenth Century*, London, 1955.—Ed.

tuations, this theory is plausible enough, although the evidence at our disposal makes it difficult to check. Certainly the influence of harvests can be detected in fluctuations in output in many of the industries for which production data are directly available, but since these were mainly industries which, in the short run at least, depended on agriculture for their supply of raw materials, it does not follow that this was entirely due to the income effects of good harvests.

Here, however, we are mainly concerned with long-term trends, and several students have argued that the effects of a series of good harvests may have been very different. For owing to the inelastic demand for foodstuffs—and especially cereals—good harvests meant, not only a rise in real wages, but a fall in agricultural incomes. In the short run this might not be important, since the losses in one year could be made good in the next. But the combination of a succession of good harvests with a stationary population may well have had such a depressing effect on the demand from the agricultural sector as to offset the stimulus which the industrial economy derived from high or rising real wages. It is true, of course, that over a period of years it may be difficult to distinguish improvements in agricultural productivity due to favourable climatic conditions from those due to technical change. The suggestion here, however, is simply that variations in the internal terms of trade between workshop and farm may have had a similar effect on the home demand for industrial goods as did changes in import and export prices on the fortunes of the export trade. And since it is probably fair to assume that the demand for cereals was less elastic than that for sugar and tobacco, it is possible that the economy as a whole may have lost more from sagging demand for industrial goods than it gained from abundant supplies of agricultural products. As Professor Habakkuk puts it: 'The low or stationary agricultural prices of the earlier decades of the century had a depressing effect on agricultural investment and indirectly on the demand for industrial goods. The rising prices over most of the second half of the century stimulated agricultural investment and led to increased demand for industrial goods; they led not so much to a shift of income between the industrial and agricultural sectors as to an increase in the income of both. . . .'[1]

---

[1] H. J. Habakkuk, Essays in bibliography and criticism. The Eighteenth Century, *Ec. H. R.*, 2nd ser., VIII, 1956.—Ed.

There appears ... to be a strong prima facie case for the view that the growth of the home market for industrial goods was closely bound up with the fortunes of the agricultural community, in much the same way as the growth of the export trade depended on the prosperity of the primary producers overseas.

Two obvious explanations may be suggested. In the first place, it should be noted that until 1750 periods of comparatively high agricultural prices were not only periods of population expansion at home, but of growing overseas demand for grain. Corn exports rose in the first quarter of the century, and again in the late forties; from the early twenties until the early forties they were virtually stationary. Exports of corn were encouraged by bounty during this period, but for the most part, the increase in the incomes of farmers, landlords and middlemen exporters associated with an increase in grain exports represented a net addition to incomes at home.

Second, and more important, however, the expectation that the redistribution of incomes arising from low corn prices should have stimulated industrial demand assumes that the marginal propensity of wage-earners and the non-agricultural sector as a whole to consume manufactured goods was in fact higher than that of farmers and landlords. If England had been a society in which the market and taste for manufactured goods was highly developed, and in which, at the same time, the agricultural community tended to hoard its gains, such an assumption might be warranted. But it was not. For centuries English agriculture had had extensive ties of varying strength with the market, and by the eighteenth century it was largely organised on a capitalist basis: the typical farmer was not a peasant toiling for his own subsistence, but an employer of wage-labour holding his land at an economic rent from men who not infrequently ploughed their profits back into agriculture, or into transport, industry and trade. Much industrial output was produced by agricultural wage-earners or their families on a domestic basis. On the other hand, it is probably true that in England, as in any other largely pre-industrial economy, the economic horizons of the mass of the population tended to be narrow, and the range of consumer goods small. Hence the demand for manufactured goods may have been relatively inelastic, and a rise in real wages may have led, not to an increase in their consumption, but to an increase in leisure—or, as contemporaries unanimously complained, to 'idleness'. Probably rising real wages did stimulate an increase in the consumption of some goods, and it is significant that the thirties and early forties witnessed the height of the gin mania. But evidently the demand for gin was not sufficient either to arrest the fall of agricultural prices or to provide the basis for rapid industrial growth.

When prices rose, on the other hand, agricultural incomes also rose and, at the same time, industrial artisans and the wage-earning population as a whole had to work harder to maintain their traditional standard of life. It is not surprising, therefore, that the rise in prices after 1743 seems to have been associated with a modest rise in total output per head. Moreover, it is important to note that the rise in the price of foodstuffs was brought about, not by a decline in agricultural output—indeed the evidence suggests that the yield of the soil in the decades after 1745 must have been substantially greater than it had been before—but mainly by an increase in the number of mouths to be fed. For a growing population and the increase in the size of families which it brought tended to transform the position of the labouring population. Not only did it give an immediate stimulus to wants, but it also meant that, as families grew up and population too continued to expand at an increasing rate, competition in the labour market began to replace the traditional scarcity. From about the middle of the eighteenth century it is possible to discern a significant change in the attitude of contemporaries towards the labouring population. Complaints of the recalcitrance of labourers diminished and some writers began to argue that high, not low, wages provided the greater incentive to industry. By 1776 Adam Smith could assert that the problem among piece-workers, at least, was not that they were idle, but that overwork tended to 'ruin their health and constitution in a few years'.

In these circumstances, food would necessarily constitute the first claim on available incomes, and since the agricultural community was thus assured of an expanding market for its produce, the significance of harvest variations began to change. Provided that farmers and landlords continued to spend or invest their additional incomes, it might make little difference to industrial demand whether the prices of food were low or high. And if the addition to total output resulting from favourable harvests was no longer offset by losses in the industrial sector we might expect the national income as a whole to rise most rapidly when the prices of food were comparatively low. This, indeed, is what the data suggest. As we have seen, it appears that the period from the mid-forties until the early sixties was one of all-round expansion in both industry and agriculture. Despite the very heavy exports of grain in the ten years after 1745 and the unprecedented expansion of population in that and the ensuing decades the rise in agricultural prices was at first comparatively modest and their average level rose no higher than in the first two decades of the century. Gradually, however, the growing population began to press against the available resources; exports of corn dwindled, and, with the poor harvests of the late sixties and early seventies, prices rose much more steeply, and Britain was for the first time compelled to import substantial quantities of grain. This brought a sharp increase in agricultural investment. Until the late fifties, the farming community evidently had little incentive to indulge in ambitious schemes of agricultural improvement.

From 1730 to 1744, the number of enclosure bills presented in Parliament had averaged about forty per decade, and in the ten years ending in 1754 the total was only forty-nine. In the next ten years, however, the number jumped to 283, and in the following decade to 531. There is no evidence that this wave of investment directly stimulated industrial demand, but it does not seem to have been accompanied by any contraction of the home market for industrial goods. High agricultural prices may have contributed to the trade recession of the early seventies, which appears to have been particularly severe in the linen trade, but in the ten years ending in 1774, the volume of industrial goods consumed at home seems to have risen more than in previous decades. At the same time, however, the rise in the internal price-level no doubt contributed to the favourable swing in the external terms of trade during this period, and hence to the stagnation in the export trade; and since the output of agriculture and of the industries dependent on the land was almost stationary, it is not surprising that our estimates suggest a fall in the overall rate of expansion in both the major sectors of the economy, certainly in relation to the rapidly growing population, and possibly also in absolute terms.

In the late seventies, the effects of enclosures began to make themselves felt. The price of corn was stabilised and, as other prices probably continued to rise as a result of the high cost of imports during the American War, its 'real' price dropped. After 1777, the wave of enclosures ebbed, and for a time, at least, arrears of rent testify to comparatively depressed conditions for the farming community. But again there seems to have been a steady growth in the home market. Despite the virtual collapse of foreign trade in the war years, the available indicators suggest that the rate of growth of even those industries which were normally most dependent on overseas markets was only slightly lower than in the previous decade. And when the return of peace brought with it a great revival of foreign trade, while prices of agricultural produce remained comparatively low, the economy experienced a new wave of expansion which was checked only by the combined effects of commercial difficulties, population pressure and bad harvests during the Napoleonic Wars.

Thus it appears that the importance which economic historians have recently ascribed to demographic factors—or, more precisely, the balance between population and other resources, and particularly land—in shaping the pattern of eighteenth-century economic growth is justified. In the early part of the century, Britain already had a relatively well-developed commercial agriculture, capable of supporting a larger industrial population than she in fact possessed. Moreover, she had acquired extensive overseas markets for the products of her industries, and colonial territories producing cash crops of foodstuffs and raw materials which complemented the products of the mother country. But since these territories were, in the strictest sense of the term, economic dependencies, largely cut off from outside influences, the expansion of the markets they provided was closely bound up with the development of the metropolitan economy. Although a large and probably growing proportion of Britain's industrial output was exported during this period the growth of her overseas trade seems to have been held back by the slow pace of advance at home. Yet there appears to have been no serious shortage of capital at this time, and, as Professor Ashton has emphasised, interest rates were generally low. Nor does slow technological advance appear to have been a limiting factor, for the pace of innovation was even slower, at any rate in the metal industries; and some of the technical developments of the first two decades of the century, such as the Newcomen engine, the use of coal and coke in the smelting of iron, and the introduction of a successful means of producing tinplate, had to wait until the fifth and later decades before they were extensively applied. On the other hand, we know that labour was scarce in the early eighteenth century, and the stagnation of population aggravated this problem and contributed to the depression of both agricultural incomes and the demand for industrial goods.

It may be asked why the scarcity of labour did not stimulate labour-saving innovations, and why low agricultural prices did not encourage the migration of capital and labour from agriculture to industry. The answer to both questions may be that to some extent they did. Certainly landlords seem to have experienced difficulty in finding tenants, and in the worst period of the agricultural depression there were some cases of vacant holdings. It has been argued that in the period from 1680 to 1740 big farmers and landlords were in the strongest position, and it is possible that the pressure of the land tax and the competition of larger and more efficient estates drove some of the lesser gentry and yeomen to abandon the land for other pursuits. We shall see in the next chapter that the first half of the eighteenth century witnessed a significant movement of population from the rural areas to London and, less strongly, to some of the industrial counties. Moreover, this was not—as it seems to have been in later decades—simply a movement of the surplus population engendered by a high rate of natural increase, for as we have already noted, the population of several of the agricultural counties actually fell. On the other hand, the wage statistics suggest that the depression was not severe enough to reduce the demand for agricultural labour sufficiently to check the upward pressure on wage rates, while a succession of favourable seasons was not likely to generate a strong movement out of agriculture.

Similar considerations apply to the course of technological change. The limited technical innovations of the second quarter of the century were indeed largely aimed at economising labour, particularly in the textile industries. But labour scarcity is more likely to induce rapid technical progress in an expanding economy than in one where demand is limited and output virtually stationary. It was not until economic expansion was well under way, in the 1760's and seventies, when the pressures of a growing population were beginning to stimulate investment in measures designed to economise other resources, such as land (enclosures) and coal (canals), that the great labour-saving inventions of the eighteenth century laid the basis for the revolution in the textile industries and the introduction of the factory system. Nor was it entirely by chance that these discoveries came when they did, for by the 1760's competitions were being held for the best inventions. There is not much doubt that the widespread improvements and innovations in agriculture, transport and industry helped to maintain if not to increase real incomes per head in the last quarter of the century. But it seems equally clear that the quest for technical improvement which gave rise to these revolutionary innovations was itself stimulated by the great upsurge of population which began a generation before.

XIX

H. J. Habakkuk, *American and British technology in the nineteenth century*, Cambridge, 1962, pp. 49–53.

Labour-scarcity might, in the third place, have stimulated technical progress. Technical progress, that is movements of the technical spectrum as opposed to movements along it, would, by increasing manufacturing productivity, raise or at least keep up profit-rates, whether the progress was manna from heaven or induced by rising labour-costs. But manna from heaven one would expect to drop more readily in England, since England initially had much larger supplies of technical knowledge. The point about labour-scarcity is that it constituted a favourable influence on technical progress which was exerted more strongly in the U.S.A. than in England. Any manufacturer had an inducement to adopt new methods which made a substantial reduction of cost for all factors. But in their early stages, many of the methods devised in the nineteenth century could not be confidently assumed to effect such a reduction: before they had been tried out in practice for some time, estimates of their costs were highly conjectural. Where the best guess that could be made of a new method was that it promised a reduction of labour but some increase of capital, the Americans had a sharper incentive than the English to explore its possibilities. This is to say that labour-scarcity encouraged not only a careful and systematic investigation of the costs of the more capital-intensive of existing techniques, but the early adoption of any additions at the capital-intensive end which resulted from inventions of purely autonomous origin, even when they were made outside the U.S.A. Friedrich List wrote in the 1820's after a stay in America: 'Everything new is quickly introduced here, and all the latest inventions. There is no clinging to old ways, the moment an American hears the word "invention" he pricks up his ears.'[1]

---

[1] M. E. Hirst, *Life of Friedrich List* (1909), p. 35.

Montgomery, writing in the next decade about the cotton-textile industry, considered that though the number of specific inventions originating in the U.S.A. was not high compared with those that came from Britain, the common stock of inventions was very rapidly integrated into the American economy.[1]

Labour-scarcity also gave Americans an incentive, not only to explore the labour-saving possibilities of autonomous inventions, but to attempt to invent new methods specifically to save labour. And if, as we shall argue later, the technical possibilities were richest at the capital-intensive end of the spectrum, the American was likely also to be better placed to make advances wherever, for any operation, he employed more capital-intensive methods than the English; that is the composition of American investment might have had a favourable effect upon its rate.

In the early decades of the century the principal effect of labour-scarcity in America was probably to induce American manufacturers to adopt labour-saving methods invented in other countries earlier and more extensively than they were adopted in their country of origin. The number of autonomous inventions was greater in the older industrial countries. But where their principal advantage was that they were labour-saving, they were more quickly adopted in the U.S.A. and labour-scarcity then induced further improvements, each additional improvement being perhaps small in relation to the original invention. And already in the early nineteenth century there were a number of important American inventions induced directly by the search for labour-saving methods and these became increasingly common as time went on.

Moreover, it was probably also easier for the Americans to adopt such methods. In England, where labour was abundant, labour-saving was likely to involve replacing, by a machine, labour that was already employed; in the U.S.A. it involved making a physically limited labour-force more effective by giving it machinery, but without displacing anyone, and with some increase in wages. There was, therefore, less opposition in America to the introduction of labour-saving practices and machines and of administrative methods for economising labour: the

---

[1] J. Montgomery, *The cotton manufacture of the United States contrasted and compared with that of Great Britain*, Glasgow 1840.

fear of unemployment was less and the likelihood greater of gaining in higher wages from the increased productivity. In England, where there was a superabundant supply of hands and therefore 'a proportionate difficulty in obtaining remunerative employment, the working classes have less sympathy with the progress of invention.'

For the same reasons, more changes in production methods came spontaneously from the workers in America than in England, particularly when the worker had been self-employed earlier in life, and most of all when he had been a farmer, for he carried over into industry the inclination to seek his own methods of doing his job better. Thus in American canal-digging, the English methods were modified by the American farmers who devised a sort of primitive, horse-drawn bulldozer, similar to a device some of them had improvised on their farms. No improvement originated among the Irish navvies who dug the English canals.

If the methods adopted or developed by the Americans did no more than offset the initial disadvantage of high labour-costs, American entrepreneurs would have been on an equality with the English. In most cases, the methods must have done less than this. But in some cases they may well have done more. In exploring the borderland of blue prints, designs and embryonic ideas and hunches which lay beyond the end of the spectrum of existing techniques it would not be surprising if the Americans hit upon some new methods which were so productive that they more than offset the high cost of labour, methods which reduced labour and capital per unit of output so greatly that they would have been the most profitable techniques even in the case of abundant labour. Very often the substantial reductions in cost came from ancillary developments and modifications made after the new technique had been operating for some time, and these benefits accrued most fully to those who had adopted the method earliest; and the process tended to be cumulative, since the successful application of machinery to one field of activity stimulated its application to another, and the accumulation of knowledge and skill made it easier to solve technical problems and sense out the points where the potentialities of further technical progress were brightest.

Furthermore, quite apart from the effect of labour-scarcity on the incentive and ability to develop superior methods, the shift of American industry towards the more capital-intensive techniques provided the American machine-making industry with an active market which stimulated inventive ability among the manufacturers of machines and machine tools and perhaps also afforded it some advantages of scale. Ability to produce a labour-saving machine in one field also made it easier to develop machines in other fields. Thus the United States developed the typewriter, not simply because in America 'copying clerks could not be bought for a pittance' but also because in Remingtons, the Illinois gunmakers, there were manufacturers available who could put ideas into practical effect.[1]

Standardisation could be applied not only to final products but to the machines which produced them. 'Wood machines' wrote an English expert 'are made in America at this time like boots and shoes, or shovels and hatchets. You do not, as in most other countries, prepare a specification of what you need . . . but must take what is made for the general market'.[2] For these reasons there were cost-reducing improvements in the production of machines. Certainly by the middle decades of the nineteenth century there were some fields where the cost of the superior machines, relative to that of simpler machines, was lower in the U.S.A. than in Britain, and this was an independent stimulus to the adoption of more mechanised techniques in the U.S.A. There were also fields in which a superior machine was available for some operations in the U.S.A. but not in England.

Once a number of industries had been established in the U.S.A., a rise in real wages in any one of them due to technical progress exerted a similar effect on choice of methods as the initial high earnings in American agriculture. Where labour is scarce, any increase in productivity and real wages in one sector threatens to attract labour from other industries which have either to contract their operations or install new equipment which will raise their productivity sufficiently to enable them to retain their labour-supply.

In England where labour-supplies were abundant the technical progress in a single industry was not likely to stimulate technical

---

[1] J. H. Clapham, *An Economic History of Modern Britain* (Cambridge, 1938), III, p. 193.
[2] J. Richards, *Wood-working Factories and Machinery* (1873), p. 171.

progress in other industries by threatening their labour-supplies. It might, of course, stimulate technical progress in other industries by threatening their markets and in some cases their supplies of raw material; but not by threatening to draw off their labour. Any tendency for wage-earners within the technically progressive industry to establish a claim upon the fruits of their increased productivity was inhibited by the existence of a reserve army of labour, and the benefits of technical progress were likely to be diffused by means of lower prices over consumers as a whole, as in the case of the English cotton-textile industry.

XX

D. E. C. Eversley, The home market and economic growth in England, 1750–80, in E. L. Jones and G. E. Mingay eds, *Land, labour and population in the Industrial Revolution*, London, 1967, pp. 207–9, 213–16, 220, 239, 249, 251–2, 255.

To lend greater precision to this contribution, and to place it in the context of material already published, it may be as well to start with the theme developed by A. H. John and others, most succinctly stated in a paper given at the Economic History Conference at Reading in 1964 and since published.[1] For our purposes, the most relevant part of this thesis is one we readily accept: that the low food prices of the period 1730–50, due to a succession of favourable seasons and agricultural improvements, allowed large sections of the working population to feed well and yet retain a margin between income and expenditure required for minimum subsistence, a margin which could be spent, and was spent, on consumer goods, thus providing the necessary buoyancy of the home market at a time when industry was just beginning to transform itself, in some sectors, by the adoption of power, division of labour, and techniques of mass production and distribution. Let us rephrase this general argument in a series of propositions (at present only to be applied to the period before 1750) which are either implied or spelled out in John's work:

(1) Agricultural production rises relative to the existing domestic and foreign markets to a sufficient degree to allow prices to remain stable or even fall compared with earlier periods.

(2) This makes it possible for a larger number of people to work in industry and live in towns without causing famine.

(3) Population rises only slowly, at any rate not fast enough to

---

[1] A. H. John, Agriculture productivity and economic growth in England, 1700-1760, *Journal of Economic History*, XXV, 1965, pp. 19 ff.—Ed.

cause food shortages, and the economically active part of the population in particular remains small enough in relation to labour demand (which may be a matter of place, skill, age or sex), at least in some areas, to keep the level of money wages high relative to food prices.

(4) The workers, or some of them, still maintain their earnings, though they could satisfy minimum needs with less work.

(5) They spend their earnings in part on manufactured commodities. The price of these rises, or the producers see that they can sell more at the same price—in either case an incentive is given to increase the scope of production.

(6) Though exports take place, and their level may be rising, this additional home demand is seen as the major stable and long-term factor in promoting industrialization.

We shall have to qualify all these assertions later, but let us first of all come to the final part of John's thesis: that this state of affairs lasted only until about 1750, and that after that date there was something of a collapse due to bad weather, and failure of agricultural productivity to keep pace with accelerated population growth and urbanization, and this led to the failure of the domestic market. If after 1750 industrialization continued, it must have been due to exports taking the place of home demand.

Against this view we now advance a different thesis: that the situation continued to be favourable to home demand from 1750 to at least 1780;[1] that exports before that date were neither at a sufficiently high level nor sufficiently stable to warrant the amount of investment that took place; that the rise in food prices was not drastic before 1780 in relation to incomes; and that in any case some rise in food prices does not necessarily squeeze the margin of expenditure on other produce; that the period from 1750 to 1780 is crucial as the 'warming-up' period just before the take-off into sustained growth; that these thirty years laid a sufficient foundation

---

[1] These breaks are artificial and have no normative meaning, but are dictated by one's precursors. For a different chronology yielding different interpretations, cf. Habakkuk and Deane, 'The take-off in Britain', ch. 4 in W. W. Rostow (ed.), *The Economics of Take-Off into Sustained Growth* (1963), p. 67.

of home consumers to enable industry to withstand the collapse of exports in the seventies; that this happened because increased real incomes tended to be spent on consumer goods rather than extra food purchases, thus still further stimulating industrial production and accelerating the movement of existing and new labour into the manufacturing sector; and that in any case the whole mechanism is to be explained not in terms of global populations, classes, or commodities, but in terms of regions and income groups.

To gain a better idea of the possible size of the new domestic markets created, we might start with some idea of national income distribution. What was the strength, in the middle of the eighteenth century, of that group of the inhabitants of the kingdom which was neither wealthy nor poor—the middle class, for the sake of brevity? Let us look again at Gregory King's famous table.[1] He assumed that there were over two and a half million people in his time in the category 'Increasing the Wealth of the Kingdom'. We can disregard the top ranks, down to the esquires, or those receiving more than £450 per annum, and we are still left with over 2·6 million people organized in households with a total income of £1 per week or more. Let us, to be on the safe side, assume that King exaggerated the incomes of the poorer freeholders and farmers, the craftsmen and artisans. If we counted only the 'persons in office', the clergy, the lawyers, the richer freeholders, the officers, etc., we still have a million people (including dependants) with incomes in the range £50–£400. Let us even exclude poor curates, pedlars, half-pay pensioners, and others unlikely to have much of a spending margin. But whichever way we look at it, we must believe that something like 10 per cent of the population were, in King's time, the nucleus of the home market. In actual fact, judging by the sort of wills we mention below, there must have been many in the class of artisans, lesser yeomen, and independent traders, publicans, and so on who were well within the 'spending group'. What the postulated growth of the home market implies is merely that this middling group should have increased in size, relatively as well as absolutely, and had a greater margin of expenditure above necessaries.

Can we estimate how much they spent? If we start again from Gregory King, we have a total of nearly £10 m.p.a. spent on

---

[1] As reproduced in Charles Wilson, *England's Apprenticeship* (1965), p. 239, or Deane, *First Ind. Rev.*, pp. 8–9.

manufactures and the products of mining and building operations, or something like £10 for the average family. But we are not concerned with a hypothetical average family. If we exclude 80 per cent of the population on the grounds of poverty, the average spending of the remaining fifth becomes £35. This sum (after allowing for food and rent) does not seem incompatible with King's view of the structure of the group in question.

Let us assume that by 1800, when the total population was about 10 million, this same age group numbered 2 million, and that another 10 per cent of the population (1 million) had been added by the process of industrialization and the growth of commerce. The growth of population and the economy would then have increased the size of the consuming group from 1 to 3 million. (We realize that this is a circular argument; it is put forward here only in order to provide a framework for later calculations.) If this group had exactly the same pattern of expenditure as their forerunners in King's time, and if prices had been constant (a not impossible assumption, though the 'basket' of goods is not constant), they should between them have purchased £30 m. worth of manufactures, etc. This happens to be what Arthur Youngs thought the value of the market was in 1770. There are a lot of ifs and buts about this sort of play with figures, yet they provide us at least with some sort of dimension for the phenomenon that has to be explained. Let us put it another way: if we do allow that 'industrial' output trebled between the end of the seventeenth and the end of the eighteenth century, and if exports of manufactures can only account for a small proportion of the total, and if the products known to have constituted the bulk of the output in 1800 were not of the type sold to the wealthy classes, what other construction can we put on the process than that the 'middle-class' of consumers expanded?

In fact, the process of structural change in the market is much more complex than this simple model suggests. First of all, we have the phenomenon of urbanization and rural specialization, which involved an unknown proportion of the population in increasing dependence on the supply of consumer goods from commercial sources as opposed to their own or their neighbours' home-made product. Examples of this sort of thing would be clothing (change from home-spun and woven), and boots, beer, eating utensils to replace the wooden home-made article, candles instead of rush-lights, furniture, fuel, and even less obvious types of expenditure, e.g. patent medicines instead of local herbs and soap in the absence of a running stream.

A much larger area for change in the expenditure pattern of any group of given real income levels arises from the change to cash wages and the urban environment. Many observers have noted the fact that urban and industrial wages were much higher than rural wages, and modern interpreters have dismissed this fact as unimportant, on the ground that the money differentials bear no relation to real wages: because in the country such a large part of total income was in kind, in food allowances, beer, rent, gardens, common rights, and so on, whereas in the towns everything had to be bought. This attitude towards the differentials tends to gloss over their significance for the structure of the market. Larger cash incomes inevitably mean more choice, and choice tends to move expenditure patterns away from the old essentials. Hence the complaints of the moralizers. In the country, so the assertions run, people had plenty to eat and a simple life. If food was particularly cheap and abundant, they ate more or worked less. They neither saved, nor did they buy other things: they had all they knew or needed. But in the towns they developed a taste for new types of goods, apart from the fact that many commodities must now be purchased. It was typical of the writers on the distress of the population at the end of the eighteenth century that they alleged misspending of incomes on inessential fripperies. We need not ask here whether this was true or not as an explanation for distress: but we can say that if it was so, then the extension of the markets went even further downwards than we have assumed. If Ure's picture[1] of cottage equipment in industrial Lancashire has any significance, the process continued even through the worst years. We do not need to go as far as this: but the existence of the charge of misspending gives us a good lower limit to our description of the consuming classes.

We now consider the whole question of how any considerable body of members of the 'middle' group of economically active people could have acquired and maintained a standard of real wages high enough to sustain the prolonged demand which we postulate as the core of industrialization: starting with a relatively cheap food supply and a shortage of labour before 1750, we postulate the existence of a margin between income and expenditure on basic

---

[1] A. Ure, *The philosophy of manufacture*, London, 1835—Ed.

necessities. Between 1750 and 1780, this margin was not reduced, and in many cases, must have become larger: (i) because food prices did not rise sufficiently to cancel out the original benefit; (ii) because relative labour shortages continued in many areas and in respect of many skills; and (iii) because employers made no concerted or conscious attempts to reduce real wages to subsistence levels. In some cases, industrial paternalism increased the demand for consumer goods. As a result, the larger labour force contains more consumers for the products of industry than ever before. Though, on our evidence, this is how the extra purchasing power was created, and how the demands were met, there is no law of nature that this must be so, or that the sequence of events forms part of an equilibrium growth situation. At any point of time the process could have been halted. Additional labour (from spare rural capacity rather than a high rate of natural increase) might not have been forthcoming at the right time and in the right place. Innovations might not have been made or adopted to ensure that output could be raised at steady or lower prices. Increments in output of a speculative kind might not have found markets at home (thanks to a reasonable distribution of incomes and a better transport system), or abroad (thanks to expanding trading horizons). In each case the impetus would have been lost.

Nor can we list here all the 'environmental' conditions for economic growth—by now we take these for granted. An equable climate, political stability, the liberty of the individual, the 'protestant ethic', the absence of heavy expenditure on defence or royal extravagances—all the favourite pre-conditions for growth are present. This background makes the process possible, though it does not ensure it. If the social and political climate of Britain in 1750 provides the necessary conditions, home demand is the main element of the sufficient cause.

We have been at pains to stress the rising or at least stable purchasing power of the home market in the period 1750–80. The question naturally arises: what was the rate of population growth, and the distribution of the increase, that permitted this state of affairs? And why did the 'Malthusian' effects not make themselves felt at this time? In other words, why did England not produce a Malthus twenty years earlier?

The short theoretical answer is that population growth at this time was 'right'—neither so small as to cause shortages of labour, or of demand for goods and services, nor so large as to reduce real wages, create labour surpluses and destroy the basis of demand. Such an answer is not incompatible with the existence of pockets of excessive or insufficient growth, with distress in some areas and great prosperity in others. Without the benefit of the results of recalculations of British population figures in the eighteenth century now being undertaken, we may base ourselves on the tables published by Deane, Cole and Mitchell as affording at any rate a consistent outline. The Cambridge calculations,[1] based essentially still on Rickman but corrected in the light of later work such as Brownlee's, give a rate of natural increase of only about one per thousand for the period 1701–50. This is, in fact, composed of a number of short-term rates: growth early in the century, stagnation or even recession 1720–30, and then accelerated growth to 1750. For the period 1750–80 with which we are here concerned the growth rate is given as 6·8 per thousand, which is very similar to that which obtained since 1730. Only after 1780 do growth rates rise to above 1 per cent to a maximum of over 1½ per cent in the early nineteenth century.

Mr. Colin Clark[2] has furnished us with an excellent model of eighteenth and early nineteenth-century population growth based on an observed rate of natural increase just quoted, and consistent with such vital rates as we do possess. He has based himself (see Table 4)[3] on the Swedish life tables of the two periods in order to give some precision to his calculations, but certainly his assumptions fit the British pattern. It will be seen that he assumes only a third of the women marrying before the age of 25, total marital fertility of just under five children per married woman, and a rate of infant and child mortality reducing a gross reproduction rate of 2·38 to a net 1·241 in the middle of the eighteenth century and 1·527 early in the nineteenth. Whilst we would not assert at this stage that these rates are correct in detail, it is useful to adduce them to show that there is a satisfactory growth model which fits in with the sort of hypotheses here advanced.

These figures are significant. The 1750–80 rate is the nearest of all those given to that obtaining in many west European countries

---

[1] P. Deane and W. A. Cole, *British economic growth 1688–1959*, Cambridge, 1962, p. 115.—Ed.
[2] *Population Growth and Land Use*, London, 1967, p. 56.
[3] Eversley, *Home market...*, *op. cit.*, p. 250.—Ed.

today. It is well below current Dutch or North American rates, which approximate more to those ruling in England round 1800. But the significant feature is that a growth rate of under 1 per cent, slowly increasing, is much more favourable to economic growth than that of the euphemistically-termed developing nations of Asia and Latin America, where 2, 3, and even 4 per cent per annum is still common. A rate of 0·7 per cent is manageable in an economy where capital resources are not yet easily mobilized, communications still in need of much improvement, and agricultural output not yet rising at the sort of speed which mechanization made possible much later. On the other hand, the total increase of one and a half million people between 1750 and 1780 was probably as high as that observed in any previous period of a hundred years, and it provided a useful labour force where it was needed. If the whole country increased by under 25 per cent in thirty years, Lancashire increased by a third, the West Riding by half, Warwickshire by just under 40 per cent.[1] But Devonshire stagnated. There is no question that the increase was absorbed: according to Miss Deane's calculations, the industrial counties gained more people by migration than by natural increase. Poverty may have been a problem, unemployment as such was unknown.

Given the differential in agricultural and industrial wages previously mentioned, which in the case of Lancashire and Warwickshire certainly meant an increase in real wages, we can say that the shift of population into the industrializing and urban counties meant an increase in consumption per head. In any case, it must be stressed again, all migration from country to town means a stimulus to industrial production, for however much the old self-sufficient community may have changed even before 1750 to a system of craft specialization, it was only with the concentration in towns that the possibility of mass production and distribution became feasible, and only with canals that prices of supplies to distant markets bore some relation to the cost of production.

If growth rates had been twice as high as they were (i.e. had the population grown by 3 m. instead of $1\frac{1}{2}$ m.), and especially if that additional growth had been due to higher fertility and lower infant mortality, it is highly likely that the standard of living of the population would have fallen. More young children mean higher

---

[1] Deane and Cole, *op. cit.*, p. 103.

dependency ratios, to use a term of modern growth analysis: more mouths to feed and fewer hands to feed them, to use Malthusian language. Larger families are, even today, poor consumers except for basic necessities. The small family (especially if the mother works) buys more luxuries, remains in better health, saves more. There can be little doubt that the equilibrium of economic growth in this period is connected with a highly convenient population growth rate. Could there have been a causal connexion? The answer is probably positive. After 1740, for the first time, more people live in a non-catastrophic world. Food, shelter, and clothing became a certain expectation. Calamitous deaths become rarer. Opportunities for upward movement become more frequent. Under these circumstances, prudence about marriage, and restriction of families, go with saving, geographical and social mobility, and reduced mortality. Reduced mortality results from better environmental conditions, the more regular supplies of necessities, and the incipient improvements in drainage, water supplies, and the rest of the familiar though overstressed catalogue of wonders of the Industrial Revolution.[1]

---

[1] This is not meant to imply any disrespect to Ashton's views in *The Industrial Revolution*—these things have some validity, though not, in the light of most recent work, as much as we all once believed.

XXI

E. C. Snow, The limits of industrial employment (II). The influence of growth of population on the development of industry. *Journal of the Royal Statistical Society*, XCVIII, Part II, 1935, pp. 241, 250–1, 255, 259–60, 262–3.

For convenience in discussing the figures I will refer to those up to the decade 1901–11 as 'pre-war' and those since 1921 as 'post-war'. . . .

Increase in population had an effect in this country quite different from that in other countries. We were relatively limited in the amount of food-stuffs we could produce. Other countries could more readily provide for the increase in population which occurred by growing more food within their boundaries. In England and Wales the amount of arable land under cultivation appears to have been at its maximum in 1870–72. The total land under cultivation continued to increase slightly, however, to its maximum in 1891. Our imports of articles of food in the middle of the century were less than £30 million per annum (and more than one-third of this was for articles—sugar, coffee, tea, etc.—which we did not produce at all), but from that time they increased rapidly. Home supplies of food at that date were about five times as great as imports, and it was probably about 1840 that we first began to rely upon imports of cereals to make up the deficiency here. Sauerbeck in his paper in the Journal in 1886, 'On Prices of Commodities and the Precious Metals', gave estimates of quantities and values of our food supplies—home production and imports—at 1848–50, 1859–61, 1872–4 and 1883–5, and revalued them on the basis of the prices of 1867–77. From his material I have constructed the following, adding certain particulars regarding population:

Limits of Industrial Employment

Estimated Value of Home and Imported Food-stuffs converted to Basis of Prices from 1867–77

Million £

	Home Production	Imports	Estimated Population of England and Wales
1848–1850	162·1	35·4	17,500,000
1859–1861	166·9	54·5	19,850,000
1872–1874	182·1	108·1	23,050,000
1883–1885	181·3	156·1	26,900,000

No figures are available for earlier periods, but we are probably not far from the truth in saying that after our population reached the 16-million level imports of food-stuffs became a necessity in order to maintain the standard of living, this occurring about 1840. It was about this date that our imports began to expand rapidly and our exports also. The total weight of the imports of food-stuffs alone for the four periods was given by Sauerbeck as follows:

Yearly Average

1848–1850	43,300,000 cwts.
1859–1861	64,700,000 cwts.
1872–1874	128,800,000 cwts.
1883–1885	177,000,000 cwts.

Over the whole period this represented an annual increase of 4 million cwts. Quite apart from the increased exports to pay for the increased imports and the railway material, etc. required for the development of the overseas countries to grow the food-stuffs, the increase in the ships required represented a very substantial amount of employment in the shipbuilding yards every year. The regular increase in our demand for ships is better indicated by the following figures of tonnage of vessels registered in the United Kingdom at the dates stated:

Yearly Average

1848–1850	3,500,000 tons
1859–1861	4,710,000 tons
1872–1874	5,845,000 tons
1883–1885	7,360,000 tons

Over the thirty-five years the annual increase in tonnage registered was well over 100,000 tons, and this was mainly brought about by the fact that we required to import 200,000 tons extra each year to feed our rapidly growing population. It was the growing population which provided the main stimulus for this manufacturing activity....

I think I have said enough about the pre-war circumstances of population and industry to make my point clear, although many more similar facts could be set out. The rapid increase in our international trading in the nineteenth century arose very largely, in my opinion, from a fortunate coincidence of three factors. The rapid increase in population was a world-wide phenomenon, but it happened that in this country (1) we had almost reached the limit of our domestic production of food and, therefore, had to import if we were to maintain the standard of living, (2) we were in possession of the industrial inventions which enabled us to make the goods which other countries needed in exchange for the food-stuffs which they could supply, and (3) we had the financial machinery which was readily able to provide the credit facilities by which the exchange of our manufactured goods and the food-stuffs and raw materials could be effected. If it had not been for the last two named factors, our increasing population would have had to live on a lower standard than it actually attained. On the other hand, if there had been no need to import large quantities of food-stuffs, as would have been the case if there had been little increase in population, the scope for the other two factors to operate would have been very much restricted. The mainspring of the development was the increase in population. The other factors, although vitally important, were ancillary to this....

In the pre-war period we adjusted our commercial and industrial machinery to provide for an annual increase of about 2 per cent. in our total food supplies, and this necessitated an annual increase of about 5 per cent in our imports of food-stuffs. Between 1911 and 1926, however, our total consumption (by weight) of food-stuffs increased by less than $\frac{1}{4}$ per cent. per annum, and the highly complicated commercial and industrial machinery which we set up on the basis of requiring an increase of 5 per cent per annum in our imported food supply is only required to produce an annual increase of less than 1 per cent. This simple fact seems to me to be at the bottom of many of the world's economic troubles. Australia and Argentina, for example, two of the countries which have supplied us with enormous quantities of food-stuffs, have organized themselves in the post-war period to expand their production more or less at the same rate as in the pre-war period. Judging by the public statements of prominent men in both countries, they do not appreciate yet the simple facts about the cessation of growth of population in this country—their chief market. They appear to think that we ought to be able to go on taking what they produce as we did in the past; we simply cannot do it unless we are prepared to see our own land go derelict. (I do not overlook the fact that there is scope for an increase in consumption per head in this country, but I am dealing with the practical facts as they are). We should welcome the opportunity of importing food-stuffs at the same rate of annual progression as in the past if it could be done, because it would lead to increase in our exports and in our shipbuilding industry, etc. The cause for the slowing up of international trade since the war is, to a large extent, due to the change of circumstances in this country. Just as the reduction in mortality with its sequel of rapid increase of population was a main cause of the great growth of our international trade in the nineteenth century, so the reduction in birth-rate with its sequel of decline in rate of growth of the population was a main cause for the slackening of our international trade in the twentieth century. If we could have taken more food-stuffs and raw materials from the rest of the world in the past few years, not only would our own exports have been better maintained, but the international trade of other countries would, in turn, have been improved. Quotas, exchange restrictions and increased tariffs are not so much causes of the reduction in international trade, but are the effects of that reduction due primarily to other causes. They have, in turn, some effect, but they are not the underlying causes. Underlying all other causes in my opinion is this question of the change in the rate of growth of population. . . .

Taking a summary view of the post-war period a prominent feature has been a substantial slackening in the rate of increase of population accompanied with a corresponding slackening in the rate of increase of imported food supplies. Our inability to take the imports of food which other countries have expected us to be able to take and so have organized themselves on the expectation of regular expansion of our market for their products, has affected our exports as well as our imports. In the case of a large number of countries the proportion of the total exports which come to this country is substantial, and the international trade of these countries in other directions is adversely affected by our inability to take from them the quantity of their products which they expected we would. There are, of course, many causes contributing to the present congestion of the international trade of the world, but one of the chief is the fact that this country has almost reached the zenith of its requirements of food-stuffs. If we draw up a list of the causes for our present troubles in international trade, high up on the list must be placed the declining birth-rate in this country, commencing more than a generation ago. I do not overlook the part played by currency considerations from 1925 to 1931 in the one direction or since 1931 in the other direction on our employment problem. But in my opinion the great change in the circumstances of growth of population has been a most potent factor in maintaining our unemployment index at a high figure for years past. It is impossible in short space to deal with all the ramifications of the question, but one illustration will show how far-reaching the effect has been. If we had been able to increase our imports of wheat in the past ten years at the same rate as before the war, stocks of wheat would have remained at reasonable dimensions, prices would have been better maintained, and the world would have been saved many of the consequences of the disastrous collapse of prices. . . .

XXII

R. and K. Titmuss, *Parents' Revolt*, London 1942, pp. 44, 46–53.

Chapter V

THE CONSEQUENCES OF DECLINING NUMBERS

So far we have discussed the future only in terms of numbers. Many people will not have been impressed by a merely statistical argument and will ask, "Does it matter?" or "Why all this fuss?" adding, "Anyway there are too many people in the country and a smaller population will mean less unemployment". This chapter sets out to answer this type of question. . . .

A declining population implies a smaller number of consumers, but more important in the first stage of the change will be the effect on consumption demand caused by the shift in the age structure. . . . The first phase in the population change is therefore one of a stationary market in place of an expanding market to which capitalism has been geared for over a hundred years, and conjointly a gradual change in the type of goods and services required.

As some industries become redundant others will be required to expand. Arm-chairs and bedroom slippers instead of children's foods is one extreme instance of the change-over from the requirements of youth to those of old age. The demand for basic necessitities, such as bread, will diminish as the need for the semi-luxuries of old age rises. Educational requirements will decline as the burden of old people increases. In fact, innumerable changes will result affecting agricultural, housing, medical, clothing and amusement policies. Broadly we may say that industry will have to be far less rigid; indeed much more flexible in adapting itself to change than it has been for the past twenty years. A more flexible industrial system will demand a much more mobile labour force—despite a higher average age. Labour mobility means not only moving from one job to another but moving from one part of the country to another. In sum, therefore, and despite increasing age, individuals will need to be more adaptable and more intelligent. Superimposed on these difficulties—difficulties which will demand by their very nature less monopoly control within the present economic system—will be the unavoidable fact that the total consumption market for both consumers and capital goods will not be expanding. One of the most important lessons to be drawn from a study of the consequences of an ageing and contracting population is the greater need for social and economic vision. The future will have to be planned and this, as we have said, will require greater intelligence, courage, power of initiative, and qualities of creative imagination. But instead of having a youthful population we shall have a relatively old one and the qualities we have named are not usually to be found in the aged. There will be no lack of painstaking enquiry: of broad experience and calm judgment. These qualities may well serve to carry out a gentle liquidation of our society in an orderly and dignified manner, but something more will be needed if we are to survive. Clearly, the longer we delay in facing this problem the more handicapped shall we be by the factor of age. In 1938 there were $10\frac{1}{4}$ million people in England and Wales aged 50 or over—one person in 4. By 1955— only 13 years ahead—there will be over $2\frac{1}{2}$ million more such persons and one individual in every 3 will be 50 or over. But, although our need for the qualities of youth will be greater, paradoxically the chances for youth to advance will be much smaller. In a rapidly expanding population (as in the nineteenth century) it was relatively easy for the so-called self-made man to rise as he had far fewer older men in front. The millionaires' success stories have in some measure been due to the age structure of the population, a reason conspicuously overlooked by the heroes of the stories. The progressive rise in average age within the group 20–65 years which is at present in motion and which is bound to go on, will result in an increasingly restrictive effect upon young people. It may be easier, on account of their scarcity, for young people to obtain jobs, but it will be far harder for them to advance. There will be an increasingly higher proportion of older persons who will hold appointments by virtue of their seniority. It will take far longer for youth to arrive at responsible and leading positions in every sphere of our social and economic life. As advancement is continuously blocked in an increasingly stratified society (for an older population will also tend to emphasise and intensify class structure) discouragement will grow; society will lose the mental attitude that is essential for social progress and community interest will shift from progress to security. This process of the dominance of old age and its interests has already been developing for some years. For example, the claim for higher old age pensions (admittedly needed) has been met, whereas a twenty-five year fight for family allowances is still short of success despite the fact that we have (as compared with the 1914–18 war) 1,500,000 fewer children for whom allowances could be paid.

The probable economic effects of a contracting population in the future can, to some extent, be measured by the influence of an expanding population in the past. The past has much to teach us, provided always that we translate the lessons we learn into twentieth-century conditions; but not if we persist in adopting the traditionally unhealthy habits of the ostrich. Most economists hold, for instance, that rapidly increasing population in the nineteenth century was a vitally important factor in raising the demands for capital and thereby promoting employment. "Increasing population, a rapid succession of inventions, and opportunities for exploiting new territories give buoyancy to the profitability of capital and provide an ever-renewed stimulus to investment...." "In assessing", said Mr. J. M. Keynes, "the causes of the enormous increase in capital during the nineteenth century and since, too little importance has been given to the influence of an increasing population as distinct from other influences."[1] This process had, too, an important psychological aspect. In the nineteenth century business men never doubted that population and markets would expand. They took expansion for granted as a perfectly natural phenomenon; it was never questioned, such was the fear of the over-population bogey. They were able to look ahead and plan ahead in terms of an ever-increasing number of consumers. For them prosperity was not just round the corner; it stretched ahead as far as the eye could see. This optimistic belief that the future would resemble the present led them to expand their plants, take risks, and generally behave in an expansionist manner, thus continually creating new avenues for employment. Increased employment led to increasing consumption which led to more employment and so on. This, then, was the "success spiral" out of which grew "success stories"; the reverse side of the medal from today's "vicious spiral" and "depression

---

[1] J. M. Keynes, Some economic consequences of a declining population, *The Eugenics Review*, XXIX, No. 1, 1937.—Ed.

stories". This expansionist atmosphere bred "confidence", that illusive something which still lingers pathetically in the minds of the City of London but which has vanished from our ken just as surely as the naughty nineties and the Brontosauri.

That business "confidence" made its exit just about the time that mass unemployment came on the stage is no coincidence. Both cannot appear in public at the same time, and, as we have said, mass unemployment has been the social phenomenon of our age. What causes mass unemployment? We cannot here indulge in an analysis of why the economic machine breaks down and why, in peace time, it is increasingly failing (1) to employ all men, and (2) to provide everyone with a decent standard of living made possible by technological and scientific advances and the increasing quantity of goods and services produced by each worker. But because we wish to know whether population trends in the future will be a blessing or a curse we will attempt a brief outline. At the outset let us emphasize something which needs to be said over and over again. Unemployment, poverty, malnutrition and misery are not caused by the sun, moon or stars or by some mysterious supernatural influence on the economic machine: all these things and the evils which dance attendance on them are man-made. This in itself is reassuring because it means that man can solve them.

Now the amount of money in your pay envelope does not depend on how much you produce in goods or provide in the form of services. The amount paid to the worker is less than the value of the things he produces, the difference being rent, interest and profit. For the system to be kept in perfect balance and to continue to function this surplus must all be re-invested in building new factories, constructing new machines, sinking new mines and so on. Thus if this perfect balance is achieved and all goods are consumed, the standard of living should rise progressively as productivity per worker increases. Capital outlay (the disposal of the surplus or what the economists call the "propensity to invest") therefore plays a key role in the economic system. But capital outlay is not undertaken by business men unless they expect an adequate level of profits. Economic recovery, in our present economic system, thus depends upon the foresight, imagination and "confidence" of a numerically small but economically all-important group of people known as entrepreneurs. Their "confidence" is a fragile thing (*a*) because no one can forecast business conditions more than a year or two ahead

(b) because they depend for their capital on banks, and on the "investing public" who may be even more influenced by short-term considerations than the business men. Unfortunately for the mass of ordinary folk, the "confidence" of entrepreneurs is exposed to a constant tendency for the "marginal efficiency" of capital—i.e. the profitability of investment—to decline. The accumulation of capital itself tends ultimately to diminish the "marginal efficiency" of capital. The more plentiful capital becomes, the lower tends to be the net yield which the next capital goods produced will give to the entrepreneur, unless counter-balancing forces simultaneously create a new and proportionate demand for net additional capital outlay. "Capital has to be kept scarce enough in the long period", says Mr. J. M. Keynes, "to have a marginal efficiency" sufficient to induce entrepreneurs to continue producing new capital goods. He points out that:

> "Of two equal communities, having the same technique but different stocks of capital, the community with the smaller stock of capital may be able for the time to enjoy a higher standard of living than the community with the larger stock; though when the poorer community has caught up the richer . . . then both alike will suffer the fate of Midas."

Thus, although from the objective needs-resources point of view, a greater quantity of socially useful capital is invariably preferable to a smaller quantity, man-made obstacles to consumption may convert this accumulation of material wealth into a cause of poverty.

Hitherto there have been counteracting forces which succeeded in keeping capital scarce enough in the long run—by expanding the demand for it—to maintain its "marginal efficiency". These forces were (a) technical advance (i.e. new knowledge embodied in inventions, improved organization of production and in a labour force trained to apply new methods); (b) steady and rapid growth of the home population (i.e. expansion of the internal consumers' market); (c) expansion of foreign trade (i.e. expansion of the number of overseas consumers embraced in the British economic system as customers or as borrowers); and (d) the rise of consuming power per head. This factor was largely a function of the first three. Prolonged stagnation of any one of these forces of expansion would, if the other factors continue to expand demand for net additions to capital no faster than before, have a depressing effect on capital outlay.

We return therefore to the vital point that the system will only work if the entrepreneurs are continually re-investing their profits in new enterprises of every kind. But the very nature of the system is such that surpluses have to be disposed of in some profitable way. Business men do not ask "Will this relieve unemployment?" or "Is it Right to produce more goods?" but "Will it Pay?" In war-time, of course, business men are forced by the Government to produce things (hence we get full employment) but, assuming no fundamental change in the system when Peace comes, the question will be "Will it Pay?" Economic depression may be regarded typically as a state of affairs in which the level anticipated by entrepreneurs appears too low to inspire in them confidence in the profitability of new net capital outlay, which, if undertaken, would, by the mechanism of the "multiplier", expand production approximately to conditions of full employment. Instead, capital and labour remain unemployed because entrepreneurs do not anticipate any profit from expanding production. The result is mass unemployment and it was only the intervention of rearmament in the 1930s that lifted Britain out of stagnation.

The argument we have advanced here has been very simply stated and we have avoided any discussion of many other factors involved in economic depression but we have tried to point out in general terms the fundamental importance of the role played by the "propensity to invest". We have seen that one of the forces which succeeded in keeping capital scarce in the nineteenth century was population expansion. This factor will no longer operate and if there are no fundamental economic changes the effect is likely to be disastrous on the employment of capital and labour.

Unemployment of labour can be divided into two main types, which are called "structural" and "cyclical". Structural unemployment results from changes in productive methods, from some industries declining in importance while others grow. The switch to war production is one example. Unessential industries decline, thus throwing people out of work and some time elapses before they are caught up in war production. In a period of contracting population, structural unemployment is bound to occur on a larger scale than hitherto and in a more intensified form for the reasons already given. Moreover, there is no certainty that people thrown out of work by declining industries will be absorbed by other industries catering for the needs of old people. Then again, every 1000 people who become unemployed by this process will, in their turn, create further unemployment to the extent of x individuals, by reducing their consumption of goods and services. If, while our population is declining, we can maintain full employment, "structural" unemployment will not be important: it will only be important if it is accompanied by "cyclical" or mass unemployment. That is to say, it will be easy to refit and retrain workers displaced by decaying industries if mass unemployment does not occur. The latter (described by some economists as "cyclical" unemployment) will, as we have indicated, result in the main from a contracting market and an over-supply of capital unable to find profitable avenues of employment. Quite apart from the effects of the war and of the period of reconstruction, our general conclusion then is that the change-over in population trend will, within the present economic structure, tend to produce more unemployment which in turn will be aggravated by the monopolistic and restrictionist practices of vested interests which are quite likely to be much more dangerous when one of the forces making for an expanding economy has disappeared.

We may mention one other vital aspect of a comparison between the economic consequence of an expanding and a contracting population. Economic mistakes under the first, resulting in a particular type of capital being in temporary over-supply, were, in such conditions, rapidly corrected. Mistakes, grave mistakes, were made; but, and this is important in our discussion of social intelligence, there was an automatic corrective in the continuous population growth. Bluntly put, we could "take a chance", and if things went wrong then no irreparable damage was done. Now there is no mechanism to cover up our mistakes. Now, if our relatively septuagenarian statesmen make mistakes they will be economically serious because they cannot rely on the birth-rate to cloak the consequences. To quote Mr. Keynes again, "Demand in an era of declining population tends to be below what was expected, and a state of over-supply is less easily corrected. Thus a pessimistic atmosphere may ensue; and, although at long last pessimism may tend to correct itself through its effect on supply, the first result to prosperity of a change-over from an increasing to a declining population may be very disastrous".

If we want an illustration of this process we need look no further than the Lancashire cotton trade. Here, the industry has been faced for many years with a contracting market but it still tried to maintain a nineteenth-century outlook. "The reason why, despite all that has been said," remarked the late Lord Stamp in the House of Lords in June, 1939, "there is very little popular apprehensiveness on the subject (population decline) is that we are still living under the social illusion of continuous expansion. You can see it in discussions by urban district councils and borough councils, and even in discussions in this august place. We have got so used for a hundred years to this continual increment that we are not yet attuned to the thought, not merely of becoming stationary, but of a reversal of the process."

XXIII

J. Jewkes, The population scare, *Manchester School of Economic and Social Studies*, X, 2, 1939, pp. 106–14, 121.

Mr. Harrod, in his recent article,[1] presents a gloomy picture of the economic effects of a fall in population. They appear to me to constitute an insecure basis upon which to erect the social policy which he advocates. Certain of these economic effects are transitional aches and pains; if we assume that the population could be stabilized at a lower level, they are, therefore, temporary in character.

Mr. Harrod argues that "in the coming decades we shall have a rapidly ageing population and the maintenance of the older members will be an increasing burden on those actively employed." On the other hand, he omits to point out that there will be a smaller number of children to be maintained by the actively employed. Enid Charles, even on the basis of a forecast that the population of England and Wales will fall to 19 millions by 2035, also estimates that the number of persons aged 15–59 years, which was 64·3 per cent of the total population in 1935, will be 62·3 per cent in 1970 and 60·1 per cent in 2035.[2] This is a decline of insignificant magnitude. Other estimates give more optimistic conclusions. Thus Colin Clark argues[3] that "owing to changing age composition, the economic productivity of the population is going to rise during the next generation" and that, even after 1975, the decline in the proportion of occupied males will be comparatively small. Two other important possible reactions must, however, be taken into account here. First, if the average size of family falls, it is not unlikely that there will be an increase in the proportion of females who are not unduly embarrassed by heavy family responsibilities and who, therefore, will be able to increase the total occupied population. Second, the increasing length of life

---

[1] R. F. Harrod, Modern population trends, *Manchester School of Economic and Social Studies*, X, 1, 1939.—Ed.
[2] Enid Charles, London and Cambridge Economic Service, Special Memorandum No. 40.
[3] Colin Clark, National Income and Outlay, p. 21.

means not only that people live longer but that they are capable of carrying on effective work to a later age. A great deal of play has been made with the idea of a 'nation in carpet slippers' but in fact, in the future, we can confidently expect that the average person will be able to delay the donning of his carpet slippers. The proportion of the occupied to the total population would then tend to increase. The presumption, therefore, is that the nation will gain, and not lose, within the next thirty years, from the changing proportion of occupied to non-occupied persons.

There is, secondly, the argument that where the population is declining, secular changes in the relative importance of industries will create greater dislocation of the labour market and make for increasing labour immobility and unemployment. The validity of this argument, of course, is not to be doubted. It really constitutes a case for a rapidly increasing population, since a stationary population is also at some disadvantage here. But this surely is a factor of minor importance, certainly not one which should count heavily in reaching fundamental decisions relating to population policy. The pressure of population, even in Great Britain in the nineteenth century, scarcely exceeded 1 per cent per annum. Population in Great Britain in the next thirty years will probably decline by less than 0·25 per cent per annum. Normal retirement of personnel from an industry through old age or death is about 2 per cent per annum. And it must not be overlooked that a rapid increase in population leading to a swift growth of certain industries may, under free enterprise, produce dislocation in the labour market because of the faulty or short-sighted judgment of individual workers. The nineteenth century was not free from periods of severe maladjustment in the labour market, ranging from the plight of the hand-loom weavers down to the periodic gluts of labour in the building trades. In any case a policy of encouraging a large domestic population can bring little relief to industries mainly concerned with export. Cannan's balanced perspective is surely the correct one: "(the approach of a declining population) will provide more rather than less reason for promoting mobility of labour ... we shall have to take more, rather than less care, than at present to secure that arrangements which seem superficially desirable do not hinder that mobility." But when Mr. Harrod seeks to magnify this point and assert that mobility of labour is likely to decrease in the future, and hence increase unemployment, it appears that he embarks upon extremely dangerous surmise. It may be true, as he suggests, that the growing importance of semi-luxury trades will increase the instability of demand and hence the need for greater mobility. It is probably true that the Unemployment Insurance Scheme has reduced mobility. And there are many other points that might have been added. For instance, since female labour is particularly immobile, any increase in its relative importance will increase general labour immobility. On the other hand, there are many factors which might normally be expected in the future to increase mobility. A higher proportion of workers are being trained in more general forms of industrial skill, particularly in machine-tending. In the future, we shall probably never have again the problem of a dislocated labour market in the degree to which we suffered from it after 1920; our export trades are relatively smaller; our industries less intensely localized. It is only to be expected that, with increasing experience, the placing work of the Employment Exchanges will become more efficient: certainly their recently enlarged experiments in the re-training of unemployed workers hold out enormous possibilities. I am not suggesting, of course, that mobility of labour in the future will be greater. In the midst of these, and many other counteracting and imponderable factors, my answer would be that I don't know. But then, I submit, neither does anyone else.

I turn now to the economic reasons for deploring a return to a smaller population. Mr. Harrod believes that a small population will result in "a net loss of production per head. The economies of large scale have not yet reached their limit in this country and a contraction of the market would lead to diminished efficiency in many fields." This, of course, is a crucial decision and Mr. Harrod, presumably, has evidence, which could not be given in one short paper, to back this decision. My own impression would be exactly the contrary. Most industries in this country consist of a relatively large number of independent firms and of an even larger number of independent technical units. Moreover, these units are of varying efficiency. I cannot think that the output per head would decrease in coal mining, in iron and steel, in cotton, in clothing, in engineering, in food or in building, if (say) the 20 per cent least efficient firms were closed down. It is difficult to think of any one important industry or public service which could not seize upon the full economies of large scale production with (say) a market of 20 million persons in an area as small as that of Great Britain. On the other side the cost of congestion in our main centres of population in the way of traffic delay and the time spent in reaching and returning from work must be considerable. Clearly, innumerable and most intricate problems involving economic, social and administrative issues would have to be settled here before any judgment, having any claim to scientific responsibility, could be arrived at. I suggest that we are not yet in a position to exercise that judgment.

Mr. Harrod seeks, even, to snatch away from us the consolation that at least a diminished population will, by forcing the less efficient lands out of cultivation, increase agricultural productivity. He believes that "the application of science to agriculture throws some doubt on whether the law of diminishing return works very strongly in the backward direction". It may be true, although I am not aware of the evidence, that increasingly scientific methods in agriculture will somewhat lessen the consequences of inherent differentials in productivity between one piece of land and another. But those differences still remain substantial. Even in a country as small as our own, Mr. Kendall has shown recently[1] what substantial variations there are in fertility, and the decline in arable area in the past ten years, county by county, confirms what most people up to now have regarded as a truism, that the least fertile land goes out of cultivation first. In the United States the yield per acre varies greatly for the same crop from one State to another. Certainly the decline in arable acreage in the United States since the war has taken place in the naturally less fertile land.[2] It is just as dangerous now to under-emphasize the importance of the law of diminishing returns as it was, in the time of Malthus, to over-emphasize it.

Mr. Harrod is particularly alarmed lest a decline in population, by leading to a deficient demand for new saving, will increase unemployment. This, again, is partly a problem of transition, although it is not wholly unrelated to the question of the size of the population. His conclusions are based upon a number of forecasts of probable secular changes in habits of saving and outlets for investment.

(a) "The channels of overseas investment are closed and are not likely soon to be re-opened." If by 'soon' is meant a decade the statement may have some probability value. But if 50 or 75 years is meant, and

---

[1] M. G. Kendall, *Journal of Royal Statistical Society*, Part I, 1939.
[2] *Recent Social Trends*, Vol. I, 109.

The Population Scare

that is the period of which Mr. Harrod must think in terms of his population policy, it would seem to have none. Who is to say that, within the next quarter of a century, there may not be enormous international investment in China, in South America, in Africa?

(b) "The new technical inventions are not notably of a capital requiring kind". Here again forecasting seems to be dangerous. But many will be surprised that the statement should be made even of the last decade.[1] It is true that there are, at present, no spectacular openings for investment such as that provided in this country in the nineteenth century by the construction of railways, but, after all, there has been practically no railway building for the past half-century. On the other hand, we have had enormous growth of investment in road transport and in the generation and distribution of electricity. Moreover a considerable number of industries provide illustrations of extremely heavy investment: branches of the chemical industry; the hydrogenation of coal; mechanization in bottle-making and flour-milling. But it is not so much the general rule as the average case that is important. There is a universal tendency towards mechanization at present which there is no reason to believe will slacken off in the future.[2] Estimates of the rate at which capital equipment is accumulating must inevitably be hazardous, but Douglas,[3] in the only elaborate calculation that has been made, indicates that, in the United States, between 1899 and 1922 there was certainly no tendency for the annual percentage rate of increase of capital equipment to slow down. And the fact that, in the United States, between 1922 and 1929 the output of durable goods and capital equipment was increasing much more rapidly than that of non-durable and consumption goods[4] should at least lead us into caution when forecasting future technical changes.

(c) A decline in population, of itself, might be expected to create a

---

[1] Mr. Harrod's view appears to run contrary to the school of thinkers who look upon increasing capital intensity as the most spectacular fact of our time and whose views as to the future social, political and economic structure of society are coloured by this supposed fact.
[2] See, as indicative of conditions in the United States, H. Jerome, *Mechanisation in Industry*.
[3] P. H. Douglas, *Real Wages in the United States*, p. 567.
[4] F. C. Mills, *Recent Economic Tendencies*, p. 280.

tendency towards long-period unemployment. When population is increasing the multiplication of capital goods of the existing types is a task which the entrepreneur confidently foresees; he has fairly definitely pre-ordained function.[1] If the population is falling, the supply of capital goods will be maintained only if different kinds of capital goods are being brought forward. Recognizing Mr. Harrod's eminence in this field of economics I express doubt on his conclusions on this point only with the greatest reluctance. But I am not convinced that, in fact, the tendency mentioned above is particularly likely to become actual since possible counteracting forces cannot be ruled out.

There is the whole question of the rate of industrial invention. For many reasons this might be expected to increase rather than decrease in the future. Improvements in the general standard of education enlarge the field of the intellectually trained from whom new ideas may spring. The increase of mechanical mindedness which normal life demands of us all may be the forcing ground for further mechanical developments. The increasing proportion of the national income devoted to industrial and scientific research might have the same effect. Moreover, once a general body of scientific knowledge exists, each new invention is not only of value in itself; it becomes possible, very often, to link it with earlier techniques and apply it almost universally. Thus the internal combustion engine makes possible, for the first time, controlled flight in the air but the engine can also be harnessed to the boat, the road vehicle, the stationary machine. The conveyance of impressions by waves makes possible the transmission of sound and of form and colour but also opens up the possibility of more complete use of existing wire telephony. Each new invention is not merely the establishment of a new plant; it is a fertilizer which leads all the existing trees to push out all their boughs and branches a little further. It is at least tenable that, in the future, the consequences of a declining population upon possible avenues for investment might well be offset by the force of invention alone.

There is, too, the question of the increasing use of durable consumption goods. It may well be that an increasing proportion of the capital equipment of the community is now taking this form and will

---

[1] See J. R. Hicks, "Mr. Keynes' Theory of Employment", *Economic Journal*, June, 1936.

continue to do so. The equipment of homes with labour-saving devices; the association of leisure pursuits with the use of machines, such as television or motor cars; the replacement of hand-work by the typewriter and the dictaphone; the more complete control of temperature and air condition within buildings, including the domestic house; the replacement of the mass-provided public services, such as the public services vehicle, and cinema by the more convenient (but probably more expensive from the capital point of view) private motor car or home cinema: here are enormous potentialities over a long period in the case of which the consumer will be clamouring for the new technique. A rapid increase in the capital intensity of private possessions is certainly not out of the question. The possibilities are the greater here since the existing inequality in the distribution of wealth means that there are numerous forms of private capital equipment now in possession of the rich which, as it were, are on show to the rest of the community who may frequently seek, by economy on consumers goods, to take advantage of that kind of equipment. So the dinner parties disappear and the eight-cylinder car is bought, or the consumption of beer declines and the motor cycle replaces it.

As a population declines it acquires, almost as a legacy, an increasing quantity of equipment per head such as more factories, more roads. Some of that equipment will almost certainly not be found worth while to maintain. But other equipment, notably roads, would almost certainly be maintained. The cost of depreciation per head of the population would rise. An increased part of national savings would, therefore, be directed into these channels; an increased proportion of the population would find employment in these fields.

Finally, it must be borne in mind that, over the next thirty years in Great Britain the decline in population will be small; that the decline in the number of adults (who exercise the important demand for capital equipment) will go on more slowly than in the case of the population as a whole and that this decline will be foreseen with some confidence and will therefore not be so serious, from the angle from which we are at present discussing it, as might otherwise be the case.

(d) If Mr. Harrod is thinking over a long period of the relation between the demand for new capital and the savings accruing, he must not leave out of account the possibility of secular changes in habits of saving. Mr. Clark, indeed, has recently startled us all by the statement that "net private saving has ceased or become negative."[1] Whether that statement is true or not, it appears that changes in habits of saving are not impossible and it is possible that they would be in a direction which would lesson the evils feared.

Finally, Mr. Harrod feels that "our country will present the mournful aspect of a deserted and derelict area, its houses uninhabited and its equipment unused." That is a value-judgment which many would not be prepared to accept. Others might be more prepared to mourn the fantastic pushing and jostling of our larger centres of population and the de-humanizing influence of constantly living in a large crowd which many of our cities enforce upon a large section of the population . . . .

I arrive at a single and negative conclusion: that scientific knowledge of the economic and social consequences of changes in the size of a population is still too fragmentary to justify our framing of any population policy, much less one which constitutes a drastic revolution in the distribution of income. It is true that more, much more, is known concerning population movements now than half-a-century ago. But it is equally clear that other questions can be formulated to which answers cannot be provided with confidence. And beyond this there are factors, which we cannot even yet formulate precisely, but which we are dimly and obscurely aware might in the long run be of overwhelming significance. It is necessary to give the benefit of the doubt to what we do not know. At the present time the need is for patient and unambitious research into population problems and not for large scale and precipitous experiment or even for Royal Commissions. Another big mistake by economists on this subject would certainly put them out of court for the rest of this century.

---

[1] Colin Clark, *National Income and Outlay*, p. xv.

XXIV

United Nations, *The determinants and consequences of population trends*, New York 1953, pp. 239, 241, 241–2, 243, 243–4, 244–5, 245, 246, 246–7, 247, 248, 248–9, 249, 250, 251, 252, 253, 253–4, 254, 255–6, 256.

3. The social and economic implications of population changes in the highly industrialized countries differ from those in the under-developed countries, not only because of differences in social and economic conditions, but also because of differences in the existing demographic trends. The existing and prospective population structures and population trends in the various countries have been outlined in Chapters VII and VIII. In general, the highly industrialized countries have a greater degree of demographic stability than the under-developed countries; their fertility and mortality rates are lower, and in many of them the rate of population increase has declined to a low level.

4. In highly industrialized countries, the economic and social effects of population changes are more complex and more subtle than in less developed countries. The indications are that in industrialized countries, demographic factors are relatively less important than other factors which bear on industrial efficiency, the development of capital equipment, and the fullness of employment. Partly for this reason and partly because of the diversity of conditions in the various industries characteristic of highly developed manufacturing and commercial economies, the economic effects of population changes in such countries are difficult to evaluate statistically. For example, the technique of comparing data on short-term population changes with time series on production, employment, or other relevant economic variables is of dubious value for this purpose. The variations in the latter series due to non-demographic factors tend to obscure the demographic influences which may be present. Long-range comparisons are inconclusive because of the lack of adequate, long-term series of statistics and because of the multiplicity of non-demographic factors which come to bear on the economy during

long intervals. Similar difficulties, if not even greater ones, hinder the analysis of the effects of population changes upon such phenomena as the development of social services, changes in social institutions and mores, and the incidence of social maladjustments and tensions.

5. In spite of the difficulties of statistical analysis, recent research in this field has produced a number of hypotheses regarding the influence of demographic factors upon the productivity of industry, the trends of investment opportunities, capital formation, the risks of unemployment, development of the social services, etc., in industrialized countries. To a large extent these hypotheses lack statistical verification, and even where supported by statistics, the conclusions are frequently open to question. Some of the hypotheses conflict with one another, but many of them find at least a fairly general acceptance. They represent a somewhat tentative, incomplete, and unintegrated body of theory which requires a great deal of further research, but may nevertheless have substantial value in the consideration of questions of policy. . . .

12. According to the findings of studies summarized in Chapter VIII the outstanding feature of recent demographic history in most of the highly industrialized countries is a decline in the rate of population growth. In some of these countries this trend has continued until the population is approaching a stationary level; in others population growth continues at a moderate rate, but at a rate below that of former times. It is possible that in the future some of the industrialized countries will enter a period of decreasing population. A considerable volume of literature is concerned with the possible social and economic effects of a declining rate of population growth and of a stationary or declining population. . . .

14. It is a widely held opinion among present-day economists that the volume of employment in a capitalistic, industrial community depends largely upon two factors: the volume of investment and the thriftiness of the community. If the economy is to operate at a high level of employment and income, the rate of investment must not be too low, nor the rate of savings too high. The decisions to invest and to save are to a considerable extent independent of each other, and the rate at which entrepreneurs wish to invest may not be the same

as the rate at which individuals wish to save. But the amounts that are invested and saved during any period must necessarily be equal, for both savings and investment are measured by the difference between production and consumption during the period. Thus, if in the light of prospective capital earnings, entrepreneurs are not prepared to make an amount of investment equal to the amount which individuals would save at a certain level of employment and income, the volume of employment and the aggregate income will be smaller. This means a smaller amount of savings, not only because the individuals will have less income from which to save, but also because the proportion which they wish to save from a smaller income is normally less than the proportion which they would wish to save from a larger income. Thus, given the rates of savings which individuals desire at various income levels, the levels of employment and income are governed by the rate of investment; alternatively, given the rate of investment, employment and income depend on the schedule of proportions of income which the individuals wish to save (often called the "propensity to save").

15. According to the "stagnation thesis", as presented by Keynes, Hansen, and their followers, a declining rate of population growth tends in two ways to diminish the volume of employment and income: (*a*) by reducing the rate of investment, and (*b*) by increasing the propensity to save.

16. It is the tendency to reduce investment which is considered to be the more important of the two factors. The argument in this connexion proceeds from the premise that a large proportion of all investment in a country with a rapidly growing population goes to provide the additional capital and durable goods needed to satisfy the increasing demand for consumers' goods. During the nineteenth century, when the population of the Western industrial countries was growing rapidly, this increase of numbers gave a constant encouragement to investment, supplementing the stimuli of new inventions and opportunities for exploiting new territories and resources. More recently, the declining rate of population growth has greatly diminished the stimulus to investment coming from that source. The era of territorial expansion also is drawing to a close. Technological innovations making for

intensive expansion of the economy may be expected to continue, but they cannot easily compensate for the closing of other investment outlets. The result is a tendency for income and employment to fall, or at least to rise more sluggishly than before; and persistent unemployment appears. If income and employment decline, bringing about a decrease of consumption, there is a further shrinkage of investment according to the so-called "acceleration-deceleration principle". According to one view, the fall of investment may be cushioned by a drop in the interest rate resulting from the reduction of income, but this view does not appear to be shared by all proponents of the "stagnation thesis"....

20. Many, but not all, of the authors who believe that a decline in population growth tends to restrict investment opportunities also maintain that the rate of saving is raised and the difficulties of maintaining full employment in capitalistic, industrial countries thus increased. The literature regarding the possible influence of population trends upon the "propensity to consume" or the rate of saving is summarized in Chapter XII. As that summary shows, the hypothesis stated above is based primarily on the results of statistical inquiries into family expenditures and savings which show that at a given income level families with fewer children save more than families with many children. It is sometimes suggested that other demographic factors, such as the aging of the population which accompanies the slackening of population growth, may tend to reduce savings. Furthermore, non-demographic factors, i.e., a fall in the interest rate, may reduce savings. However, the importance of these offsetting factors is uncertain. Some writers have concluded that the net result is likely to be an increase in the rate of saving, and some have suggested that, even where there may be a decline in the rate of savings, it is generally not sufficient to counterbalance a marked decrease in the rate of investment....

21. The pessimistic views stated above have by no means gone unchallenged. Some of the critics have denied that a decline or cessation of population growth will depress investment or that it will stimulate over-saving. Others emphasize non-demographic causes of persistent unemployment.

22. Some of these critics, while admitting that population growth in the past has been a very important source of investment opportunities, reject the conclusion that the cessation of growth means under-investment. They claim that adequate alternative investment outlets exist in known but unexploited techniques. These alternatives are not new; they have existed for generations, but population growth in the past created opportunities which were more lucrative at that time. The "stagnationists" are accused of assuming too close a relation between the number of consumers and total consumption; per capita purchasing power may be far more important than the size of the population. The level of real per capita incomes may continue to rise even if total population declines; thus investment outlets may still expand. . . .

26. The argument that population decline or slackening population growth tends to increase the rate of saving is disputed by many writers, and even by some who accept that part of the "stagnation thesis" relating to investment. For example, Terborgh, while believing that the tapering off of population growth tends to reduce investment opportunities, indicated that this has no serious consequences, since reduced investment is balanced at least in part by reduced savings. While a substantial fraction of all saving is motivated by investment in particular capital goods, such as automobiles, household equipment, etc., that fraction vanishes when such goods cease to be purchased. Therefore, the decline in the component of capital formation attributable to population growth results in a partially compensatory reduction in saving.[1] Furthermore, as mentioned in Chapter XII, an increase in the proportion of aged persons within the population may tend to increase the dissaving in the community, leaving a reduced fraction of the total saving to be absorbed in capital formation. Also, increased community expenses for social services to the aged may reduce the proportion of the national income available for savings. In addition, it has been noted that the saving differentials found in statistical studies dealing with the relationship between propensity to consume and family size were too small to warrant the conclusion that a trend toward smaller families creates serious investment-savings

---

[1] G. Terborgh, *The bogey of economic maturity*, Chicago, 1945.—Ed.

discrepancies. Furthermore, the spread of the small family system is not necessarily accompanied by a decline in the propensity to consume for the community as a whole, since the propensity to save may increase as the pattern of living and other relevant conditions are altered.

27. Most critics of the thesis under discussion emphasize non-demographic causes of unemployment. Perhaps the group considered as critics should include all authors who have endeavoured to explain the long-range trends in demand for labour without referring to population trends. . . .

28. The discussion up to this point relates to the question of how a diminution in the rate of population growth may affect savings, investment, and employment if other things remain equal. But other things may not remain equal; their changes may offset the deleterious effects, if any, of the declining rate of population growth. Some authors believe that an acceleration of technological progress may offset any reduction of investment opportunities due to the population trends, others doubt that technological advances will be rapid enough to have that effect. Expansion into new territories, particularly in the form of large investments in under-developed countries, is often regarded as a simultaneous solution for the savings-investments problems of industrialized countries and for the developmental problems of under-developed countries. Many economists, however, consider it unlikely that an adequate solution can be found in this way, because they believe that only limited amounts of capital can profitably be invested in the under-developed countries, and that such investments utilize few savings that would not be employed otherwise. It is sometimes said that a reduction of the interest rate would permit radical changes of technique involving large capital outlays, and would encourage greater consumption of the products of highly capitalized industries. The contrary view is also frequently stated, to the effect that the rate of interest does not greatly influence consumption patterns or the willingness of entrepreneurs to invest. Attention is called to the possibility of public investments designed to compensate for deficits in private investments, and of tax and fiscal policies aimed at achieving a more equitable distribution of incomes and thereby reducing the

rate of saving. Other means of bringing investments and savings into balance, such as changes in wage rates, have also been suggested. ...

33. The preceding summary of findings relating to the "stagnation thesis" makes it plain that economists do not agree as to the effects of a declining rate of population growth on investment and savings and thus on the trend of employment. The controversy over this question is far from being settled. ...

34. It seems to be fairly well agreed that, if a slow rate of population increase (or a decrease of population) does have an adverse effect in this connexion, its effect can be minimized or offset by remedies other than population policy measures. On the other hand, if the population trend does play an important part in the problem of maintaining full employment, measures to encourage population growth would be advantageous from this point of view. There is a need for more investigation, especially historical investigation, of the influence of population growth upon investment and saving.

35. The discussion of the "stagnation thesis" deals chiefly with the possible effects of population trends on the problem of unemployment due to an inadequate demand for labour. Consideration must also be given to the losses caused by maladjustments of demand and supply in particular industries, giving rise to what has been called "structural unemployment". The consensus of opinion among writers concerned with this topic is that, other things being equal, the risks of such maladjustments are likely to be somewhat greater under conditions of a stationary or declining population than when the population is growing rapidly.

36. First, it is generally believed that the risk of over-development in particular industries is greater when the population is stationary or declining than when the population is growing considerably. Myrdal has pointed out that the risk of wasteful disproportions and maladjustments in capital investments, and of subsequent losses, increases when the rate of population growth falls. As long as population grows rapidly, over-production in any line of economic activity is likely to be corrected quickly, as there seldom is an absolute decline in demand for the products of any particular industry. But with a

stationary or diminishing population, the argument runs, shifts in consumers' demand will mean reduction in demand for certain consumers' goods, and in accordance with the "deceleration principle" a subsequent contraction of demand for the corresponding capital goods may occur. . . .[1]

38. Further, it is held that adjustments to over-capacity in some industries can be more easily effected under conditions of rapid population growth. When the population is growing, the distribution of the labour supply can often be corrected without transferring workers already established in the contracting industries, by directing young people entering the labour market into the expanding industries. . . .

42. The importance of the conclusion that problems of structural unemployment are likely to be aggravated by a decline in the rate of population growth must not be exaggerated. The population trend is only one factor, though an important one, which may influence demand and supply in particular industries. Further, the problem of structural unemployment should be considered in relation to that of general unemployment. If unemployment is not general, the factors tending towards structural unemployment may not be of great importance. In any case, the tendency in that direction can be resisted, though it cannot be entirely overcome, by positive action.

43. A third type of unemployment, that which is associated with the business cycle, has also been attributed, to some extent, to changes in the rate of population growth. . . .

44. The argument is that, during the upswing of the business cycle, rapid population growth and the increase in the number of "consuming units" contribute to the growth of consumption and deter any rise in the rate of savings. At the same time, the growth of population results in the diverting of a large part of consumers' expenditures toward products which require heavy capital outlays. In both of these ways it tends to support and extend the expansion of income and employment. On the other hand, in a community

---

[1] G. Myrdal, *Population: a problem for democracy*, Cambridge (Mass.) 1940.—Ed.

with a declining population, the phase of expansion is more likely to come to an end before a state of full employment is reached. Furthermore, during the depression phase an increasing population tends to stimulate consumption (e.g. by some pressure on residential construction), whereas in a contracting population this stimulant for consumption will be absent. . . .

47. The effects of slower population growth on labour supply have also been mentioned in support of this hypothesis. It is said that during a period of cyclical expansion the annual increments in labour supply (and the labour reserves accumulated during the preceding depression) push back the limits which a shortage of labour would impose on the expansion. During the depression, when there is already a large amount of unemployment, an increase in labour supply does not appear to directly affect the level of economic activity. An increased labour supply is unlikely to have much effect on wages, and any effects it may have in this respect are not likely to contribute to recovery. On the other hand, in the case of a declining population where the labour supply is contracting, the prosperity period is likely to be a shorter duration due to the limitation of labour supply than in the case of an expanding population. On the whole, labour supply is considered as a limiting rather than a positive factor in affecting the level of economic activity. . . .

49. The population trend may be conducive not only to the total unemployment of a portion of the labour force, but also to "underemployment", that is, to employment in jobs which occupy only a part of the workers' available time or permit only the partial utilization of their productive capacities. The latter form of waste of human resources is sometimes called "concealed" or "disguised" unemployment, and may be caused by any of the conditions which produce total unemployment, including structural maladjustments, cyclical fluctuations, or persistent deficiency of the general demand for labour. If a slackening rate of population growth tends to increase the volume of total unemployment by aggravating any of these conditions, an increase in the extent of under-employment is also likely to occur. . . .

54. The influence of population growth on the rate of the size of the labour force to the total population and on various characteristics of

the labour force relevant to its productive efficiency, has been treated in Chapter XI. The findings of studies reviewed there show that the decline of population growth in the highly industrialized countries has tended, on the whole, to raise the ratio of the labour force to the total population and thus to raise per capita income. This effect has been brought about primarily by the aging of the population which accompanied the declining rate of population growth. In the future, however, unless the population again begins to grow rapidly, its age-composition in some countries is likely to assume a form which implies a relatively small labour force in proportion to the total population, and serious problems of old-age dependency.

55. Declining population growth and the accompanying changes in age-composition are also likely to facilitate the education and training of the labour force, and thus to increase labour force productivity. These favourable influences may perhaps be offset to some extent by a loss of efficiency and adaptability due to the increasing proportion of workers past middle age; but the potential importance of that loss has not been clearly demonstrated.

56. If a nation's stock of natural resources and man-made capital equipment is taken as given, it is evident that the smaller the population the larger will be the per capita quantity of these assets and, ceteris paribus, the higher the level of per capita output. As the rate of population growth falls, many assets which were formerly required to satisfy the needs of large annual increments in the number of consumers are freed for use in supplying the labour force with a larger per capita quantity of materials and equipment. The Economics Committee of the British Population Commission pointed out that if the British population were still growing at the "Victorian rate" of 1·2 per cent per year, an amount equal to 5 per cent of the national income just prior to World War II would have to be spent annually, merely to maintain at its present level the per capita amount of capital equipment. With a stationary population, this capital could be used to raise per capita output. A purely static analysis thus indicates that slow growth or decline of population is favourable to rising per capita output, so far as its effect on the per capita quantity of productive assets is concerned.

57. The advantage of slow population growth in this connexion is

Consequences of Population Trends

particularly apparent as regards the per capita supplies of those natural resources which cannot be readily replaced or increased. As shown in Chapter XIII, unless efficient and economical substitutes for such resources can be found, the increasing use of them required by a growing population tends to raise costs and thus to hamper an increase in per capita output. The position of the highly industrialized countries with reference to mineral reserves and sources of energy, discussed from a world-wide point of view in Chapter X, is particularly pertinent. It is possible that in some of the industrialized countries a denser population would facilitate the exploitation of certain hitherto unused natural resources, perhaps at a declining per unit cost. It seems evident, however, that the slower the population grows in most of the industrialized countries, the more advantageous will be their future position with regard to irreplaceable natural resources.

58. With regard to man-made capital equipment, on the other hand, it is possible that the decline in the rate of population growth tends to diminish the rate at which such equipment is accumulated over a considerable period of time. As shown in this chapter, many contemporary economists believe that the decline of population growth tends to increase the risk of unemployment; in that way it may diminish production, income, and the quantity of capital formed during a period of years. Furthermore, it is possible that slow population growth and aging of the population may tend to prolong the use of out-moded and nearly out-worn capital goods, thus reducing the efficiency of production.

59. The findings of studies summarized in Chapter XIII indicate that there are three ways in which population growth may influence per capita output through its effects on economic organization and techniques: (a) by making possible a greater division of labour; (b) by permitting the realization of economies of large-scale production; and (c) by stimulating or retarding technological progress.

60. So far as the division of labour and economies of scale are concerned, the cessation of population growth evidently involves

the sacrifice of at least a part of whatever reductions of cost and increases in per capita output could be achieved in those ways. However, the literature reviewed in Chapter XIII indicates that the economies of scale which may result from population increase have not yet been thoroughly analysed even in conceptual terms. Their probable magnitude under the conditions existing in particular countries is a little explored field of study....

62. Findings of studies reviewed in Chapter XIII indicate that the influence of a declining rate of population growth upon technological progress is not known. Certain authors believe a decline in population growth stimulates technological progress; others believe its influence is inhibiting or negligible....

66. Whether the decline in the rate of population growth observed in many highly industrialized countries is advantageous on the balance, is not easy to determine. The answer depends on the relative weight given to certain opposing influences, and may differ for individual countries....

69. Many authors, including some of those who believe that slower population growth is advantageous as well as certain others who consider it disadvantageous on the balance, concluded that the population of most of the highly industrialized countries could vary within rather wide limits without any appreciable change in per capita output of the population of these countries....

70. As explained in Chapter VII, an aging of the population has taken place in most of the highly industrialized countries during the last fifty years or more, and is expected to continue at least for several decades into the future. The aging is due primarily to the decline of fertility, leading to a progressive decrease in the percentage of children in the population and a corresponding increase in the percentage of persons in the higher age brackets. This process may be hastened by the decline of mortality, resulting in an increasing proportion of the children born who will survive to adulthood and old age. In some countries the aging process has also been accelerated by emigration, which has removed from the population a substantial number of young adults. Certain of the economic and social effects of the aging

tendency will be summarized here in order to present a general view of the social and economic problems associated with this demographic trend. . . .

72. The influence of aging of the population upon the size of the dependency load, as measured by the relative numbers of economically active and inactive persons, has been considered in Chapter XI. The findings of studies reviewed there show that the process of aging, in its early stages, tends to reduce the burden of dependency by cutting down the ratio of children too young to work to the total number of persons in the productive age groups. At a later stage, the relative number of persons too old to work may increase faster than the relative number of children is reduced, with the result that the ratio of dependants to the economically active population rises. Until recently, the aging of the population in most of the highly industrialized countries has been such as to reduce dependency; in consequence, most of them are at present in an advantageous position so far as the ratio of the economically active to dependent age groups is concerned. Many of them have been in that position for a long time, and can be expected to remain there for a long time to come, with only relatively minor changes in the ratio. However, if aging continues, their position in this respect will deteriorate, for the percentage of aged dependants will eventually mount much faster than the percentage of children falls. Some countries have already begun to pay the penalty of a sharply rising ratio of dependants to producers. . . .

78. Not only the size of the economically active population, but also the efficiency of the workers and the amount of time they are willing to put in working may be affected by the aging of the population and the concomitant aging of the labour force. The summary of literature presented in Chapter XI indicates, however, that the possible influence of aging in these connexions has not been fully investigated. Some authors believe that a decline in the proportion of young workers, who are considered to be superior in strength, energy, adaptability and speed, implies a reduction in the efficiency of the labour force. Others are of the opinion that any losses in these qualities will be more than compensated for by the greater skill, dependability and wisdom which come with age and experience. Studies of the relative efficiency of workers of different ages in

various types of jobs have not been adequate to resolve this controversy. Likewise, the existing data are not adequate to establish whether or not aging tends to reduce the amount of time which the members of the labour force are willing to work per day, per week, or per year.

79. Some authors believe that the efficiency, not only of the workers, but also of their machines, tools, and other capital equipment tends to decline as population ages. This is thought to occur because the need for renewing equipment is not felt so strongly in a country where the average age is relatively high, as in one with a younger population.

80. The flexibility of the economically active population is also believed to be affected by the aging process. Numerous writers have considered the probable effects of changes in the age composition upon geographic or inter-regional mobility and upon occupational mobility and adaptability. Most writers have concluded that younger men and women are the most mobile and adaptable groups in the population; therefore, a decline in their numerical importance in the labour force will result in less flexibility, unless counterbalancing measures appear.

81. Evidence is presented later to the effect that younger people are more apt to migrate to new areas than are older people. This being the case, it seems likely that industrial readjustment can be achieved more easily when the labour force is composed of a relatively large proportion of young workers who can be expected to respond to employment opportunities in other areas. Daniel's study of labour migration in Great Britain, for example, shows that for a given economic incentive young people move more readily than older people.[1] One reason advanced for this tendency is that older workers are more likely to have ties which deter their moving to new areas.

82. Occupational and industrial mobility within a given area may also be affected by the age factor, since older workers are considered to be less adaptable and less able to change occupations than are

---

[1] G. H. Daniel, Labour migration and age composition, *Sociological Review*, 31 3, 1939.—Ed.

younger workers. This point of view is advanced because it is believed that older workers, having acquired specialized skills, in many cases cannot be easily retrained for other jobs requiring different skills.

83. This reduction in flexibility which appears to accompany the aging of the labour force is likely to increase the danger of structural unemployment. As indicated earlier, it becomes increasingly necessary with a declining population, to shift workers from one industry or occupation to another, but at the same time such shifts become more difficult as the average age of the labour force rises. That older workers are less adaptable is demonstrated by statistics of unemployed workers classified by the duration of their unemployment, which characteristically show much longer durations of unemployment for workers past middle age than for younger workers. For these reasons it is sometimes said that the aging of the labour force, together with changes in employment practices that work to the disadvantage of the older men, threatens to create a large and growing body of permanently unemployed and unemployable persons. These fears, however, may easily be exaggerated. The United Kingdom Royal Commission on Population observed that the average age of the economically active population has increased in the past, apparently without catastrophic effects on the volume of unemployment. The Commission, nevertheless, noted the greater difficulty and waste with which structural changes in the economic system have been carried out in recent decades, possibly owing in part to the changes in the age distribution. . . .

86. The possible effects of the changing age composition upon the "propensity to consume" and the "propensity to save", and upon the demand for various types of consumers' goods, have been discussed in Chapter XII. So far as the general rates of saving and consumption are concerned, the findings are not conclusive. A majority of the authors who have studied the question believe that the increase in the percentage of persons past middle age tends to lower the rate of saving since many such persons live on accumulated savings and the community incurs large expenditures for services to them. On the other hand, some authors maintain that the increase in the proportion of aged persons tends to raise the rate of saving, because old people consume less than young adults. It has

also been pointed out that a decrease in the proportion of children in the population tends to increase savings because parents spend a smaller proportion of their income on children. Consequently, it would appear that neither a very young nor a very old population is most favourable to a high rate of saving, but rather a population with a large proportion of adults of working age. These hypotheses, however, have not been adequately verified by statistical analyses of expenditures and savings in relation to age. It seems evident in any case that the age composition of the population has much less to do with the per capita rates of consumption and saving than do a number of non-demographic factors, notably those which control the level and distribution of income.

87. Non-demographic factors also are the principal causes of change in the consumption of specific goods and services. Nevertheless, the findings reviewed in Chapter XII leave little doubt that the distribution of consumers' expenditure among various types of goods and services is affected at least to some extent by the aging of the population.

XXV

Arthur Young, *Political Arithmetic. Containing Observations on the Present State of Great Britain; And the Principles of Her Policy in the Encouragement of Agriculture*, London, 1774, pp. 61-9.

The national wealth increased the demand for labour, which had always the effect of raising the price; but this rise encouraged the production of the commodity, that is, of man or labour, call it which you will, and the consequent increase of the commodity sinks the price. Increasing the demand for a manufacture does not raise the price of the labour, it increases the number of labourers in the manufacture, as a greater quantum or regularity of employment, gives that additional value to the supply, which creates the new hands. Why have the inhabitants of Birmingham increased from 23,000 in 1750, to 30,000 in 1770? Certainly because a proportional increase of employment has taken place. Wherever there is a demand for hands, there they will abound: this demand is but another word for ease of subsistence, which operates in the same manner (the healthiness of one, and the unhealthiness of the other allowed for) as the plenty of land in the back country of America. Marriages abound there, because children are no burthen—they abound in Birmingham for the same reason, as every child as soon as it can use its hands, can maintain itself, and the father and mother need never to want employment, that is, income—land—support. Thus where employment increases (Birmingham) the people increase: and where employment does not increase, (Colchester) the people do not increase. And if upon an average of the whole kingdom employment has for a century increased, most certainly the people have increased with it. . . .

Let any person go to Glasgow, and its neighbourhood, to Birmingham, to Sheffield, or to Manchester, according to some writers, every cause of depopulation has acted powerfully against such places: how then have they increased their people? Why, by emigrations from the country. It would be very difficult for any person to shew me a depopulation in the country comparable to the increase of towns, not to speak of counter tracts in the country that have doubled and trebled their people: But why have not these emigrations been to other towns, to York, to Winchester, to Canterbury, &c.? Because employment does not abound in those places—and therefore they do not increase. Does not this prove that in every light you view it, it is employment which creates population? A position impossible to be disproved; and which, if allowed, throws the enquiry concerning the depopulation of the kingdom into an examination of the decline or increase of employment.

But so much land may be thrown into grass, and consequently so much employment cut off, that depopulation may ensue. Impossible; this cause can never operate beyond those lands, more proper by nature for grass than tillage, for if it did, it would at once counteract itself; corn would then rise to a price beyond the proportion of meat, and of course it would be more profitable to plough, than to lay down. This is a circumstance that ought to shew the enemies of inclosures that they are fighting against a chimera—they complain of meat being dearer than corn, in the same breath that they say the country is depopulated by converting arable to grass.—What a contradiction is this; meat being what they call so dear, is a clear proof that a greater proportion of land is not laid to grass than is broken up for corn, otherwise corn instead of being cheaper than meat would be dearer.

I shall carry this idea yet farther. I have considered an increased demand, which raises the value of a commodity, to be the means of increasing the quantity of that commodity, by encouraging the production of it; and I have applied it to beef, to mutton, to wheat, and to labour. I remarked that lessening the quantity in the market while the demand continued the same, operated as an encouragement, and presently supplied more than the usual quantum: it is the same with population. You fight off your men by wars—you destroy them by great cities—you lessen them by emigrations—most infallible method of increasing their number—PROVIDED THE DEMAND DOES NOT DECLINE. This is exactly the same thing, as rendering beef scarcer by the slaughter of calves, and wheat by exportation—take a quantity from the market, certainly you add to the value of what remains, and how can you encourage the reproduction of it more powerfully than by adding to its value?

What are the terms of complaint for depopulation in this kingdom?—People scarce—labour dear;—would you give a premium for population, could you express it in better terms? The commodity wanted is scarce, and the price raised; what is this but saying, that the value of MAN is raised. Away! my boys—get children, they are worth more than ever they were. What is the characteristic of a populous country? Many people, but labour dear. What is the mark of a country thinly peopled? Few people, and labour cheap. Labour is dearer in Holland than in any part of Europe, and therefore it is the most populous country in Europe.

Dr. Price says,[1] that for the last 80 years, there has not been one great cause of depopulation which has not operated among us. What is the great encouragement of population? Ease of acquiring income. It is of no consequence whether that income arises from land, manufacture, or commerce; it is as powerful in the pay of a manufacturer, as in the wilds of America. What is the great obstacle to population? Difficulty of acquiring income. Here then we have a criterion, by which to judge of the population or depopulation of any period. If you view the country and see agriculture under such circumstances that the farmer's products will not pay his usual improvements, and consequently, dismissing the hands he formerly kept. If the manufactures of the kingdom want a market, and the active industry, exerted in them, becomes languid, and decays. If commerce no longer supports the seamen she was wont to do. If private and public works, instead of entering into competition for hands with the manufacturer and the farmer, stand still amidst numbers who cry in vain for work.—If these effects are seen, a WANT OF EMPLOYMENT will stare you in the face, and that want is the only cause of depopulation that can exist. Have these spectacles been common in the eyes of our people since the revolution? Are they common at present? Does not the great active cause, EMPLOYMENT, operate more powerfully than ever? Away then with these visionary ideas, the disgrace of an enlightened age—the reproach of this great and flourishing nation.

Sir James Stewart[2] has an observation similar to the idea which I am now explaining, that if Africk's sons were all returned her, who can suppose she would be the more populous? But he founds this

---

[1] R. Price, Essay containing an account of the progress from the Revolution. . . . , in W. Morgan, *The Doctrine of Annuities and Assurances on Lives and Survivorships, Stated and Explained*, London, 1779.—Ed.

[2] Sir James Stewart, *An Inquiry into the Principles of Political Economy*, London, 1767, 2 vols.—Ed.

idea on the quantity of food in the country: but I mean to throw the point of food out of the question, taking it always for granted, if a man gains employment which gives him the value of food, that he will never go without it. Increase your people as much as you please, food will increase with them. Notwithstanding the increase of people which must have taken place in this kingdom since the revolution, added to the waste of luxury, and also exportation, yet the price of corn has fallen.—Population merely for want of food, will not stop till every acre of the territory is improved to the utmost.

XXVI

S. Laing junior, *National Distress; its causes and remedies*, London, 1844, pp. 67–70, 74–80.

In the large towns and manufacturing districts, where the condition of great masses of the population is, as we have already seen, extremely wretched, the rate of increase is so high, as to show that, independently of immigration, a very rapid multiplication is taking place. In Lancashire the rate of increase between 1831 and 1841 is 24·7 per cent, while in Westmorland it is only 2·5, and in Cumberland 4·8. In the great manufacturing towns, whose condition has been described in the Sanitary Reports, the rates of increase have been as follows:

	Population in 1821	Rate of Increase 1821 to 1831	Rate of Increase 1831 to 1841	Population in 1841
Manchester and Salford	133,788	36·6	43·3	262,136
Glasgow	147,043	37·6	27	257,592
Liverpool	118,972	38·8	35	223,054
Leeds	83,796	47·2	36·8	168,869

In all the accounts of the manufacturing population we find the same complaint repeated, of improvident marriages among the classes whose earnings are most insufficient and precarious. In the reports of the hand-loom weaver commissioners we have a great deal of detailed evidence, showing both the fact of a rapid increase of population accompanying destitution, and the manner in which this fact is brought about. Mr. Fletcher, after having described the condition of the poorer class of ribbon weavers in the neighbourhood of Coventry as miserable and demoralised in the extreme, goes on to say, that 'improvident marriages are much more common than in years past, so much so that an usual age of marriage with the young men is twenty, and sometimes earlier'; and again, that 'improvident marriages are prevalent throughout the weaving population'. Mr.

Miles says of the weavers of the west of England, 'that they marry younger than any other class of people'; and Mr. Keyser, speaking of the silk weavers of Macclesfield, describes both the effect and cause of this accelerated increase of population among a class reduced to the extreme verge of destitution, in the following terms:— 'A numerous family, which, to a man otherwise employed, would be considered an incumbrance, is rather a source of consolation to the poor weaver, whose children, even about eight or nine years of age, are capable of earning nearly sufficient to pay for their maintenance. This consideration induces early marriages and generally large families'. Another witness states, 'Beggarly Bisley has long been a proverb, and the improvidence of the people has been as conspicuous in the way in which they have kept their children at home, hanging on a miserable and uncertain pittance, in preference to sending them out to work for their bread elsewhere'. Similar evidence abounds of the tendency to improvident marriages among the distressed population of the manufacturing districts generally, and also among such portions of the agricultural population as are most wretched and degraded. In fact, an accelerated rate of increase in the population is a necessary result of poverty down to the point where literal starvation arrests its progress, and how low this point lies, the instance of Ireland sufficiently attests. While lumper-potatoes can be had for food, and a corner of a cellar with a bundle of mouldy straw for lodging, it is a demonstrated fact that population will continue to increase at a rate five times more rapid than in countries where every peasant lives under his own roof and cultivates his own estate. The reasons are obvious; directly the labourer is placed in a situation where he has nothing to look forward to—no hope of being able to better his condition by restraint—no definite period of establishment in life as a master-workman, or independent proprietor, to mark the prudent and customary era of marriage—all the natural checks on the instinctive appetite are withdrawn, and he marries, as a matter of course, as soon as he feels the inclination. The great check on premature marriage in every class is the 'public opinion' of that class, which requires a certain income and establishment in life before marrying, under penalty of losing caste and being looked upon as silly and imprudent. When the standard prescribed by the 'public opinion' of the class has sunk so low that, as Mr. Fletcher says of the weaving population of Nuneaton, men commonly marry 'without a home to go to', or 'with a bed consisting of chaff, held together by bricks, and covered with a wrapper', for sole stock of furniture, it is evident that all moral check on population is at an end, and that the evil must, of necessity, go on propagating itself, until either typhus fever and famine make a clearance, or the moral and physical condition of the people is raised by exertions from without. . . .

On the whole, therefore, we may take it as a demonstrated fact, that misery, up to the extreme point of famine and pestilence, instead of checking, tends to increase population. This fact, so contrary to the theoretical conclusions at which Malthus arrived, may afford us a clue to the means of escape from the consequences with which his inexorable theory of population threatened to envelope us. It is true that there is a principle in population which makes the mechanical theory of society defeat itself, and proves to demonstration that no permanent amelioration, even of the physical condition of society, can be looked for from economical causes alone. It is true that where a neglect of moral duties has led to the moral degradation of large masses of the community, there is a tendency in population to bring things to a crisis, and to compel society to do its duty under pain of destruction. But it is not true that this tendency is of the nature of an universal and irresistible decree of fate overruling human efforts. It is not true that if we relieve distress and diminish vice and misery, population rushes in like a spring-tide to efface the puny lines which we have traced in the sand. On the contrary, it is distinctly true, that duty and expediency, the means of raising the condition of the labouring classes, and the means of rightly proportioning their numbers to the supply of food, go hand in hand, and that in applying ourselves zealously to the task imposed upon us by religion and humanity, of relieving immediate distress, and promoting the welfare and improvement of the poorer classes, we are at the same time adopting the only effectual means of limiting the morbid and unhealthy increase of a destitute population. . . .

The great increase of population during the last sixty years has been accompanied by a total revolution in the course of industry, and in the habits, employments, and manner of life of the mass of the people. Until the latter half of the last century we were essentially an agricultural nation, exporting grain, and producing more than was required for the home consumption. Our manufactures were considerable, especially that of woollens, but conducted entirely on the domestic system, and to a great extent connected with agriculture. The raw material was spun into yarn by the distaffs and spinning-wheels of the whole female population, and made into cloth by a number of small manufacturers or master weavers, who generally occupied small farms, and had two or three looms in the house, on which they employed themselves and families, and a journeyman or two. During harvest time and the intervals of employment the whole household were sent to work out of doors, and the loom was resumed with the approach of winter and the renewal of demand. This system was first broken up by the wonderful inventions in machinery which signalised the close of the eighteenth century, and by the general application of steam as a motive power. The spinning-jenny, invented by Hargraves, in 1767; Arkwright's spinning-frame, invented in 1769; and Crompton's mule, invented in 1775, completely superseded domestic spinning, and substituted the factory, built at an immense outlay of capital, employing hundreds of hands, turning thousands of spindles, and producing yarn by the hundreds of thousands of miles, for the hum of the wheel, by every cottage fireside. The deluge of yarn thus poured upon the world gave, for a time, an extraordinary impulse to all the other branches of domestic manufacturing, and especially to weaving. The invention of the power-loom, however, and of improved methods of effecting the different processes of manufacture by the application of machinery, soon completed the revolution which had been begun by the spinning-jenny. The 'factory system', including under one comprehensive term the system of minute subdivision of labour, separation of the different processes of manufacture, application of machinery, and concentration of capital and productive power, came into general operation in all the great branches of manufacture, of which spinning and weaving constitute the staple process: viz., the cotton, woollen, linen, and silk.

The result of these changes, as far as production is concerned, has been almost miraculous. In 1800, the quantity of cotton wool taken for consumption was 54,203,433 lbs.; in 1840 it amounted to the enormous quantity of 592,965,504 lbs. During the same period the export of cotton goods has increased tenfold in quantity, and that of cotton yarn and twist, twenty-fold. In the year 1840, 790,631,997 yards of cotton cloth were exported, of the declared value of £16,302,220, and 118,470,223 lbs. of cotton twist and yarn, of the declared value of £7,101,308. The total value of the entire annual produce of the cotton manufactures was estimated in 1824, by Mr.

Huskisson, at £34,000,000, and is probably now upwards of £40,000,000. In the other manufactures production has increased less rapidly, but still at an enormous rate. The annual value of the produce of the woollen manufacture in 1840 may be estimated at not less than £20,000,000; that of linen manufacture at £10,000,000, and that of silk manufacture at £10,000,000. So far the factory system has been completely successful. It has increased the power and cheapness of production beyond anything that could have been anticipated, and it seems capable of almost indefinite improvement in these respects. Every day fresh improvements in machinery, and in the organisation of the combined efforts of labour and capital, are enabling us to produce more rapidly, and more cheaply, and the period does not seem far distant, if indeed, it has not in some branches of manufacture already arrived, when production will have attained the maximum limit of which it is capable, and be checked by the physical inability of the world to consume all that is produced. In another point of view, the factory system has also been completely successful. It has, in less than half a century, doubled the population, and far more than doubled the wealth and resources of the nation. If we are not at this moment a department of the grand empire, receiving laws from a prêfet of Napoleon the First or Second, we may thank the factory system for the creation of the money-power which enabled us to contend successfully with the overwhelming military force of France. We may thank the factory system also, in a great measure, for the general diffusion of wealth throughout English society, and for the great development of a middle class of tradesmen, mechanics, and artizans. So far, the factory system fully deserves the praises which have been heaped upon it by Macculloch, Baines, and other distinguished political economists, whose admiration of the stupendous conquests achieved over brute matter has broken out into something resembling poetical enthusiasm.

But the question has another side. Along with these great and undoubted advantages, the factory system has been attended with great and undoubted evils, which fully justify the indignant denunciations launched against it by humane and benevolent men. In the first place, the destruction of the old system of domestic manufacture was in itself a great evil. The advantages of this system are clearly and forcibly stated in a report of a committee of the House of Commons in 1806:

It is one peculiar recommendation of the domestic system that a young man of good character can always command the means of establishing himself as a little master-manufacturer, and rising to a situation of comfort and independence. Another advantage is, that any sudden stoppage of a foreign market—any failure of a great house—or any other of those adverse shocks to which our foreign trade, especially, is liable in its present extended state, has not the effect of throwing a great number of workmen out of employ.

The moral advantages of the domestic system are also strongly pointed out 'in encouraging domestic habits and virtues; keeping families and apprentices under the eye of their natural master, and promoting the health and morals of a large and important class of the community'.

The factory system is, on all these points, diametrically opposite. The capitalist and operative are separated by a wide gulf which it is becoming every day more and more difficult to pass. The constant incentive to prudence and good conduct afforded in the former case, by the prospect of being able to rise a step in the social scale, and to secure a more permanent and respectable position than that of the journeyman or day-labourer, is cut off, and the consequence is too often seen in reckless improvidence and dissipation, even among workmen whose money wages are comparatively high. The position of the workmen is also vastly more insecure, the new system tending to make production a speculative affair, independent of consumption; commerce a gambling transaction, fluctuating with every political rumour and monetary derangement, from New York to Canton. The full development of the system of unlimited competition and production threatens to make trade a succession of feverish oscillations, destroying all sense of stability and security in the life of the operative, and almost of necessity infecting him with the reckless and dissolute spirit of a gambler. The congregation of workmen in large masses, and the general transfer of manufacturing industry to crowded cities, are also results of the factory system, which could hardly fail to lead to extensive demoralisation and misery, unless a very strong moral feeling had been abroad to counteract the disadvantageous influences to which the operative was thus exposed. How completely such a moral feeling has been wanting on the part of employers, government, and of the upper classes generally; and how entirely the masses of population called into existence have been left destitute either of personal or public superintendence, is sufficiently apparent from the evidence already quoted. To speak in plain terms, the avarice of the employer has been the only law, and the axiom has been universally acted upon that whatever is profitable is right.

These inherent difficulties of the factory system have been greatly aggravated by the introduction of two enormous evils, infant and female labour. Steam power and machinery having superseded the necessity of physical force in most of the operations of the factory, and the labour of children and women being a much cheaper instrument than that of men, it became an object with producers to substitute it as far as possible. Being left at full liberty by the legislature to buy labour like cotton wherever they could get it cheapest, they succeeded to such an extent that the employment of adult male labour may almost be said to be superseded. In 4213 factories which produce the bulk of the enormous production in the four staple manufacturers of cotton, wool, flax, and silk, out of 422,209 hands employed, only 96,752 are males above 18 years of age; while 244,821 are females, of whom 162,256 are below 21.

Without entering into the disputed question, how far the gross enormities attested by evidence before the factory committee of the House of Commons in 1832, are a fair unexaggerated picture of the general working of the factory system, it is evident from the above figures that the system is radically unsound. Even if we concede to its advocates that the accounts of revolting cruelties practised on helpless infants, gross immorality resulting from the unrestrained intercourse of the sexes at the age of puberty, and general deterioration of the physical appearance and health of the factory population from exhausting labour, are partly exaggerated and partly applicable to a state of things which was always an exception to the general rule, and which has now almost entirely ceased to exist; still the fact remains, that the general result of the factory system has been to substitute the labour of young girls for that of men. This is a great evil. The emancipation of the female sex from the regular labour of productive industry, and their appropriation to the domestic duties of life, is justly reckoned one of the greatest achievements of European civilisation. The factory system reverses this process, and makes a retrograde step towards the barbarism of savage life. The girl who commences working in a factory at 9 or 10 years of age, and from the age of 13 upwards, is employed within the mill for twelve hours daily, must necessarily grow up uneducated, in a sense of the word of which the mere deprivation of intellectual instruction can convey no idea. What can she know of sewing, baking, cooking, the care of children, and the thousand details of domestic economy, upon which the comfort and respectability of the labouring man's home depend infinitely more than upon the amount of money wages? What can the ties of family be between a mother who hastens from her accouchement to the mill, and children who are left in infancy to the care of some old woman hired for a couple of shillings a week, and who, at the age when parental discipline is most required, find themselves independent workmen, earning, perhaps, better wages than their father? Accordingly, all accounts of the manufacturing districts concur in complaints of the moral evils engendered by these causes among the factory population; of the relaxation of domestic ties, the want of management and economy of parents, and the insubordination and premature independence of children. The practical operation of the system in one of the principal manufacturing towns is thus summed up by an intelligent and disinterested witness, from whose report to the poor law commissioners we have already quoted.

"1. The congregation of all ages, and of every grade of character without the means of classification.
2. The early loss of parental control by the pecuniary means which are acquired.
3. The employment of female labour, whilst men are unemployed.
4. The utter inability of the wives of the operatives to obtain their requisite domestic acquirements, by which the homes of future husbands may be made more attractive than society abroad."

Even if these evils could be in some measure palliated, the crowning evil attendant on infant labour, in the abstract, would still remain—viz., that it tends to create a mass of population who are thrown upon the world destitute, like so much used-up material, at the very time when they ought to be commencing the career of active life. The official tables, showing the numbers employed at different ages, are conclusive as to the fact, that many thousands of hands annually are thrown off by the factories simply because they have outgrown employment. There are in round numbers 270,000 hands below twenty-one employed in factories, while the whole number, male and female, about twenty-one, is only 150,000; it is evident, therefore, that, one year with another, 40,000 or 50,000 persons, trained from early childhood to factory labour, must be cast adrift. What becomes of them? All other employments are full; and even if they were not, it is difficult for a person trained for ten years to a particular pursuit to learn a new trade, and begin life afresh at twenty-one, even if he has a stock of physical vigour and elasticity of which the poor factory child is too frequently deprived. Can we wonder that, in spite of the admonitions of political economists, hand-loom weaving at 5s. a week is still taken up as a resource by thousands? Can we wonder that the cess-pool of unemployed wretchedness in our large manufacturing towns is always full with this copious stream pouring into it, in addition to the torrent of Irish and agricultural misery?[1]

---

[1] Or can we wonder that population increases with undue rapidity, and that poor starving wretches, cut out from every legitimate means of industry, take to the manufacture of children as the only article for which there is a demand.

XXVII

P. Gaskell, *Artisans and Machinery. The moral and physical condition of the manufacturing population considered with reference to mechanical substitutes for human labour*, London, 1836. Reprinted, London, 1968, pp. 137–8, 140–1, 143–4.

The simplicity of the first machines adapted for spinning, and their small size, fitted them for being tended by children. The localities in which the mills were at first erected for the convenience of water power, were often remote from towns or villages, from which alone an adequate supply of hands could be obtained: hence, in the early period of mill labour, apprentices, from six to twelve years of age, were almost the only workers. These apprentices were chiefly taken from the workhouses of large towns, such as London, Birmingham, &c. and from foundling hospitals, and transmitted in droves to the different mills, where, in many instances, it is to be feared they suffered very severely. Villages, however, sprung up in the vicinity of the mills, and the parents of children very naturally took advantage of their labour, and hence free labourers became superadded, and, in time, displaced the apprentice system to a considerable degree.

The construction of the first mills was, of course, fitted only for small machines; they were consequently small, and the rooms in them were low, and of very contracted dimensions, and very little precaution was used, either as to ventilation or temperature. The time of labour was extended to twelve hours, with very little interval; the immense profits which accrued from their produce pushing aside all ulterior considerations. Nor was this all: unsatisfied with the day labour, the night was almost uniformly spent by one portion of the hands in the mill; the owners or occupiers thus securing twenty-three hours out of the twenty-four for making their machinery valuable.

There cannot be a question but that child-labour, urged to this extent, and under these circumstances, was prejudicial in every way, and gross immorality was one result. . . .

The machines for spinning were, day after day, becoming more bulky, and requiring greater skill and exertion for producing fine numbers, so that adults gradually found their way to them. The application of steam as a moving power, which became general from 1801 to 1804, produced a great change in all respects. It did away with the necessity for so much water power, and hence mills were more commonly built in towns or populous districts, favourable as to coal, &c., and where a population was at hand for their occupation. The uniformity, the increased rapidity of motion, and the greater size of the machines, called in some departments for active labour, and grown-up men and women were now largely engaged in spinning:—but still children formed the majority of hands, many processes being better calculated for them than for adults. But they were not put to work quite so young, few before ten years of age—an age, in fact, which the masters found to be as soon as they could be properly useful. . . .

Yet a change is rapidly taking place in the condition of the operatives, and a disposition is developing itself to have recourse to the labour of women and children in preference to adults. The causes which have led to this are, the great improvements which are taking place in machinery, and its application to an infinite variety of minute operations, requiring the nicest management, the requisite power being given by steam. Nearly the whole of the hands employed in the silk factories are females, as well as in the Scotch flax, cotton, and woollen mills. . . .

The necessity for human power thus gradually yielding before another and more subservient one, has had, in the first place, the effect of rendering adult labour of no greater value than that of the infant or girl; the workmen are reduced to mere watchers, and suppliers of the wants of machinery, requiring in the great majority of its operations no physical or intellectual exertion; and the adult male has begun to give way, and his place been supplied by those who in the usual order of things were dependent upon him for their support.

XXVIII

J. R. McCulloch, *The principles of political economy*, Edinburgh, 1825, pp. 157–60.

Much has been said respecting the extraordinary mortality of large manufacturing establishments. The ready communication of contagion where people are crowded together—the want of sufficient ventilation—the confinement of children—and the positive unhealthiness of some particular processes, are circumstances from which most writers have been led to infer that the mortality in manufacturing cities must be unusually great, without giving themselves the trouble to inquire whether the fact really was so. The returns under the population acts have shown the fallacy of these opinions. The proportion of manufactures to the whole population of Great Britain was vastly greater in 1810 and 1820 than in 1780; and yet, notwithstanding the extraordinary increase of what we have been in the habit of considering unhealthy employments, the average mortality in England and Wales in 1810 was only one in every 52, and in 1820 only one in every 58 of the existing population, whereas in 1780 it was one in every 40! The diminution of mortality has been going on gradually since 1750; and has doubtless been owing partly to the greater prevalence of cleanliness and sobriety among the poor, and the improvements that have been made in their diet, dress, and houses, partly to the drainage of bogs and marshes, and partly, and since 1800 chiefly, perhaps, to the discoveries in medical science, and the extirpation of the small-pox. But whatever may be the causes of this increased healthiness, there is abundant evidence to show that they have not been counteracted by the extension of manufactures. On the contrary, the healthiness of the inhabitants of cities and towns, where manufactures are almost exclusively carried on, has increased in a much greater proportion than the healthiness of the inhabitants of the agricultural districts. In Manchester, for example, where the average mortality in 1770 was one in 28,[1] it is now

---

[1] Dr. Percival's *Observations on the State of the Population in Manchester*, p.4.

reduced to less than one in 43; and a similar improvement has taken place in Glasgow, Paisley, and all the other large manufacturing towns. It is certain, too, that much of this diminution of mortality is a direct, and not an indirect consequence of the improvement and diffusion of manufactures. Every one knows of what vast importance it is to health that the poor should have the means of providing themselves with comfortable clothes at a cheap rate. And this is one of the many advantages which improvements in manufacturing industry always bring along with them. The reduction in the price of cotton goods only, occasioned by the greater facility with which they are now produced, has enabled the poorest individuals to clothe themselves in a warm, clean and elegant dress; and has thus been productive of an increase of comfort and enjoyment, of which it is extremely difficult for us, who have so long experienced its beneficial effects, to estimate the extent.

XXIX

J. Kennedy, *Observations on the Influence of Machinery upon the Working Classes of the Community*, Manchester, 1829, pp. 3–9.

My object in the present paper is to state my opinion of the influence of machinery, and to lay before the society a few hints on the advantages consequent on the introduction of mechanical and scientific improvements into the various and widely-extended departments of our Manufactures.—In the first place, the object of all manufacturing machinery being the substitution of some power in the place of human labour, its immediate tendency is to diminish the necessity for manual exertion, or to render it less burdensome, and as a direct consequence of this to enable the younger and more delicate members of the community to perform those operations, which only the skilful and robust were wont to execute. Hence it is that wind, water, and steam, have been applied as moving power in the place of human or horse labour, and that women and children are enabled to execute those tasks, which formerly required the ingenuity or the strength of men.

While, by this important change in our manufacturing system, the more laborious operations are made no longer to depend entirely on human exertion, the extension of mechanical improvements causes a new division of labour, which is advantageous in some important respects to the operative members of the community.

Not only is great skill required in the construction of those beautiful machines, which are intended to diminish human labour, but a demand is thus created for the exertion of industry and skill in the superintendence of the newly-invented machine. No mechanical contrivance is so perfect as not to require continued attention, nor is there any, the efficacy of which does not materially depend on the care and dexterity of the over-looker. This is particularly the case, when the movements of the machine are of a complicated or delicate nature. Such are the various engines employed in the cotton and woollen, the silk and linen, manufactories; these, while they abridge human labour in many respects, create a demand for it in other directions, and thus the older and more experienced members of families find abundant employment.

Much labour and ingenuity and expense being incurred in the invention and construction of machinery, the owner of a costly improvement naturally wishes to employ it as far as he can to his individual advantage. He is desirous of obtaining some adequate remuneration for the money he has expended or the talent he has excited, in order to possess himself of a machine calculated to supersede in some degree the operation of mere manual labour. But still the machine itself must be worked, and this cannot be done without human labour employed at least in its superintendence. Now the price, he will pay for the labour required, will be in proportion to the necessity he feels for it, arising from its productiveness and from the demand for the manufactured article thus furnished. And as the ingenuity and skill required in the superintendence of complex machinery are not of ordinary attainment, the wages of persons thus employed will bear a proportion to the value of their labour. Hence it will appear, that in all cases the employed necessarily partake in every improvement that is made in machinery, and have their full share of interest in all new inventions.

The extended classification of labour is an advantage to the working classes themselves, and contributes in various ways to their comfort, convenience, and profit.

The farther this classification of human industry is carried, the more any individual branch of trade or manufacture becomes dependent on the subordinate branches of this subdivision of labour. All the departments being thus subservient to and dependent on each other; the very lowest (those I mean which require the least exertion of skill or industry,) have still their relative value; and whilst the highest degree of ingenuity and dexterity will be applied where it is most wanted, and will be sure of a proportionate remuneration, the inferior kinds of labour will furnish employment to a very large class of the community, whose services could not have been required, had not the invention of machinery rendered them available. Every new machine may, in fact, be considered as a source of individual advantage to the artizan, on whose skill or industry alone its productiveness must ultimately depend, and, so far from decreasing the value of human labour, the discovery and application of mechanical contrivances to the various departments of our manufactures has, in reality, created a new and perpetually increasing demand for it.

In proportion as machinery is improved in simplicity, and becomes more uniform in its action or motion, a lower class of labour is required for its management; and as women and children are thus enabled to produce these fabrics, which it formerly required all the ingenuity, skill, and labour of the very best workmen to furnish, the latter are set at liberty from the mere drudgery of manufacturing employment, and are at leisure to engage in those more difficult and delicate operations, which the perpetual multiplication of machinery renders necessary.

Such appears the direct tendency of the introduction of machinery; it places men in a condition very different from that state of things, in which the wealthy few could and did purchase the lives and liberties and rights of the many.

Instead of being thus absorbed, capital is more justly and properly applied, and is the means of extensive benefits not to a particular class of society, but to the whole community.

Surplus wealth can now be invested, and is so, not in purchasing the fee-simple of a human being, but in the fee-simple of a machine, which relieves man from the severest slavery of labour, and enables the delicate, the feeble, the young, and the infirm, to earn a comfortable livelihood by dexterity of hand, and the ingenious application of the higher faculties of the mind. Machinery brings into exercise and competition the intelligent powers of man; mere hand and slave labour engages only his animal force.

Wealth invested in machinery improves the condition of man, and enlarges his capacities and means of happiness; but in former days it had the effect of increasing slavery and of debasing the human character. Look even at the present condition of the West India islands, and all those foreign possessions, where machinery has not been introduced to supersede the necessity of human labour, or at least to lighten it. Wealth accumulated there is invested in an increased number of slaves who are stimulated to exertion by the goad, that they may furnish luxuries for their fellow-men. Accumulating wealth in England is employed in producing comforts, by the aid of machinery, of which all are partakers; in contributing to the advancement of the human mind; and in making man, what he was intended to be, a moral agent. While the operative classes of the community are benefited by circumstances, which open to them continually new markets for their labour, and a higher rate of remuneration for it, the great mass of mankind also experience from the same cause important advantages.

The products of manufacturing industry are obtained at a lower price, and of superior quality; and those articles, which were once regarded as the peculiar accommodations of the higher classes of society, are now placed within the reach of all. There is not, perhaps, a more striking feature in the recent improvements that have taken place in this country, than the increased comforts enjoyed by the working classes, particularly as these are intimated by their better food and clothing, and the more convenient furniture of their humble dwellings. And these are so necessarily connected with an improved condition of health, that they may serve to account in a great degree for that lengthening of human life, which has been recently reported to us by the statist and political economist.

XXX

G. Talbot Griffith, *Population problems of the age of Malthus*, 2nd ed., London, 1967. pp. 255-8.

In a recent work on The Population Problem it is stated that the great increase of population which began in this country with the Industrial Revolution was merely 'the response to increase in skill'.[1] If this is interpreted in a broad way, it was probably the primary cause. Behind all this increase there loom the advances in the industries of the country, which progressed in response to the increase of skill; in so far, therefore, as many of the influences which tended to increase the population in this period would not have been called into operation but for the economic demand from our own people, and would all have been powerless to maintain a greatly increased population without the increase in the opportunities of employment which the growing industries supplied, to that extent the increase of the population was the response to the increase of skill. There existed features in the increase, connected with the economic organisation of the country, which are not necessarily bound up with the increase of skill, though they depend on the expansion of industry. Apprenticeship first of all declined and was then swept away by legislation, with the result that one great obstacle to early marriage was removed, while the change of housing arrangements in the country removed another. Trades and industries of a heavy unskilled kind which did not require apprenticeship as a training, and which for various legal reasons were outside these regulations, grew up, and these were mostly trades in which the full earning power was reached at an early age, with the result that there was no great inducement to postpone marriage. The watertight structure of society was destroyed both in the industrial and in the agricultural districts. The manufactures supplied an ever widening market, and improved transport and methods of agriculture enabled farmers to supply the wants of people other than their immediate

---

[1] Carr Saunders, *The Population Problem*, p. 308.

neighbours. In addition to these changes in the economic organisation of the country, which tended to increase the population, the administration of the Poor Laws, with its system of allowances from the rates in aid of wages, was looked upon at the time as a fruitful source of the increase. In contemporary reports and literature it enjoyed more prominence than any other single cause, though it is probable that its actual effect was not so potent as was represented. These are all factors which would tend to raise the marriage rate and the birth rate; the marriage rate rose until 1790, and the birth rate rose steadily from 1710 to 1790.

The increase of skill and the greater opportunities for employment to which it led, encouraged another source of increase; the population of Ireland was increasing at a rate even more rapid than that which obtained in this country, and chiefly as a response to inadequate and unsafe encouragements; and the opportunities in this country provided many Irish with a livelihood in various more or less unskilled occupations, and by the immigration added a considerable number to the population. The comparative absence of any increase of skill in Ireland during this period and the great increase in its population should act as a warning against ascribing too much in England to the influence of an increase in skill; that is, against ascribing without due consideration the increase to the Industrial Revolution.

In addition to these causes of increase which were connected with the industrial aspect of the country, another lay in the medical improvements of the time. The period saw the rapid development of the hospital movement, and the beginning and remarkable growth of the dispensaries. Medical education and scientific investigations were improved. Sanitary science and right principles in the treatment of such scourges as fever which thrived under insanitary conditions were advanced, though not necessarily for strictly scientific reasons. For our purpose, however, the important thing is the reduction in mortality which resulted whatever the scientific principles involved may have been. The practice of midwifery was greatly improved: certain diseases which in former times had been serious sources of mortality were reduced or abolished, and smallpox was greatly lessened after the middle of the period by the introduction of vaccination. Many of these improvements were based on empiricism; the greater care for cleanliness and hygiene which was displayed, was in unconscious harmony with the scientific discoveries which came later, and it may well be that this was the greatest single achievement of the medical improvements of the period. Many things may have contributed to this. Cleanliness is not cheap, and the growth of wealth may both have created the desire and enabled the ideal to be realised. The increased use of soap, combined with the substitution of easily washed cotton goods for the heavy and rarely washed woollen goods, which followed the comparatively recent growth of the cotton industry, may have assisted. The greater communication with India and the East where habits of cleanliness were enforced as part of the regulations of a caste system, and where in some cases the climate rendered them more essential, may have been an additional influence. The religious enthusiasm of the Wesleyans and the precept that 'cleanliness is next to godliness', may also have had their share, and in his Constitutional Code Bentham outlines a Ministry of Health of a very elaborate kind, which reflects the attitude of the Benthamite group to the question.

The increase of medical skill, combined with such things as a decline in the consumption of alcohol and an improvement in the food supply resulting from certain phases of the agricultural revolution, which led to a decline in the death rate and to a prolongation of life, worked hand in hand with the increase of industrial skill, with the increased opportunities of employment to which this gave rise and with the changes in the economic organisation tending to encourage early marriage, to increase the population. Either of these would have been seriously handicapped without the other; the increased wealth of the country and the increased opportunities of employment afforded by the industrial development were at once the bedrock on which the medical improvements were built and the justification for the demand for a large population, and the industrial improvements were enabled to take effect with less strain on the country than would have been the case had there been no medical improvements.

XXXI

P. Mantoux, *The Industrial Revolution in the Eighteenth Century*, Reprinted, London, 1966, pp. 341-6, 349, 354-5.

The rapid and continuous growth of population is not a phenomenon peculiar to our industrial civilization. It can and does occur in quite other surroundings, as for instance in China, where the system of small holdings and intensive agriculture supports the densest population in the world. We may add that the extraordinary increase of population in Western countries which has taken place in the last hundred years cannot be attributed to one cause alone. It is encouraged by everything which tends to add to general prosperity and individual security. But what must be pointed out is that no such increase was noticeable before the era of the modern factory system. Nowadays a stationary or slowly increasing population causes surprise and anxiety. A hundred and fifty or two hundred years ago the opposite fact would have caused astonishment. In his Observations on the State of England, written in 1696, Gregory King thus predicted how the population of England would increase during the coming centuries: 'In all probability the next doubling of the people in England will be in about six hundred years to come, or by the year of our Lord 2300, at which time it will have eleven millions of people.... The next doubling after that will not be, in all probability, in less than twelve or thirteen hundred years, or by the year of our Lord 3500 or 3600. At which time the Kingdom will have 22 millions of souls... in case the world should last so long.'

Gregory King was an optimist. During the whole of the eighteenth century the accepted theory was that the population of England was decreasing, and people talked as though it was a fact which had actually been proved, while statesmen like Lord Shelburne and Lord Chatham publicly expressed the fears they felt on this score. This supposed evil ascribed to most various causes: to the excessive increase of armed forces, to the wars, to emigration, to over-taxation, to the rising price of foodstuffs, to the engrossing of farms. But as the increasing wealth of the country became more apparent an opposite theory was put forward, which argued, a priori, that an increase of population must go hand in hand with economic progress. Some curious discussions took place on the subject between 1770 and 1780, at the very time when the new factory system was beginning to display its wonderful creative activity.

These discussions were only possible because of the lack of any reliable statistics. The first official census of population in England was taken in 1801. Before then people had to rest content with more or less plausible estimates. These were based either on taxation returns, which contained the enumeration of hearths or houses, or on parish registers, in which a record of christenings, marriages and burials was kept. From these data calculations were made of the average number of inhabitants per house or of the birth and death rates, and these figures became the basis for multiplication sums. This was Gregory King's method. Under the date of March 25th, 1690, he had found in the hearth tax returns the figure of 1,319,115 houses. That total number could, he thought, be divided into several categories. There were the houses in London, those in the suburbs of London, those in other towns in England and Wales, and finally those in the villages and hamlets. He assumed that a house in each category contained a certain number of inhabitants, which varied between four and five and a half. By this figure he multiplied the number of houses in the corresponding area. Adding the results together, he arrived at a total of 5,318,000 souls. By throwing in the strength of the land and sea forces, and an additional number to make up for probable omissions in the registers, he reached the figure of 5,500,000 inhabitants.

It is obvious that arbitrary assumptions played a considerable part in such computations. Moreover, the figures themselves, although taken from authentic documents, were far from reliable. Even the best kept parish register could only supply incomplete returns, for there was no compulsory registration of births, marriages and deaths. It was still mainly a religious matter, the Church in each parish registering the christenings, the marriages and the burials of its members. But the Church took no account of nonconformists, who in some districts were very numerous, sometimes even more numerous than members of the Church of England. The figures, too, which were taken from taxation registers, are open to doubt. The Treasury officials who were responsible for the making of these registers regarded them from a purely practical point of view. For them, houses which paid neither hearth nor window tax did not exist, and as a rule they did not even trouble to count them. Such documents, taken just as they stood and read without criticism, were bound to lead those who utilized them to the most unfounded conclusions.

These were the documents used to prove that the population of England was decreasing. The main argument, which was developed at great length by Richard Price in his Essay on the Population of England (1780), was as follows: In the reign of William III there were in the kingdom, exclusive of Scotland and Ireland, about thirteen hundred thousand houses. By 1759 this figure had fallen to 986,482, by 1767 to 980,692, and by 1777 to 952,734. How was it possible to avoid the conclusion that the population of England was decreasing? It must have fallen twenty-five per cent in less than a century. Price overlooked only one detail. The figures on which he based his comparisons were taken from different sources. The earliest figure was taken from the hearth tax registers. But in 1696 the hearth tax had been abolished and its place taken by a tax on house property, which was based on the number of windows. This new tax had resulted in the creation of a new set of statistics, the figures of which did not agree with the data of an earlier period. Hence a sudden and apparently inexplicable drop. According to the hearth tax register in 1690 London had a total of 111,215 houses. According to the window tax registers in 1708 it had only 47,031. Must we therefore assume that about the beginning of the eighteenth century some sudden disaster, unobserved by contemporaries and unknown to history, had destroyed half London? This reduction ad absurdum is enough to show the ridiculous fallacy of this method of making estimates, a method finally condemned by Arthur Young in his Political Arithmetic.

It is, nevertheless, unlikely that the depopulation theory would have been attacked merely on the ground of statistical method had not visible signs of general prosperity suggested a presumption in favour of the opposite theory. How was it possible to believe that a country was growing weaker and losing its people, when its activity and its resources grew greater every day? Arthur Young wrote:

"View the navigation, the roads, the harbours, and all other public works. Take notice of the spirit with which manufactures are carried on.... Move your eye on which side you will, you behold nothing but great riches and yet greater resources.... I have proved the nation to be in possession of a vast income, highly sufficient for all demands, to possess a vigorous agriculture, flourishing manufactures, and an extended commerce; in a word, to be a great industrious country. Now, I conceive that it is impossible to prove such points without proportionally proving the Kingdom to be a populous one. It is in vain to talk of tables of births, and lists of houses and windows, as proofs of our loss of people: the flourishing state of our agriculture, our manufactures, and commerce, with our general wealth, prove the contrary."[1]

This was, of course, only an impression. In order to turn it into a proven fact, sources of information were needed which, in those days, were not available. People like William Eden, Howlett and Wales[2] made the mistake of adopting the methods they had themselves so justly criticized, and their conclusions were no more convincing than those of their opponents. Others for want of facts to prove their case relied on abstract reasoning, like the economists whose disciples they were, and, from what had at first only been an opinion, they ultimately evolved a theory.

That theory is implied in the lines we have just quoted from Arthur Young, and is explained and developed in other passages of the same book. According to him the increase of wealth and the growth of population are interdependent facts. Wherever men can make a living they increase and multiply: 'It is employment that creates population. There is not an instance in the whole globe of an idle people being numerous in proportion to their territory, but, on the contrary, all industrious countries are populous, and proportionably to the degree of their industry. When employment is plentiful and time of value, families are not burdens, marriages are early and numerous.... It is an absolute impossibility that, in such circumstances, the people should not increase.... The increase of employment will be found to raise men like mushrooms.' The fear that undertakings might grow too quickly and that there would be a shortage of labour was purely imaginary: 'No industrious nation need ever fear a want of hands for executing any of the most

---

[1] A. Young. *A Six months tour through the North Of England*, 4 vols, London, 1770.

[2] W. Eden, *Four letters to the Earl of Carlisle*, 1781. J. Howlett, *An examination of Dr. Price's essay*, 1781. W. Wales, *An inquiry into the present state of the population of England and Wales*, 1781.—Ed.

extensive plans of public or private improvement. It would be false to assert that such plans could anywhere be executed at a given expense, or at a certain rate of wages, but wherever employment exists, that is, money to be expended, workmen can never be wanting.... Let but the requisite money be found, men can never be wanting....'

As the population grew its centre of gravity moved, and the direction of this movement is a sufficient indication of its cause. If, on the map of England proper, a line is drawn from the mouth of the Humber to that of the Severn, following approximately the Jurassic hills north and west of the London geological basin, that line will divide two regions of more or less equal size. The one on the north-west includes today almost all the great centres of English industry: the Midlands, Yorkshire, Lancashire, the Northumbrian and Durham coal deposits, and the manufacturing centres round Manchester, Liverpool, Leeds, Sheffield and Newcastle. The south-eastern part has a less concentrated and less active economic existence. Few large cities are to be found there apart from London, whose gigantic growth corresponds to that of a world-wide Empire. But on the other hand that part of England is full of ancient towns, proud of their colleges, their castles and cathedrals, but stunted and sleepy, as though wrapped in themselves within their old walls. The contrast, which it is enough to mention, is most clearly marked by statistics. In 1901, just a hundred years after the first census, the seventeen north-western counties had a population of 16,718,000 inhabitants. The twenty-four south-eastern counties had only 14,254,000, of which nearly a third (exactly 4,536,000) were in the County of London. The first group contained twenty-one towns with a minimum population of a hundred thousand, of which three had a population of over 500,000 and twelve of over 200,000. The second group contained only eight, including London and two of its suburbs, West Ham and Croydon. The average density of population in the north-west was 720 inhabitants to the square mile, while in the south-east it was 530, or if we exclude the County of London, only 360.

It was otherwise in the eighteenth century. On the following maps[1] we have tried to indicate the distribution of population in 1700, 1750 and 1801. The documents attached to the 1801 census have enabled

---

[1] P. Mantoux, *The Industrial Revolution in the Eighteenth Century*, reprinted, London, 1966, pp. 350-3.—Ed.

us to make this attempt, which is not open to the same objections as the estimates of the seventeenth and eighteenth centuries: this kind of construction seems to us reasonably justified when undisputable and complete data supplied by an official census are available for purposes of comparison.[1] The point which at once arrests attention on looking at the first of these maps is the low average density of the population as compared with today. Apart from London and its immediate neighbourhood, not a single county had 160 inhabitants to the square mile. The distribution of population is clearly marked. The most densely populated counties formed a continuous zone, running from the Bristol Channel to the Suffolk coast. That narrow strip of country contained over three-fifths of the whole population of England. The northern counties were sparsely populated, Lancashire and the West Riding of Yorkshire having only 80 to 110 inhabitants to the square mile.

In 1750 the trend of population towards the north and west had begun to show itself. It seemed to be moving towards the Atlantic, drawn thither by the development of the maritime trade and the growing wealth of Liverpool and Bristol. The most densely peopled district formed a triangle with its broad base in the West, and stretching northwards to the county of Durham. By 1801 the whole face of the map had changed. London, with its suburbs, forms on that map an isolated patch in the angle facing the Continent, while a dark band, widening out towards the north, stretches over the midland and western counties to the foot of the mountains in Cumberland and Wales. Had it not been for London, with her 900,000 inhabitants, the north-western group would even at that date have rivalled that of the south-east, for it had a population of 3,895,000 as against 4,711,000. Let us now turn to the map showing the distribution of the population of England in 1901. Here we find the same characteristics, more marked but quite recognizable. From 1801 to 1901 the trend is continuous and the direction always the same. In 1700 it had not yet begun.

What is the meaning of this migration towards the north and west? To understand it a more detailed study becomes necessary. Look for instance at Wiltshire, which was typical of the ancient

---

[1] See Abstract of the Answers and Returns to the Population Act, 41 Geo. III, I, 11ff. ('Observations on the Results'). Little difference will be found between our maps and those drawn up by Professor Conner (*Journal of the Royal Statistical Society*, LXXVI, 289-91).

order of things, with cottage industries scattered throughout the country and little towns where employers and merchants lived. In 1700 Wiltshire, with 130 persons to the square mile, was the third most densely populated county after Middlesex and Surrey. Its population hardly varied during the eighteenth century: in 1750 it had fallen to 127, and in 1801 had risen again to 133 to the square mile. In some purely agricultural counties, as in Rutland or Lincolnshire, the final result was about the same, after more marked fluctuations: in a hundred years their populations only rose from 104 to 109 and from 65 to 75 inhabitants to the square mile. Let us now turn our attention to those districts where the new industries were developing and where machine industry and large-scale undertakings were making their appearance. Warwickshire and Staffordshire, both contiguous to the mining and metal-working Birmingham district, had a population of 224,000 in 1700, of 285,000 in 1750, and of 447,000 in 1801. Thus the population had nearly doubled: but in Lancashire it had become almost three times as great, for from 240,000 inhabitants the figure had risen to 672,000 It is a significant fact that three-quarters of this considerable increase took place in the second half of the century.

Then it was indeed that, wherever it could develop under favourable conditions, the factory system brought about the rise of these mighty centres of population, whose monstrous growth is still going on under our own eyes. At first they were rather less concentrated, as were the industries round which they were growing up: it was the steam engine which finally fixed and consolidated them. The early factories, with machinery worked by water-wheels, were usually outside the towns. Yet they had to be near a town, as serious difficulties of communication and transport made it essential for them to be close to a market both for buying and selling purposes. Labour was needed, not only for the actual work in the factory but also for the subsidiary domestic industries without which work in the factory could not be carried on, for there was a period before the invention and the general use of the power loom when cotton and wool, which were machine spun, had to be hand woven, and the country weavers were too scattered to meet the requirements of the industry. Thus, even before the time of the steam engine, it became possible for the centres of the factory system to find their geographical position and to develop with a rapidity which foreshadowed their future greatness.

XXXII

E. C. Snow, The limits of industrial employment (II). The influence of the growth of population on the development of industry. *Journal of the Royal Statistical Society*, XCVIII, Part II, 1935, pp. 244–50.

The Cause of the Increase in Population in the Nineteenth Century

It has frequently been said that it was the industrial development in this country following a number of important inventions in the eighteenth and nineteenth centuries which enabled a continuously increasing population to be maintained. The figures show that this state of continuously increasing population arose mainly from the decline in the death-rate. I think it is of some importance to try to know what was the truth regarding the cause of the growth of population in the nineteenth century, and for this reason I have examined the statistical material in some detail. The decline in the death-rate was directly associated with improved hygienic and medical knowledge and practice. A descriptive statistical history of the various stages in the decline, bringing out the association between the downward movement and the specific advances in medical and hygienic practice, would be enlightening, and nobody is more competent than our own President to give us such a description. Why was there no decline in mortality in the thirty years or more prior to 1870? If the development of industry was the main cause of the decline of mortality it is difficult to explain a number of the facts brought out by an analysis of the statistics. I have analysed some of the mortality data (I admit, not completely) with a view to ascertaining how the decline occurred in the different age groups, and also what was the experience of other countries, most of them at that time purely agricultural countries and none of them of the same degree of industrialization as this country. As shown above, the general death-rate in this country, so far as the figures indicate, commenced to fall in the decade following 1870. The fall started in the population of ages 5 to 25 and it continued to rise in the older age groups for some time afterwards. The facts are collected together in the tabular statement below, which will readily explain itself.

England and Wales
Mortality in Age Groups in Decennial Periods
Death-rate 1841–1850 = 100

Age	1841–1850	1851–1860	1861–1870	1871–1880	1881–1890	1891–1900
MALES						
0–5	100	102	103	96	86	88
5–10	100	93	89	73	58	47
10–15	100	95	89	73	58	48
15–20	100	95	88	74	61	54
20–25	100	93	89	77	60	63
25–35	100	96	100	94	78	68
35–45	100	97	105	108	97	90
45–55	100	99	106	110	106	104
55–65	100	97	104	110	109	110
65–75	100	97	99	103	104	104
75+	100	98	98	100	96	95
All ages	100	98	100	97	89	86
FEMALES						
0–5	100	103	104	95	85	86
5–10	100	95	88	71	59	49
10–15	100	93	83	69	57	47
15–20	100	94	84	69	56	47
20–25	100	94	88	75	61	49
25–35	100	95	93	82	70	58
35–45	100	94	94	90	82	74
45–55	100	95	97	97	94	92
55–65	100	95	98	101	100	100
65–75	100	96	97	100	99	100
75+	100	98	98	99	94	93
All ages	100	98	98	92	84	81

The striking difference between the fall in certain age groups and the rise in others is apparent. Even in the last decade of the nineteenth century the mortality at ages over 35 was higher than in 1850–60. There was no general movement in the second half of the nineteenth century towards declining mortality. Rather there were two movements, one leading to a rapid decline in mortality at ages under 35, and the other leading to a moderate increase in mortality in later life. It is difficult to reconcile these facts concerning the decline in mortality with the hypothesis that some general factor, such as growth of industrialization, was the cause of the decline. This hypothesis does not explain why the death-rate commenced to fall with juveniles (but not infants) and young people before it did with others. The simplest explanation is that there were certain factors quite outside the ken of industry which affected the incidence of the diseases peculiar to the various stages of life.

But perhaps the best general evidence bearing on this question is afforded by the comparison of the movements of the death-rates in this country with those in other countries, nearly all of which differed substantially from this country in their industrial development. Particulars of death-rates going back to 1841–50 are available for a number of countries, while for a few others the figures are available from 1861–70. In the statement below I give a comparison of these rates for various countries. In each case the rate for 1861–70 is taken as 100 and those of the other decades expressed as indices on that basis. It will be seen that there is a general similarity between the movements of the indices for the various countries. The index for England and Wales in 1871–80 was 5 per cent. below that for 1861–70. For a number of other countries there was also a decline in this period, although in some cases the figure was higher. In the next decade, however, most of the indices were well below the 100 mark and a number of them were not far removed from the 85 of England and Wales.[1] In the last decade of the century the similarity was even more marked, the figure of 81 for England and Wales being equalled or improved on by eleven of the countries named. The inference I draw from these figures is that from the period 1871–80 there were some factors operating which led to decline in mortality in most of the countries of the world, without any regard to the degree of industrialization in those countries. In agricultural countries, such as Australia and many parts of Europe, the movement in mortality was similar to that in this country and to the most industrialized countries of Europe. It is difficult, accordingly, to see how the decline in the death-rate in England and Wales can properly be attributed to the growth of industry in this country. What were the factors affecting the health of all the countries of the world more or less equally need not be discussed here, but the point I want to emphasize is that there was no difference between this

---

[1] Only in respect of some of the American statistics were the indices appreciably higher than in 1871–80. It should be remembered, however, that registration of births and deaths in the United States was very backward, and I suspect that the increase in mortality recorded in the table was due more to improvements in registration than to anything else.

Limits of Industrial Employment

country with its rapidly developing industry, and many others which remained almost completely agricultural.[1]

Indices of Death-rates in Decennial Periods
Death-rate 1861–70 = 100

Country	1841–1850	1851–1860	1861–1870	1871–1880	1881–1890	1891–1900
England and Wales	100	98	100	85	95	81
Scotland	—	—	100	98	87	85
Denmark	103	104	100	97	93	88
Norway	101	95	100	94	94	91
Sweden	102	107	100	91	84	81
Austria	108	102	100	103	96	87
Prussia	102	102	100	99	91	81
Bavaria	93	93	100	104	95	85
Saxony	101	96	100	104	100	85
Wurttemberg	99	94	100	98	82	75
Baden	102	96	100	103	86	81
Hesse	93	92	100	100	90	78
Hamburg	—	103	100	111	102	84
Alsace-Lorraine	95	95	100	105	95	85
Holland	103	101	100	96	82	72
Belgium	100	92	100	93	84	79
France	99	101	100	100	94	91
Spain	—	—	100	—	103	96
Roumania	—	—	100	120	105	112
Connecticut	—	92	100	101	108	107
Massachusetts	—	94	100	102	101	97
Vermont	—	—	100	104	111	115
New South Wales	—	—	100	94	89	75
Victoria	—	114	100	90	91	82
Queensland	—	—	100	91	87	64
South Australia	—	—	100	101	89	78
Tasmania	—	—	100	110	107	89
New Zealand	—	—	100	93	79	76

[1] Registration of deaths in this country commenced only in 1841. Particulars of death-rates in the Scandinavian countries, however, are available back to the beginning of the nineteenth century (and in the case of Sweden back to the middle of the eighteenth century). For these countries the mortality figures given above are extended back in the next table.

For each of the three countries there was a continuous fall in the death-rate from the beginning of the century to the end. The similarity of the figures for England and Wales to those of the Scandinavian countries in the period from 1841 to the end of the century suggests that the experience of the first forty years was also similar, and that in England and Wales the death-rate may have fallen more or less continuously from the beginning to the end of the century.

Mortality in Scandinavian Countries in Decades from 1751
Death-rate 1861–1870 = 100

	Sweden	Norway	Denmark
1751–1760	136		
1761–1770	138		
1771–1780	144		
1781–1790	138		
1791–1800	128		
1801–1810	138	140	119
1811–1820	128	118	108
1821–1830	117	105	110
1831–1840	113	112	116
1841–1850	102	101	103
1851–1860	107	95	104
1861–1870	100	100	100
1871–1880	91	94	97
1881–1890	84	94	93
1891–1900	81	91	88

As further evidence of the view that world-wide factors were more important than national factors in affecting demographic movements, I would refer shortly also to the data of the birth-rate in many countries. These data are available to the same extent as for the death-rate. The following table gives particulars of movements of the birth-rates in the same form as given above for death-rates, while the statement in the footnote[1] gives the additional information for earlier years for the Scandinavian countries.

The birth-rate did not move continuously in the same direction in all countries, but there is a distinct similarity in the movements in the different countries. In many of them the birth-rate was higher in the years 1861–80 than in the twenty years earlier or later. Just as in the case of the death-rates, although the relation is less marked, there was little difference in the movements between the birth-rates in industrialized England and Wales and in many agricultural countries and countries differing from this in other respects. The factors affecting variations in the birth-rate in that period were not associated in any direct sense with industrial development, but were much the same all over the world.

It may seem that in quoting all these figures of foreign birth and death rates over the past century I am unduly labouring the point.

---

[1] Birth-rates in Scandinavian Countries in Decades from 1751 Birth-rates 1861–70 = 100.

Indices of Birth-rates in Decennial Periods
Birth-rate 1861–1870 = 100

Country	1841–1850	1851–1860	1861–1870	1871–1880	1881–1890	1891–1900
England and Wales	93	97	100	101	92	85
Scotland			100	100	92	87
Denmark	100	106	100	102	104	98
Norway	99	107	100	100	100	98
Sweden	99	104	100	97	93	86
Austria	99	97	100	101	98	96
Prussia	99	98	100	102	98	96
Bavaria	92	90	100	109	100	99
Saxony	97	98	100	106	103	98
Wurttemberg	100	88	100	106	88	84
Baden	103	89	100	105	90	90
Hesse	97	89	100	105	91	93
Hamburg		91	100	119	112	106
Alsace-Lorraine	100	92	100	106	96	94
Holland	92	93	100	101	96	91
Belgium	97	95	100	101	94	91
France	104	100	100	97	91	84
Roumania			100	106	125	123
Connecticut			100	109	102	106
Massachusetts			100	101	99	106
New South Wales			100	93	83	73
Victoria		93	100	81	77	69
Queensland			100	88	85	72
South Australia			100	89	86	69
Tasmania			100	97	111	98
New Zealand			100	101	84	66

	Sweden	Norway	Denmark
1751–1760	115		
1761–1770	110		
1771–1780	105		
1781–1790	102		
1791–1800	106		
1801–1810	98	89	101
1811–1820	107	97	100
1821–1830	110	108	102
1831–1840	100	96	98
1841–1850	99	99	100
1851–1860	104	107	106
1861–1870	100	100	100
1871–1880	97	100	102
1881–1890	93	100	104
1891–1900	86	98	98

But I think they throw valuable light upon the development of the nineteenth century, and if they do not give convincing proof, they afford strong evidence for the view that the population of this country would have expanded considerably last century even if there had been little or no industrial development. In the main, the great industrial inventions were able to bear fruit because of the rapid increase in population. It was increase in population which helped industry rather than industry helping increase in population. Of course, I do not go so far as to say that these industrial developments did not directly lead to some increase in population. Obviously, the fact that surgical and hygienic equipment have greatly improved as a result of the inventions of industry has directly contributed in reducing the death-rate. But these were, in my opinion, minor reactions (in their effect on population). The main stream was some world-wide factor or factors which influenced the death-rate and led to increase in population in which the industrial inventions were able to thrive.

XXXIII

R. Wallace, *A dissertation on the numbers of mankind in antient and modern times: in which the superior populousness of antiquity is maintained*, Edinburgh, 1753, pp. 19-21, 22-4, 30-1.

5. As mankind can only be supported by the fruits of the earth and animal food, and it is only by agriculture, fishing and hunting, that food can be provided, to render the earth as populous as possible, these arts must be duly cherished, especially agriculture and fishing.

Hence, the more persons employ themselves in agriculture and fishing, and the arts which are necessary for managing them to greatest advantage, the world in general will be more populous; and as fewer hands are employed in this manner, there will be fewer people. 'Tis of no consequence in this argument, how the people are employed otherwise, nay tho' they are employed in arts which may increase the riches and numbers of particular nations, if they are not employed in such as are necessary for providing food.

Among arts of this latter kind, we include not only such as are immediately, but such likewise as are absolutely necessary for this purpose, tho' perhaps more immediately subservient to other ends; such as, the arts of preparing all necessary tools of the best sort, and even cloaths and houses, and whatever tends to preserve health and strength for labour. But we exclude all those arts which tend wholly to ornament and delicacy: and tho' perhaps it is impossible (nor is it necessary in the present argument) to distinguish precisely, which art is for ornament, and which for use; yet we can easily distinguish en gros. And in proportion as the arts for ornament or those for use do most prevail, there shall be, in general, fewer or more inhabitants in the world.

For if 10,000, or any other determinate number, be employed merely in works of ornament, and their labour does not serve for multiplying food, there must be a certain number, by whose labour, in providing food, these 10,000 must be supported. Now if these 10,000 instead of labouring for ornament alone, were employed directly in providing food, they might not only provide for themselves, but likewise for a certain number of others; by which greater numbers might be supported on the whole. In order therefore to have the greatest possible number of inhabitants in the world, all mankind should be employed directly in providing food; and this must always be the case till the whole earth shall be cultivated to the full. But whenever the earth shall happen to be as richly cultivated as is possible, then will there be room for those arts that tend only to ornament, since such as are employed in the more necessary labour of providing food, must be able to purchase it for a much greater number than themselves. . . .

Hence it follows likewise, contrary perhaps to what many may apprehend, that trade and commerce, instead of increasing, may often tend to diminish the number of mankind, and while they enrich a particular nation and entice great numbers of people into one place, may be not a little detrimental upon the whole, as they promote luxury and prevent many useful hands from being employed in agriculture. The exchange of commodities and carrying them from one country to another by sea or land, does not multiply food; and if such as are employed in this exchange, were employed in agriculture at home, a greater quantity of food would be provided, and a greater number of people might be maintained.

The same principle will teach us, that huge and overgrown cities, which are nurseries of corruption and debauchery, and prejudicial in many other respects, are in a particular manner destructive to the populousness of the world, as they cherish luxury, entice great numbers of all ranks to resort to them, and drain the rest of a country of useful labouring hands, who otherwise would be employed in agriculture and the most necessary arts.

Nor do the operose manufactures of linen and woollen, toys and utensils of wood or metals or earth, in which so many hands are employed in a commercial nation, contribute so much to the increase of the people as many are apt to apprehend: and it is not always true, that in proportion as manufactures are numerous and flourishing, a country must of course be more populous than in times of greater simplicity.

In general, living must be cheaper, where fewer things are wanted, and what is needed may be most easily purchased. Where-ever living is cheapest, and a family can be most easily supported, there will be more frequent marriages and greater numbers of people. Where scarce any thing is needed but simple food, a simple garment, and a little plain furniture, living will be cheapest. This agrees best to a state, where few mechanic arts are in use, and men are chiefly addicted to agriculture.

But operose manufactures of linen and woollen for cloaths and furniture of houses, a variety of utensils of wood and metals, and all the refinements of an opulent and trading nation, tend to multiply mens wants, make the most necessary and substantial things dearer, and in general increase the expences of living. Food and cloaths, houses and a little furniture are necessary to all. And if a nation be laborious and industrious, these necessaries of life will be in such abundance, that almost every one will have them at an easy rate; and while the people preserve their simple taste, and continue to be industrious, they will multiply prodigiously. But when this simplicity of taste is lost, which must always happen in proportion as operose manufactures increase: tho' they continue to be industrious, yet more of the people will apply themselves to less necessary manufactures, and fewer to provide what is more substantial; and as the proportion of those who apply to elegant manufactures increases, and fewer hands are employed in providing food, necessaries will become more scarce; toys abound, and become more necessary for the bulk of the people. This will still keep them dear, tho' they are in plenty. Hence living even in the most simple manner will become more expensive. Consequently mankind be less able to support families, and less encouraged to marry....

The taste of mankind, in the most early times, most certainly was simple, and without refinement. We may even suppose the actual existence of a time, when men lived on the spontaneous fruits of the earth, and the milk and flesh of animals; when agriculture scarce was known, or was extremely imperfect. This taste however could not continue always; the world would become refined by degrees, agriculture would come more into esteem, and be improved. But it would not be improved alone: other arts would advance likewise. There is a connexion among them, whence they cannot be entirely separated, but must appear together, if any of them approaches to perfection. Hence, as agriculture advanced, other arts would advance likewise; the most necessary would be first improved, and afterwards the less necessary, those, to wit, that tended more to refinement than use. The taste for simplicity being original, would long prevail; after it was lost in some things, it would continue in others; and the world would be old before the highest refinement, and most enormous luxury could take place. In fact, it will be found, that what would appear rustic and inelegant to many thought mighty polite at present, and would be called great simplicity, remained long among the antient nations: yet objects were never wanting to excite industry, to provoke emulation and ambition, and distinguish the rich from the poor. This is certainly the natural order and progression of things. 'Tis impossible to conceive, that various arts and manufactures would not be daily invented and improved along with agriculture. But we must also admit, that the highest refinement and greatest luxury would come last into fashion. In short, I cannot help apprehending, that while the antient simplicity remained, and men continued to employ themselves in agriculture and the subservient arts, and did not divert to arts more elegant than necessary, nations would become more populous; and as luxury prevailed, they would increase more slowly, and their number at length would begin to diminish.

XXXIV

T. R. Malthus, *First Essay on Population 1798*, with notes by James Bonar, Reprinted for the Royal Economic Society, London, 1926, pp. 305-21.

Little or no doubt can exist, that the comforts of the labouring poor depend upon the increase of the funds destined for the maintenance of labour; and will be very exactly in proportion to the rapidity of this increase. The demand for labour which such increase would occasion, by creating a competition in the market, must necessarily raise the value of labour; and, till the additional number of hands required were reared, the increased funds would be distributed to the same number of persons as before the increase, and therefore every labourer would live comparatively at his ease. But perhaps Dr. Adam Smith errs in representing every increase of the revenue or stock of a society as an increase of these funds. Such surplus stock or revenue will, indeed, always be considered by the individual possessing it, as an additional fund from which he may maintain more labour: but it will not be a real and effectual fund for the maintenance of an additional number of labourers, unless the whole, or at least a great part of this increase of the stock or revenue of the society, be convertible into a proportional quantity of provisions; and it will not be so convertible, where the increase has arisen merely from the produce of Labour, and not from the produce of land. A distinction will in this case occur, between the number of hands which the stock of the society could employ, and the number which its territory can maintain.

To explain myself by an instance. Dr. Adam Smith defines the wealth of a nation to consist in the annual produce of its land and labour. This definition evidently includes manufactured produce, as well as the produce of the land. Now supposing a nation, for a course of years, was to add what it saved from its yearly revenue, to its manufacturing capital solely, and not to its capital employed upon land, it is evident, that it might grow richer according to the above definition, without a power of supporting a greater number of labourers, and therefore, without an increase in the real funds for the maintenance of labour. There would, notwithstanding, be a demand for labour, from the power which each manufacturer would possess, or at least think he possessed, of extending his old stock in trade, or of setting up fresh works. This demand would of course raise the price of labour; but if the yearly stock of provisions in the country was not increasing, this rise would soon turn out to be merely nominal, as the price of provisions must necessarily rise with it. The demand for manufacturing labourers might, indeed, entice many from agriculture, and thus tend to diminish the annual produce of the land; but we will suppose any effect of this kind to be compensated by improvements in the instruments of agriculture, and the quantity of provisions therefore to remain the same.

Improvements in manufacturing machinery would of course take place; and this circumstance, added to the greater number of hands employed in manufactures, would cause the annual produce of the labour of the country to be upon the whole greatly increased. The wealth therefore of the country would be increasing annually, according to the definition, and might not, perhaps, be increasing very slowly.

The question is, whether wealth, increasing in this way, has any tendency to better the condition of the labouring poor. It is a self-evident proposition, that any general rise in the price of labour, the stock of provisions remaining the same, can only be a nominal rise, as it must very shortly be followed by a proportional rise in provisions. The increase in the price of labour therefore, which we have supposed, would have little or no effect in giving the labouring poor a greater command over the necessaries and conveniences of life. In this respect they would be nearly in the same state as before. In one other respect they would be in a worse state. A greater proportion of them would be employed in manufactures, and fewer, consequently, in agriculture. And this exchange of professions will be allowed, I think, by all, to be very unfavourable in respect of health, one essential ingredient of happiness, besides the greater uncertainty of manufacturing labour, arising from the capricious taste of man, the accidents of war, and other causes.

It may be said, perhaps, that such an instance as I have supposed could not occur, because the rise in the price of provisions would immediately turn some additional capital into the channel of agriculture. But this is an event which may take place very slowly, as it should be remarked, that a rise in the price of labour, had preceded the rise of provisions, and would, therefore, impede the good effects upon agriculture, which the increased value of the produce of the land might otherwise have occasioned.

It might also be said, that the additional capital of the nation would enable it to import provisions sufficient for the maintenance of those whom its stock could employ. A small country with a large navy, and great inland accommodations for carriage, such as Holland, may, indeed, import and distribute an effectual quantity of provisions; but the price of provisions must be very high, to make such an importation and distribution answer in large countries, less advantageously circumstanced in this respect.

An instance, accurately such as I have supposed, may not, perhaps, ever have occurred; but I have little doubt that instances nearly approximating to it may be found without any very laborious search. Indeed I am strongly inclined to think, that England herself, since the revolution, affords a very striking elucidation of the argument in question.

The commerce of this country, internal, as well as external, has certainly been rapidly advancing during the last century. The exchangeable value, in the market of Europe, of the annual produce of its land and labour, has, without doubt, increased very considerably. But, upon examination, it will be found, that the increase has been chiefly in the produce of labour, and not in the produce of land; and therefore, though the wealth of the nation has been advancing with a quick pace, the effectual funds for the maintenance of labour have been increasing very slowly; and the result is such as might be expected. The increasing wealth of the nation has had little or no tendency to better the condition of the labouring poor. They have not, I believe, a greater command of the necessaries and conveniences of life; and a much greater proportion of them than at the period of the revolution, is employed in manufactures, and crowded together in close and unwholesome rooms.

Could we believe the statement of Dr. Price,[1] that the population of England has decreased since the revolution, it would even appear, that the effectual fund for the maintenance of labour had been declining during the progress of wealth in other respects. For I

---

[1] R. Price, Essay containing an account of the progress from the Revolution, and the present state of the population in England and Wales, in W. Morgan, *The doctrine of annuities and assurances on lives and survivorships, stated and explained*, London, 1779.—Ed.

conceive that it may be laid down as a general rule, that if the effectual funds for the maintenance of labour are increasing, that is, if the territory can maintain, as well as the stock employ, a greater number of labourers, this additional number will quickly spring up, even in spite of such wars as Dr. Price enumerates. And, consequently, if the population of any country has been stationary, or declining, we may safely infer, that, however it may have advanced in manufacturing wealth, its effectual funds for the maintenance of labour cannot have increased.

It is difficult, however, to conceive that the population of England has been declining since the revolution; though every testimony concurs to prove that its increase, if it has increased, has been very slow. In the controversy which the question has occasioned, Dr. Price undoubtedly appears to be much more completely master of his subject, and to possess more accurate information than his opponents. Judging simply from this controversy, I think one should say, that Dr. Price's point is nearer being proved than Mr. Howlett's.[1] Truth, probably, lies between the two statements, but this supposition makes the increase of population, since the revolution, to have been very slow, in comparison with the increase of wealth.

That the produce of the land has been decreasing, or even that it has been absolutely stationary during the last century, few will be disposed to believe. The inclosure of commons and waste lands, certainly tends to increase the food of the country; but it has been asserted with confidence, that the inclosure of common fields, had frequently had a contrary effect; and that large tracts of land, which formerly produced great quantities of corn, by being converted into pasture, both employ fewer hands, and feed fewer mouths, than before their inclosure. It is, indeed, an acknowledged truth, that pasture land produces a smaller quantity of human subsistence, than corn land of the same natural fertility; and could it be clearly ascertained, that from the increased demand for butchers meat of the best quality, and its increased price in consequence, a greater quantity of good land has annually been employed in grazing, the diminution of human subsistence, which this circumstance would occasion, might have counterbalanced the advantages derived from

---

[1] J. Howlett, *An examination of Dr. Price's Essay on the Population of England and Wales; and the doctrine of an increased population in this Kingdom, established by facts*, Maidstone, 1781.—Ed.

the inclosure of waste lands, and the general improvements in husbandry.

It scarcely need be remarked, that the high price of butchers meat at present, and its low price formerly, were not caused by the scarcity in the one case, or the plenty in the other, but by the different expence sustained at the different periods, in preparing cattle for the market. It is, however, possible, that there might have been more cattle a hundred years ago in the country, than at present; but no doubt can be entertained, that there is much more meat of a superior quality brought to market at present, than ever there was. When the price of butchers meat was very low, cattle were reared chiefly upon waste lands; and except for some of the principal markets, were probably killed with but little other fatting. The veal that is sold so cheap in some distant counties at present, bears little other resemblance than the name, to that which is bought in London. Formerly, the price of butchers meat would not pay for rearing, and scarcely for feeding cattle on land that would answer in tillage; but the present price will not only pay for fatting cattle on the very best land, but will even allow of the rearing many, on land that would bear good crops of corn. The same number of cattle, or even the same weight of cattle at the different periods when killed, will have consumed (if I may be allowed the expression) very different quantities of human subsistence. A fatted beast may in some respects be considered, in the language of the French economists, as an unproductive labourer: he has added nothing to the value of the raw produce that he has consumed. The present system of grazing, undoubtedly tends more than the former system to diminish the quantity of human subsistence in the country, in proportion to the general fertility of the land.

I would not by any means be understood to say, that the former system either could, or ought, to have continued. The increasing price of butchers meat, is a natural and inevitable consequence of the general progress of cultivation; but I cannot help thinking, that the present great demand for butchers meat of the best quality, and the quantity of good land that is in consequence annually employed to produce it, together with the great number of horses at present kept for pleasure, are the chief causes, that have prevented the quantity of human food in the country, from keeping pace with the generally increased fertility of the soil; and a change of custom in these respects, would, I have little doubt, have a very sensible effect on the quantity of subsistence in the country, and consequently on its population.

The employment of much of the most fertile land in grazing, the improvements in agricultural instruments, the increase of large farms, and particularly, the diminution of the number of cottages throughout the kingdom, all concur to prove, that there are not probably, so many persons employed in agricultural labour now, as at the period of the revolution. Whatever increase of population, therefore, has taken place, must be employed almost wholly in manufactures; and it is well known, that the failure of some of these manufactures, merely from the caprice of fashion, such as, the adoption of muslins instead of silks, or of shoe-strings, and covered buttons, instead of buckles and metal buttons, combined with the restraints in the market of labour arising from corporation, and parish laws, have frequently driven thousands on charity for support. The great increase of the poor rates, is, indeed of itself, a strong evidence, that the poor have not a greater command of the necessaries and conveniences of life; and if to the consideration, that their condition in this respect is rather worse than better, be added the circumstance, that a much greater proportion of them is employed in large manufactories, unfavourable both to health and virtue, it must be acknowledged, that the increase of wealth of late years, has had no tendency to increase the happiness of the labouring poor.

XXXV

T. R. Malthus, *An essay on the principle of population*, 6th ed., 1826, reprinted London, 1890, pp. 419–20, 423–5.

It must be allowed then, that the funds for the maintenance of labour do not necessarily increase with the increase of wealth, and very rarely increase in proportion to it.

But the condition of the lower classes of society certainly does not depend exclusively upon the increase of the funds for the maintenance of labour, or the means of supporting more labourers. That these means form always a very powerful ingredient in the condition of the labouring classes, and the main ingredient in the increase of population, is unquestionable. But, in the first place, the comforts of the lower classes of society do not depend solely upon food, nor even upon strict necessaries; and they cannot be considered as in a good state unless they have the command of some conveniences and even luxuries. Secondly, the tendency in population fully to keep pace with the means of subsistence must in general prevent the increase of these means from having a great and permanent effect in improving the condition of the poor. And, thirdly, the cause which has the most lasting effect in improving the situation of the lower classes of society depends chiefly upon the conduct and prudence of the individuals themselves, and is, therefore, not immediately and necessarily connected with an increase in the means of subsistence.

With a view, therefore, to the other causes which affect the condition of the labouring classes, as well as the increase of the means of subsistence, it may be desirable to trace more particularly the mode in which increasing wealth operates, and to state both the disadvantages as well as the advantages with which it is accompanied.

In the natural and regular progress of a country to a state of great wealth and population, there are two disadvantages to which the lower classes of society seem necessarily to be subjected. The first is, a diminished power of supporting children under the existing habits of the society with respect to the necessaries of life. And the second, the employment of a larger proportion of the population in occupations less favourable to health and more exposed to fluctuations of demand and unsteadiness of wages.

A diminished power of supporting children is an absolutely unavoidable consequence of the progress of a country towards the utmost limits of its population. If we allow that the power of a given quantity of territory to produce food has some limit, we must allow that as this limit is approached, the increase of population becomes slower and slower, the power of supporting children will be less and less, till finally, when the increase of produce stops, it becomes only sufficient to maintain, on an average, families of such a size as will not allow of a further addition of numbers. This state of things is generally accompanied by a fall in the corn price of labour; but should this effect be prevented by the prevalence of prudential habits among the lower classes of society, still the result just described must take place; and though, from the powerful operation of the preventive check to increase, the wages of labour estimated even in corn might not be low, yet it is obvious that, in this case, the power of supporting children would rather be nominal than real; and the moment this power began to be exercised to its apparent extent, it would cease to exist.

The second disadvantage to which the lower classes of society are subjected in the progressive increase of wealth is, that a larger portion of them is engaged in unhealthy occupations, and in employments in which the wages of labour are exposed to much greater fluctuations than in agriculture, and the simpler kinds of domestic trade. . . .

It must be allowed then, that in the natural and usual progress of wealth, the means of marrying early and supporting a family are diminished, and a greater proportion of the population is engaged in employments less favourable to health and morals, and more subject to fluctuations in the price of labour, than the population employed in agriculture.

These are no doubt considerable disadvantages, and they would be sufficient to render the progress of riches decidedly unfavourable to the condition of the poor, if they were not counteracted by advantages which nearly, if not fully, counterbalance them.

And, first, it is obvious that the profits of stock are that source of revenue from which the middle classes are chiefly maintained; and the increase of capital, which is both the cause and effect of increasing riches, may be said to be the efficient cause of the emancipation of the great body of society from a dependence on the landlords. In a country of limited extent, consisting of fertile land divided into large properties, as long as the capital remains inconsiderable, the structure of society is most unfavourable to liberty and good government. This was exactly the state of Europe in the feudal times. The landlords could in no other way spend their incomes than by maintaining a great number of idle followers; and it was by the growth of capital in all the employments to which it is directed, that the pernicious power of the landlords was destroyed, and their dependent followers were turned into merchants, manufacturers, tradesmen, farmers, and independent labourers;—a change of prodigious advantage to the great body of society, including the labouring classes.

Secondly; in the natural progress of cultivation and wealth, the production of an additional quantity of corn will require more labour, while, at the same time, from the accumulation and better distribution of capital, the continual improvements made in machinery, and the facilities opened to foreign commerce, manufactures and foreign commodities will be produced or purchased with less labour, and consequently a given quantity of corn will command a much greater quantity of manufactures and foreign commodities than while the country was poor. Although, therefore, the labourer may earn less corn than before, the superior value which every portion which he does not consume in kind will have in the purchase of conveniences, may more than counterbalance this diminution. He will not indeed have the same power of maintaining a large family; but with a small family he may be better lodged and clothed, and better able to command the decencies and comforts of life.

Thirdly; it seems to be proved by experience, that the labouring classes of society seldom acquire a decided taste for conveniences and comforts till they become plentiful compared with food, which they never do till food has become in some degree scarce. If the labourer can obtain the full support of himself and family by two or three days' labour; and if, to furnish himself with conveniences and comforts he must work three or four days more, he will generally think the sacrifice too great compared with the objects to be obtained, which are not strictly necessary to him, and will therefore often prefer the luxury of idleness to the luxury of improved lodging and clothing. This is said by Humboldt to be particularly the case in some parts of South America, and to a certain extent prevails in Ireland, India and all countries where food is plentiful compared with capital and manufactured commodities. On the other hand, if the main part of the labourer's time be occupied in procuring food, habits of industry are necessarily generated, and the remaining time, which is but inconsiderable compared with the commodities it will purchase, is seldom grudged. It is under these circumstances, particularly when combined with a good government, that the labouring classes of society are most likely to acquire a decided taste for the conveniences and comforts of life; and this taste may be such an event to prevent, after a certain period, a further fall in the corn price of labour. But if the corn price of labour continues tolerably high while the relative value of commodities compared with corn falls very considerably, the labourer is placed in a most favourable situation. Owing to his decided taste for conveniences and comforts, the good corn wages of labour will not generally lead to early marriages, yet in individual cases, where large families occur, there will be the means of supporting them independently, by the sacrifice of the accustomed conveniences and comforts; and thus the poorest of the lower classes will rarely be stinted in food, while the great mass of them will not only have sufficient means of subsistence, but be able to command no inconsiderable quantity of those conveniences and comforts, which, at the same time that they gratify a natural or acquired want, tend unquestionably to improve the mind and elevate the character.

On an attentive review, then, of the effects of increasing wealth on the condition of the poor, it appears that, although such an increase does not imply a proportionate increase of the funds for the maintenance of labour, yet it brings with it advantages to the lower classes of society which may fully counterbalance the disadvantages with which it is attended, and, strictly speaking, the good or bad condition of the poor is not necessarily connected with any particular stage in the progress of society to its full complement of wealth. A rapid increase of wealth indeed, whether it consists principally in addition to the means of subsistence or to the stock of conveniences and comforts will always, coeteris paribus, have a favourable effect on the poor; but the influence even of this cause is greatly modified and altered by other circumstances, and nothing but the union of individual prudence with the skill and industry which produce wealth can permanently secure to the lower classes of society that share of it which it is, on every account, so desirable that they should possess.

XXXVI

A. Alison, *The principles of population and their connection with human happiness*, Edinburgh and London, 1840, pp. 137-8, 139-41, 181, 182-3, 186-7, 187-8, 189-90, 192.

2. The vast and constantly increasing surplus of agricultural produce which accumulates in every country with the progress of society, and the increasing powers of production which agricultural skill have in every age communicated to human industry in the later stages of society, uniformly and invariably, in densely peopled and opulent communities, lead to the accumulation of mankind in great cities. In such situations, unless the prevalence of manufactures and the operation of the factory system have given a forced and unnatural encouragement to early marriages, the moral causes of restraint, from the progress of luxury, and spread of artificial wants among all classes, necessarily become extremely powerful. But even if it should be otherwise, and pernicious institutions should force on in such situations, in particular great towns, a vast increase of births, the unhealthiness incident to the situation of the children necessarily occasions such a mortality among them, as effectually prevents these births leading to any considerable addition to the numbers of mankind. . . .

The difference between the rate of mortality in large, and still more in great manufacturing towns and rural districts or villages, is always considerable, often so great as to be attended with the most important effects. The average rate of mortality over all England is 1 in 51: whereas in Glasgow, from 1821 to 1837, it has been progressively increasing, till, from an annual decease of 1 in 39·89, in the first of these years, it had sunk so low as 1 in 24·63 in the last. Of this prodigious mortality, which Dr. Cowan justly calls 'unequalled' in any city in Britain,[1] part is without doubt to be ascribed to the factory system, and prevalence of habits of intemperance among the people, which will hereafter form the subject of an ample commentary; but

---

[1] R. Cowan, *Vital statistics of Glasgow*, Glasgow, 1838.—Ed.

part of it is to be attributed to the physical effect of the atmosphere on the health of those of tender years, decisive evidence is to be found in the fact, which the same able and indefatigable observer has established, that during all these years, from 50 to 55 per cent. of this great mortality took place among children under ten years of age. Even in London, where such extraordinary efforts are made to preserve the health of the people, the annual mortality is 1 in 41, being 20 per cent. greater than that of all England; while in Edinburgh it ranges, of late years, from 1 in 25 to 1 in 32,—probably less than half of that of all Scotland.

The statistical researches which have been made over all the other countries of Europe exhibit the same general result as to the effect of great towns in diminishing the rate of increase. In the whole of England, the annual rate of mortality below ten years of age increases just in proportion as manufactures are established, that is, as great towns are prevalent; and diminishes as the people are devoted to rural occupations; while the same is observed in Holland, Belgium, and France. It is superfluous to overload these pages with similar details, drawn from other countries of Europe; for the fact is so evident, and is so completely within every one's observation, that it would have required no illustration, if it had not lain at the foundation of an important provision of nature relative to the increase of mankind, which makes the inhabitants of great towns almost always unable to support their own numbers, and renders those great emporiums of opulence, if due provision for the humbler classes is not made, the charnel-houses of the human race. . . .

IV. These considerations lead to another most important limitation to the demand for labour, in the later stages of society, arising from the division of labour, and the inventions and improvement of machinery.

In simple times, and in agricultural states, almost every article, whether of subsistence or accommodation, is produced by human labour. Not only is the produce of the fields raised and converted into the form required for subsistence by the toil of the husbandman, but the manufactures which are exchanged for his surplus produce are wrought into various forms by the manual labour of the artisan. . . .

If this state of things had continued after capital had begun to accumulate, and the demand for labour had increased with the extension of the wants of men, the most dangerous consequences to public prosperity must have ensued. If the same amount of labour were requisite to provide the articles of necessity and convenience, in the later as the earlier stages of society, it is impossible to say how soon every state would have arrived at the limits of its increase. The whole encouragement arising from the extension of the wealth and numbers of mankind, being brought to bear directly upon the demand for labour, population would advance with too rapid strides, and society would arrive at a stationary condition before the limitations provided to the principle of increase could be developed. Fortunately this can never occur, in consequence of the operation of causes which begin to be felt even before their effects are required in the world.

Coëval with the birth of society, there spring up a succession of causes which retard the effect of an increasing desire for the productions of industry, and operate with increasing force as mankind approach a stationary condition.

The separation of professions which arises so early in the progress of mankind, is the first circumstance which limits the effect of increasing wealth on the demand for labour. The division of employment is soon found to facilitate every species of industry: the advantages of an undivided attention to a particular pursuit are so great as to force themselves upon the attention of men in an early period of civilization. The consequence of this change is, to prevent the increase in the demand for the productions of human industry from giving the same impulse to population, which it would have done, if no such cause had interfered to intercept its effects. If ten men are enabled, from the separation of employments, to do the work of twenty, it is quite clear that the encouragement to population arising from the augmented vent for its produce, is reduced to one-half of what it otherwise would have been. . . .

With the division of labour there springs up the invention and improvement of machinery, which comes in the progress of wealth to have the most important effects upon the demand for labour. The application of machinery to manufactures is early perceived to be an advantage; but it is the pressure of taxes, and the high money price of labour, which set human ingenuity at work to improve the powers thus acquired. Without such assistance the manufacturer finds himself unable to withstand the competition of states where the money wages of labour are lower, and the farmer to meet the foreign grower in the supply of the home market. Necessity, the mother of invention, overcomes this disadvantage by the machinery which improved art produces, and the ingenuity which mechanical knowledge developes. To such improvements no limit can be assigned. With the progress of science, and the extensions of art, the substitution of machinery for human labour is carried to an inconceivable extent....

It is hardly possible to estimate the effect of this substitution of machinery for human labour on the progress of population, in the opulent and advanced stages of society. It pervades every branch of industry, and operates with increasing force as the growth of wealth raises the money wages of labour, by affecting the price of subsistence. It has been calculated by experienced persons, that, if the whole cotton manufactures of Great Britain were wrought by the human hand, without the assistance of machinery, they would require two hundred millions of labourers: whereas hardly 800,000 are at present employed in that manufacture. The same diminution in the demand for labour arises from the extension of machinery in a greater or less degree to every branch of industry....

It is the perception of this fact which renders these improvements in machinery so great an object of jealousy to the manufacturing classes, and gives rise to so many dissensions between them and their employers, in seasons of public distress. Nothing can be more mistaken, however, than the idea which they entertain, that, if they could only get quit of the obnoxious engines, the demand for the produce of their industry would be wholly felt by the working-classes. If the machinery of Britain were destroyed, the export of its manufactures would almost entirely cease. The saving of expense produced by its use alone enables our manufacturers to counteract the high price of labour and the weight of taxes, and to compete with strangers in the supply of the foreign market. But for these advantages, they would be unable to retain the supply of their own people. So far from machinery, therefore, being really hurtful to British industry, it alone enables our labours to maintain their ground against the exertions of rival states. It is the operation of a law of Nature, destined to restrain the demand for labour in the advanced stages of society, which really is felt by the British operatives; and this law, in its effect on population, no human exertions are able to avoid; for its influence upon the price of the produce of industry can be avoided only by effecting a diminution in the number of hands employed in the working up of highly wrought articles. It is probable, that, whatever extension the exportation of our manufactures may receive in future years, there will be no corresponding increase in the number of our operative workmen. They may possibly not be able to maintain their present numbers. Human ingenuity will daily extend the application of machinery to the different branches of industry, and the produce of the national labour will be augmented without a proportional increase in the number of its working-classes. Judging from the past, there is no reason to believe that mechanical improvement has reached its final limit. It appears rather commencing a career to which imagination itself can affix no termination. . . .

The substitution, therefore, of steam-power looms for manual labour, of mechanical contrivance for human multiplication, is a most fortunate change in the progress of society, and more particularly to be desired in a country such as Britain, whose political greatness is intimately connected with its manufacturing superiority. Such improvements are not only necessary to counteract the effect of the depreciation in the value of money, and consequent rise in the money wages of labour which follows a state of commercial prosperity, but highly beneficial in thinning the ranks of the manufacturing classes, and preventing that undue multiplication of their numbers from which the most dangerous consequences may be anticipated.

XXXVII

United Nations, *The determinants and consequences of population trends*, New York, 1953. pp. 173-4.

During modern times the factors affecting population distribution have been undergoing several major types of changes which have interacted to alter considerably both the relative numbers of people in various regions of the world and the distribution of population within countries. First, technological advances and changes in the industrial structure of the world economy have freed a large proportion of the people from their former dependency upon the land and other place-bound natural resources. Second, the changes in technology and in consumers' wants have re-enforced the tendency for economic opportunities and population to be concentrated in certain localities, particularly in the great metropolitan agglomerations. Third, the desires of the people and the policies of governments with reference to the growth and distribution of national populations have been shifting; and there has recently been an increased degree of governmental control, especially in the countries with planned economies. Fourth, the pattern of geographical variations in birth and death rates has been changing; recently the rates of natural increase have been falling in highly industrialized countries and rising in economically less developed countries and the rates have been higher in the rural than in the urban areas of many countries. The effects of intra-national differences in rates of natural increase have been greatly modified by migration within countries, particularly by migration from rural to urban areas, bringing about a rapid population growth in the cities of many countries in spite of low urban rates of natural increase. At the international level, however, migration has recently had little influence; the changing relation of birth and death rates have been the dominant factors of change in the relative sizes of population in the different countries.

The power of land and other natural resources to determine the distribution of population has diminished with the progress of industrialization. Man is no longer dependent upon the organic products of land, to the extent that he was formerly. Similarly, in the case of mineral resources, although the Industrial Revolution initially increased their population-pulling power and although they continue to be of fundamental importance in modern economies, they no longer govern the location to the former extent. The proportion of the labour force engaged in agricultural and mining activities is today smaller than formerly. An increasingly large proportion of the equipment utilized today is man-made and can therefore be produced and located wherever man decides. In consequence of these changes, the proportion of the labour force of industrialized countries, the location of which is relatively independent of land and natural resources, may well be two or three times what it was in the beginning of the Industrial Revolution.

Among the circumstances contributing to the increasing concentration of population on a few sites, four in particular may be mentioned. First, improvements in transportation have diminished the cost of moving raw materials and sources of energy to manufacturing centres. Second, technological change has increased economies of scale, agglomeration, etc., which makes for the spatial concentration of economic activities. Third, the proportion of the national income expended for services and manufactures not heavily dependent on place-bound resources has steadily increased as per capita income has risen. Fourth, the mobility of labour within countries has increased. These four changes, together with those described in the preceding paragraph, have greatly diminished man's dependency upon land and natural resources and have extended his range of choice in economic activities, at least when he acts collectively. These changes, however, have entailed or have been accompanied by changes in production necessitating a high degree of concentration of population at the sites chosen.

Prior to the Industrial Revolution, when agriculture was man's main activity in nearly all countries, the population distribution in each country tended in the course of time to become more or less adjusted to variations in the quality of the land. According to George, the typical result was an uneven distribution; population was heavily concentrated on lands which could produce large returns with minimum equipment, while other lands which were inferior in quality or which could yield large crops only with substantial capital equipment, were less densely settled.[1] However, in comparison with the distribution which subsequently evolved in the countries that become highly industrialized, this pre-industrial distribution of population was one of relatively uniform density over wide areas. Such massing of population as occurred 'was a function of the geography of food production and of maritime and inland water transport'. Usher concluded that the limiting average density in 'relatively large areas' in such an economy was about 125 persons per square mile, both in mediaeval Europe and in the under-developed agrarian regions of the modern world.[2]

Prior to the nineteenth century manufacturing developed (*a*) where agriculture was capable of producing a surplus of food for the support of a non-agricultural population or (*b*) where there was a relatively immobile labour supply, which deriving only a bare subsistence from the accessible agriculture resources, undertook the production of goods that could be exchanged elsewhere for the means of existence. The existence of a food surplus near the area of manufacturing was a necessary condition, since the cost of transporting food was greater than that of transporting raw materials. The existence of a supply of labour in excess of what the agricultural resources of a region could support at a level above bare subsistence made for low wages and thus provided an advantage to entrepreneurs locating where this relatively 'cheap' labour was to be had. 'Cheap' labour deriving from this same condition continues as an incentive for the location of industry in certain areas today.

The Industrial Revolution not only greatly increased the magnitude of urban concentrations but also, together with the improvement of agricultural techniques and equipment, altered the pattern of rural population distribution. The rural population became more mobile, its numbers were reduced by migration to the cities and its distribution became more nearly uniform as land which had previously supported little or no population was brought under cultivation.

With the progress of the Industrial Revolution the importance of

---

[1] P. George, *Introduction à l'étude géographique de la population du monde*, I.N.E.D., Travaux et documents, Cahier no. 14, Paris, 1951.—Ed.

[2] P. Usher, The history of population and settlement in Eurasia, *The Geographical Review* (U.S.A.), XX, 4, 1930.—Ed.

Consequences of Population Trends

localized food and labour surpluses declined. The cost of transporting food became less important as a limiting factor, for while the consumption of food per head (expressed in weight) remained relatively constant, that of fuel, materials, and other factors increased. Labour could be attracted with increasing ease from elsewhere. In consequence, the greater densities of population present in the world today came to be found at or near sources of energy. Furthermore, as the new technology developed, the world trading area initially limited chiefly to the maritime fringes of the continents, came to encompass the vast interiors. By the latter part of the nineteenth century some of the industrialized areas had developed population densities exceeding 450 persons per square mile, nearly four times the maximum for the earlier agrarian economy.

XXXVIII

First Annual Report of the Registrar-General of Births, Deaths and Marriages in England. (Abstracts of 1837–8), London, H.M.S.O., 1839, pp. 108, 110–12.

Diseases of Towns and of the Open Country

Different classes of the population experience very different rates of mortality, and suffer different kinds of diseases. The principal causes of these differences, besides the sex age, and hereditary organization, must be sought in three sources—exercise in the ordinary occupations of life—the adequate or inadequate supply of warmth and of food—and the different degrees of exposure to poisonous effluvia and to destructive agencies. The subsequent tables will exhibit the influence of the contaminated atmosphere of cities. . . . The fatality of every class of diseases, and of almost every disease, is augmented

TABLE E:
DEATHS by Twelve Classes of Fatal Diseases in City and in County Districts

	Cities	Counties
Population	3,553,161	3,500,750
Epidemic, endemic, and contagious diseases	12,766	6,045
Sporadic Diseases		
Of the nervous system	7,705	3,607
Of the respiratory organs	12,619	7,847
Of the organs of circulation	590	309
Of the digestive organs	3,476	1,832
Of the urinary organs	219	161
Of the organs of generation	460	265
Of the organs of locomotion	262	154
Of the integumentary system	62	55
Of uncertain seat	4,396	3,730
Age	2,924	3,102
Violent deaths	1,370	929
Not specified	1,104	1,657
Total Deaths	47,953	29,693

in the concentrated city population, but in very different degrees. This will be more evident in a tabular form, in which the facts of the two sets of observations are consolidated.

The concentration of the population in cities doubles the deaths from the two first classes of disease; the ratio of deaths having been as 1 to 2·11, and 1 to 2·13; and upon reference to the individual diseases in Tables C., D., it will be observed that the augmentation in the latter class occurs principally in convulsions and hydrocephalus:—Deaths by convulsions, counties 1,347, cities 3,723, ratio 1 : 2·76; by hydrocephalus, counties 559, cities 1,540, ratio 1 : 2·75. It has already been intimated that convulsion is a frequent intercurrent symptom in diarrhoea and diseases of the epidemic class in infants; it may exist, however, as an independent affection, and in that case has clearly, as well as hydrocephalus, with which it is allied, an epidemic character. A similar remark will apply to pneumonia and bronchitis, of which 1,209 cases were registered in the counties, 2,865 in the cities; ratio 1 : 2·37. The pulmonary inflammation was, in many cases, developed in the course of measles, influenza, and other diseases of the first class. The three following diseases, which principally affect adults between the ages of 15 and 65, show that unhealthy places augment the fatality of diseases in different degrees.

	Counties	Cities	Increase per cent. in Cities
Deaths by consumption	5,857	8,125	39
Deaths by childbirth	217	372	71
Deaths by typhus	1,564	3,456	221

This gives the classification a peculiar property. Wherever the absolute mortality is low, the number of deaths in the epidemic class is less than the number in the pulmonary class; and, on the contrary, wherever the deaths in the first class exceed or equal those in the third, it may be affirmed that the absolute mortality is high.

The occupations in cities are not more laborious than agriculture, and the great mass of the town population have constant exercise and employment; their wages are higher, their dwellings as good, their clothing as warm, and their food certainly as substantial as that of the agricultural labourer. The Poor Law Inquiry, and successive Parliamentary Committees, have shown that the families of agricultural labourers subsist upon a minimum of animal food, and an inadequate supply of bread and potatoes. The source of the higher mortality in cities is, therefore, in the insalubrity of the atmosphere.

Every human being expires about 666 cubic feet of gas daily, which, if collected in a receiver, would destroy other animals; and is constantly producing, in a variety of ways, the decomposition of animal and vegetable matter, yielding poisonous emanations in houses, workshops, dirty streets, and bad sewers. The smoke of fires, and the products of combustion are also poisonous. All gases and effluvia, like odours, are diffusible; they have a certain force of diffusion, which Professor Graham has expressed numerically; and all the emanations from human habitations in the open country mingle, almost as soon as they escape, in the currents of the atmosphere. But locate, instead of one individual to a square mile of land (the supposed density of population in the uncultivated forests of America and the steppes of Asia), 200,000 individuals upon a square mile, as soldiers in a camp, and the poison will be concentrated 200,000 fold; intersect the space in every direction by 10,000 high walls, which overhang the narrow streets, shut out the sunlight, and intercept the movements of the atmosphere; let the rejected vegetables, the offal of slaughtered animals, the filth produced in every way decay in the houses and courts, or stagnate in the wet streets; bury the dead in the midst of the living; and the atmosphere will be an active poison, which will destroy, as it did in London formerly, and as it does in Constantinople now, 5-7 per cent. of the inhabitants annually, and generate, when the temperature is high, recurring plagues, in which a fourth part of the entire population will perish. But the health will be little more impaired by residence upon 1 than upon 100 square miles, if means can be devised for supplying the 200,000 individuals with 200,000,000 cubic feet of pure air daily, and for removing the principal sources of poisonous exhalations. The latter object is partly accomplished by paved, even streets, by the scavenger, by an abundant supply of water, by large well-constructed, trapped sewers, and by domestic habits of cleanliness; but it is difficult to perceive how volatile impurities can be removed, and how a stream of uncontaminated air can be supplied where the sun cannot heat the earth and air, where there are no open squares, or the streets are narrow, or the houses are only separated by courts, or built in *cul de sac*.

XXXIX

Report from the Committee on the "Bill to regulate the labour of children in the Mills and Factories of the United Kingdom": with the Minutes of Evidence, Appendix and Index, London, 1833, pp. 512–13, 514.

CHARLES TURNER THACKRAH Esq. called in, and examined.

10467. What is your profession?—A general practitioner in medicine and surgery at Leeds. . . .

10470. How long have you paid attention to the condition of individuals employed in mills and factories, and other laborious pursuits?—At intervals, since the year 1823.

10471. From that period you have been in the habit of renewing the subject in your own mind, and continuing your observations upon it?—I have.

10472. Have you written upon the subject?—I have.

10473. A work expressly confined to the consideration of the effect of arts, trades, and professions on health and longevity?—I have.

10474. A work that has attracted a considerable degree of notice in your profession?—I believe it has.

10475. You have seen no cause to alter any of the opinions you have expressed in that work?—None, materially; seeking truth only, I have had to correct errors in the details of particular departments, but I do not remember that I have had to alter any general principle or deduction.

10476. What is your opinion of the effects produced upon the health, the welfare, and longevity of those employed under the factory system as at present pursued?—My opinion is, that the factory system reduces the nervous power, in other words the vigour of the constitution, that it renders persons more feeble, more subject to suffer from attacks of disease; and finally, that persons constantly so employed are shorter-lived than others. There may be other points, but these strike me at this moment as the principal.

10477. Have you made calculations substantiating the latter fact, namely, the shorter duration of human life in manufacturing than in agricultural districts?—I have, from the census of 1821.

10478. You found that the facts published in that document entirely confirmed your opinions regarding the effect on human longevity of those particular pursuits?—They did, decidedly. My attention was first called to the subject of employments as affecting health, from remarking the sickness and disease that prevailed in large towns, and especially in certain occupations. This led me to inquire into the cause, and my inquiries convinced me that a greater amount of disease exists in manufacturing than in agricultural districts; and it was at a subsequent period that I referred to the population returns; these confirmed my views, by exhibiting a greater mortality in the manufacturing than in the agricultural.

10479. So that the opinions which you, as a medical man, had previously formed, were fully substantiated by the facts which you found in the census of 1821?—Yes.

10480. You have stated, in your publication, those facts in reference to this particular inquiry?—I have; I compared the three Ridings of Yorkshire; but if the first, the East, were thrown out, the contrast would be more distinct, since the East Riding contains some evils peculiar to itself, and unconnected with my inquiry. In comparing the West Riding, the manufacturing district, with the North, the agricultural, it appears that in the former the number of persons between 40 and 50 years of age in 1,000 is less than in the North; and when we go to other ages further on, from 50 to 60, 60 to 70, and so on, the proportion of persons living in the West Riding very greatly diminishes; in other words, that the people in the West Riding have decidedly shorter lives than the people in the North Riding.

10481. Do you think that children suffer more than adults from the factory system?—I would say, on the whole, that they suffer considerably more; children appear to bear dusty occupations with much less annoyance than adults; difficulty of breathing is rare among them, but this exception from disease I conceive to be more apparent than real; the children I believe to be considerably injured; and although they do not show disease in the lungs, or any great change in their general health at an early period, yet such individuals rarely become strong adults; and at a subsequent period they are more liable to consumption, and other serious affections of the lungs, than persons of like station, who are not employed in such dusty occupations.

10482. So that you think that the constitution may be undergoing very serious and even permanent injury, without the magnitude of that injury being decidedly apparent in the youthful period of existence?—Certainly you express my meaning fully; in fact, from childhood to puberty diseases are not frequent. This period of life is comparatively healthy.

10483. The diseases of that period you do not consider to be so constant and so fatal as at other periods?—I do not. This observation applies to society at large, and accounts for the comparative freedom from disease of children placed in unhealthy situations.

10484. Do you conceive that at that particular period the human constitution is more tenacious of life?—It is very tenacious of life.

10485. You would not therefore conceive it would be any just answer to those who, like yourself, declare that the factory system, as it is ordinarily pursued, is injurious to health and tends to shorten life, if it were asserted, that at the period of existence alluded to no great excess in mortality should become apparent?—Certainly not; that would by no means satisfy me; I should consider it no answer whatever to the general statement on the subject; I am well aware that the actual extent of mortality in factories is small among children; I have been often told, in reference to particular mills, that there is but a small per-centage of deaths in the course of the year; but this statement has not answered my objection, being aware that mills in general do not produce immediate and direct mortality; their chief effect on the operatives, in my opinion, is the undermining the health, the destroying the constitution, and the rendering people liable to attacks of disease to which they would not have been subject, or under which they would not have succumbed, if they had been in other situations. With few exceptions, the diseases developed in mills are chronic rather than acute. . . .

10489. Will you state to this Committee what you conceive to be the general effects of labour too long continued in the atmosphere of mills and factories, generally considered, leaving out of the question any particular dusty manufacture ?—I should say a reduction of vital power proportionate to the length of that confinement, and with this reduction of vital power a series of evils to the constitution, chronic maladies, and an inability to resist acute ones, and a shortening of life.

XL

Report from the Select Committee on The Health of Towns; Together with the Minutes of Evidence taken before them, and An Appendix and Index, London, 1840, pp. 71-2, 73, 74-5.

1259. Chairman.[1] You have a general acquaintance with the district inhabited by the poorer classes in Manchester?—I have; in the autumn of 1838 I was down there at the time that Captain Jebb was making inquiries as to the petition for a charter to Manchester, and I availed myself of the opportunity that his duties afforded, of inquiring at the different houses into the truth of the signatures, to take an opportunity to go into the houses, and see in what state they were; I first knocked at the door, and then walked in.

1260. In the course of that inquiry, did you have an opportunity of seeing many of the habitations of the lower classes?—Yes, I had, in all the poorer districts.

1261. What is their state with respect to drainage, and cleansing, and ventilation, and the comfort of the dwellings amongst those classes?—With regard to the drainage, by which I must understand that underground sewerage common in large towns, I can know scarcely anything of it; and the Committee will readily acknowledge that I could not, when I mention that the town-council of Leeds, in their own admissions upon the same subject just now, could not find out whether one half the streets of their town were or were not drained.

1262. I meant with respect to surface drainage, whether in that respect they were dirty and wet, or appeared to have underground communications?—The town presents very varying appearances; on the Ancoates side it is much improved by the commissioners of police, who have put down some paving of some kind, more or less;

---

[1] Examination of Joseph Fletcher, Esq., 30 March 1840.—Ed.

but in Irish Town, by the Medlock, and in certain other districts of the town, the old absence of pavement still remains, and in these streets the whole surface, except a little narrow slip, by which people may walk from house to house along the sides, is occupied by a great mass of filth and rubbish, pools of water and refuse, and everything you can conceive to be the offal from houses the habitations of such people.

1263. Is that applicable to several of the most populous districts?—Yes, it is.

1264. Then the smell in hot weather would be very offensive?—Exceedingly offensive, and still more injurious from the houses of that class in Manchester having generally no thorough draught; the houses stand back to back, the partition wall having a separate row of dwellings on each side, without back offices.

1265. Is not that mode of building very injurious to the health of the inhabitants?—Yes, no doubt: the Committee may imagine a partition wall between street and street, and across the end of the street, and enclosing a space so completely, that the inhabitants breathe the foul atmosphere exuded from this filth incessantly.

1266. That is the case with many of the districts in Manchester?—Yes, it is most conspicuously so in the lowest part of the town called Irish Town; the streets are not so filthy in other districts, but as to the want of a thorough draught the houses are quite as bad.

1267. In those districts there is a neglected heap of filth in front of the house, and at the back a wall enclosing whole masses of houses?—Yes.

1268. Can you imagine anything more likely to be injurious to the health of the inhabitants?—No, I cannot.

1269. What is the effect; is there a great deal of fever there?—I have not any statistics of disease in Manchester, nor shall we get them till the office of the registrar-general has been at work some time; but it must have a most injurious effect: judging from the appearance of the people it certainly has; a great deal of their pallid and care-worn appearance is not so much to be attributed to the factory system, as it is to be attributed to the sweeping together of large masses of people, with little intelligence, under circumstances so unfavourable; and the evils under which they suffer are produced from causes arising in the towns rather than from injurious influences in the processes of the cotton manufacture.

1270. Occupied as they are in the cotton manufacture, you think if their dwellings were constructed better, and those points which are so neglected were attended to, that their general health would probably be much better, and you do not see anything in that occupation, if properly regulated, to affect them?—Assuredly not, if I may judge from the appearance of persons in the employment of benevolent masters in the rural districts. I have the pleasure of knowing some of the largest manufacturers in Lancashire, and there are instances of some having the largest works, whose people and mills present the appearance, the one of health, and the other cleanliness, with good ventilation, which I should be happy to see in the persons and workshops of every district.

1287. As you suggested just now, that there should be a thorough draught through the streets, do you think a similar regulation should be made as to the construction of the houses themselves?—Yes.

1288. Chairman. For instance, so as to prevent their being built back to back?—Yes. if you think it right so far to interfere with the cupidity of the builders, and the acquiescence of ignorant people, there is not the least doubt you may execute it.

1289. Do you not think that some such regulations, duly considered and properly executed, would be highly beneficial to the inhabitants of all those densely-peopled towns? —I cannot express in terms sufficiently strong my conviction of the utility of some such measure; for the growth of our manufactures, and the sweeping together of vast populations, have been equally so sudden, that the people were not brought up in or prepared for the new circumstances in which they have been placed; and unless you render them assistance by municipal organization, for the purpose of good regulation, which they cannot attain for themselves, they must suffer severely. Unless the whole community combine to render the town healthy, and the place well regulated, the most frightful disorders must necessarily arise from a population so feeble and ignorant [sic]—feeble morally, and ignorant to secure their own interests—being so suddenly swept together, commonly from a rural origin. . . .

1292. Do you not think that that neglect of comfort and decency in their dwellings you have described in this way, has the effect in many instances of driving them to drinking, as a temporary relief from their misery?—The drinking that prevails in the large towns prevails under many influences. I should be unwilling to attribute it to actual distress, because the factory population of Manchester, with all the evils and disorders under which they are labouring, have paid among them a very large amount of wages, and what might be saved from their expenditure in spirits would go a great way towards improving their condition in other respects.

1293. Do you not think that their discomfort of all kinds, described as you have described it, has the effect of driving them to reckless courses in the way of drinking?—The general want of domestic comfort will have that effect; but the want of comfort at home arises very much from moral causes: the woman is absent from home during the day working at the mill; she has not made the home comfortable, and the discomfort of home has very greatly arisen from that circumstance.

1294. And the want of convenience at the back of the house, and the want of ventilation, all contribute to the discomfort of home?—Yes; and perhaps in the same degree to the inclination to be absent from it. . . .

1296. Mr. Cowper.] What remarks have you made with respect to the physical appearance of the poor people employed in those large towns compared with those employed in the country?—They are pallid in appearance, and are slender and thin, and there is a want of that appearance of animal spirits which generally distinguishes an agricultural people. . . .

1308. You say that a great deal of the want of comforts of home arise from the absence of the women?—Yes.

1309. Are the women at all familiar with those circumstances that make a home comfortable?—It depends upon what their previous habits have been; the young women employed in the factory in early life, turn out generally bad housewives, and their places present an appearance of disorder; it is not a home that they have; it is a house, but not a home.

1310. Would it not be desirable to mix something of household instruction in all those schools where the females go, so that they might learn something of cleaning the house or cookery, so as to make the husband's home comfortable?—No doubt; but without disputing its utility, the girls, according to the present system, go so early to the manufactories, that they may, before they become wives and mothers, have lost all ability to do anything but sew.

1311. Chairman.] At all events such instructions might be beneficial to them?—Yes, undoubtedly.

1312. Do those remarks you have made with respect to the necessity of enforcing, by some mode or other of legislative enactment, the inspection of dwellings and the regulation of drainage apply themselves generally to other manufacturing towns, with the particular circumstances of which, however, you may not be so familiar?—In every large town I have been in, I have seen circumstances that induce me to think that the same observations apply to all our great manufacturing towns, those especially in the north.

1313. All those great manufacturing towns which have risen up with large populations in the last 30 or 40 years; do you think the same observations apply to them?—Yes; the population has been brought together under municipal institutions, calculated for a rural people. Manchester has had to this day merely a manorial constitution; that is, until the day it got its charter. Bolton is under merely a court leet. These towns have had nothing but the old leet jurisdictions.

1314. The improvements had not kept pace with the increase of the population, and the necessities of the inhabitants?—Their municipal institutions are quite unfitted for masses of people so large.

XLI

D. Noble, *Facts and Observations relative to the influence of Manufactures upon Health and Life*, London, 1843, pp. 38–9, 40–1, 41–5.

I conceive indeed, for my own part, that the great mass of disease constantly witnessed in the districts where manufactures prevail, and so often laid to their account, comes rather from the great town than the factory system. The instances just given, to show the futility of mere speculative or analogical reasoning in the decision of such matters, suggest strongly the importance of deducing no inference whatever, except such as shall flow rigorously from the positive facts of the case; facts numerous in themselves, and selected upon some principle involving neither partiality nor fallacy. Such a proceeding I shall strive to maintain in the attempt to exhibit the accuracy of the position which I have just laid down, that the sanatory ills afflicting large masses of our manufacturing population result from other causes than those to which they have often been attributed.

It must certainly be conceded that a high degree of civilisation is not unattended by some prejudicial circumstances. Among the more prominent of these in modern times must be regarded the rapid springing into existence of great towns, which, owing to the circumstances under which this occurs, arrange themselves in many cases at utter variance with the requirements of health on the part of those by whom they are to be inhabited. . . .

The whole of this subject has of late, however, received the fullest and most circumstantial investigation from Mr. Chadwick, the secretary to the Poor-Law Commission, whose 'Sanatory Report' must ever be regarded as a standing monument of its author's ability, zeal, industry, and public spirit. . . .[1]

Amongst other valuable contributions, Mr. Chadwick has collected certain statistical tables which throw a flood of light upon the vexed

---

[1] *Report from the Poor Law Commissioners on an Inquiry into the Sanitary Conditions of the Labouring Population of Great Britain*, 1842.—Ed.

question forming the subject of the present publication; and these tables I shall in the sequel employ as illustrative of what I have before advanced. They were framed from careful analysis of the death registration books by the clerks of the several poor-law unions, who at the same time act as superintendant registrars. And here, before advancing further, I would submit a few remarks relative to the value of the evidence furnished by our national system of registration; more especially as I propose in the ensuing pages to make very considerable use of the results obtained from this source, not only in determining the average duration of human life in particular localities, but also in attempting to form some approximation to accuracy with respect to the influence of factory employment in the production of diseases especially laid to its account.

The system then of registering every death, in every part of this kingdom, with the age and occupation of the deceased, and with the cause of death so far as practicable, must be allowed by all to constitute a most important auxiliary in the prosecution of all such inquiries as the one in which I am at present engaged, as also in the investigation of certain characteristics of epidemic and contagious diseases. In very minute medical inquiries, or in what is called special pathology, little or no aid can be drawn from this source; but when the object is to determine the general character of diseases prevalent in various divisions of the kingdom, or to estimate the agency of many outward causes in the induction of early mortality and fatal diseases at all ages, the facts to be gathered from judicious analysis of the registration books become of the utmost importance. The great defects to be noticed, and those of a character admitting of some correction, consist in the causes of death being generally recorded upon no better authority than the verbal report of parties giving the required information to the registrar,—parties who, unprovided with any medical certificate, furnish their answers, in many cases, in the vaguest and most unmeaning terms, so that a considerable acquaintance with popular phraseology becomes necessary to allow of an approach to the real meaning. Yet, in spite of these drawbacks, very satisfactory and practically useful analyses may be made, and the tables planned and obtained by Mr. Chadwick, some of which I am about to exhibit, as well as the highly successful efforts of Mr. Farr in classifying the causes of death, as shown in the appendices to the Registrar-General's Reports, bear witness to the truth of this proposition. The facts arranged and compared are collected upon a principle that applies generally, and are thus exempt from that ordinary source of fallacy in dealing with matters of this kind, the partial selection of uncomparable facts.

In speaking of the sanatory condition of the factory operatives, I have stated my own belief that, on several accounts, their position was unfavourable to health and longevity; but that, in this respect, they differed but little, if at all, from other classes of workpeople who were exposed to the same injurious influences, excluding the effects, whatever they be, flowing especially from the factory system; now, Mr. Chadwick's tables show that the value of life at birth is greater in the rural than in the town districts; and that, on the average, the families of professional persons and gentry attain a higher age than do those of tradesmen and farmers; and that these latter again have better chances of life than the working classes. Now these facts are most valuable, as showing the source of many fallacies that have arisen in the discussion of such questions as the present one; they show that a high average mortality may prevail in a particular locality, not because it is the seat of some special department of industry, but because its labouring population, irrespective of the particular employment, may unduly preponderate. They show that, as a rule, the lower the position of any individual in the social scale, the less favorably situated may he be presumed to be in relation to the conditions of true health; and, upon detailed examination, they show that, as the peculiar evils of the 'great-town system' abound, the value of life diminishes accordingly; and, assuredly, Mr. Chadwick's figures do not make an unduly unfavourable exhibition of the towns where manufactures prevail, when contrasted with non-manufacturing towns similarly conditioned in all other respects.

I shall, here, select a few examples, in illustration of what has been just set forth; thus, in the returns of the average age of death amongst the different classes of people in manufacturing Manchester and agricultural Rutlandshire; the figures stand so:

	Manchester	Rutlandshire
Professional persons and gentry, and their families	38	52
Tradesmen and their families (In Rutlandshire, farmers and graziers are included with shopkeepers)	20	41
Mechanics, labourers, and their families	17	38

Now, if in the exhibition of the relative mortality of the two districts, no account were taken of the different positions in life of the various classes of the population, but the low average of life in Manchester set forth in comparison with what obtains in Rutlandshire, manufactures in all probability would be referred to as the cause of such a state of things; and, indeed, this was the actual mode of proceeding adopted by Mr. Sadler's committee; certain returns, very imperfect in themselves, were adduced, and contrasted with others not for their professed purpose legitimately comparable, because not similarly related with the exclusion of the factory system to the other possible causes of disease and early mortality.

The analysed results of our national system of registration have now clearly demonstrated that, in this country, a densely-populated district is less favourable to life than one but thinly inhabited; and the figures just quoted show that, so far at least as the instance extends, the result occurs, in a greater or less degree, in all ranks of life; and thus, in Manchester, where human beings are densely congregated, influences unfavourable to longevity extensively prevail; for we see that the value of life with the most favoured classes is not greater than with the least favoured in Rutlandshire. If it had appeared that in the higher grades there was little variation in the average age of death in the two localities, the difference in the pursuits of the workpeople in these places might to some extent have confirmed the idea regarding the specially injurious tendencies of manufactures; but the above facts, with many others of a like character, go to show that the evil appertains to towns rather than to factories.

XLII

P. Stocks, The effects of occupation and of its accompanying environment on mortality, *Journal of the Royal Statistical Society*, CI, Part IV, 1938, pp. 669–71, 678–80, 685–6, 688, 689–90.

Occupational and Industrial Mortality in Different Parts of England and Wales, 1851–1923

Dr. Stevenson, in the paper referred to above, made the following pertinent observation:[1]

> "The problem, however, of taking differences of occupation into account simultaneously with those of geographical situation and urbanization is not easy of solution. Even the largest occupation groups in the census classification, such as coal-miners, clerks, or agricultural labourers, are of such a size that if divided simultaneously by situation (in any degree of detail) and by urbanization, the numbers available for comparison, after the indispensable further subdivision by age, would frequently be insufficient to yield significant results. The tabulator of statistics is indeed constantly faced by the difficulty that his returns will not bear the degree of subdivision theoretically desirable".

This difficulty explains, perhaps, why the early tabulations of occupational deaths in detail of area which were carried out by the Registrar-General for 1851, 1860–1, and 1871 were not continued. The 14th Annual Report tabulated in 75 pages the census populations and deaths of males over 20 years of age for the year 1851 in over 300 occupations in each geographical division, county and town district, but notwithstanding all this material, the Report made no comment upon local characteristics of occupational mortality. The Supplement to the 25th Annual Report contained a more detailed tabulation at 12 separate ages of the deaths of males in a great variety

---

[1] T. H. C. Stevenson, The vital statistics of wealth and poverty, *J.R.S.S.*, XCI, Part II, 1928.—Ed.

of occupations and industries during 1860-1 in 11 geographical divisions and the aggregates of town districts in those divisions, but the whole of this tabulation of 115 pages was dismissed by Dr. Farr in four characteristic sentences, as follows:

> "As in the case of towns, so it may be said of men of unhealthy occupations; the mortality is susceptible of reduction by the investigation and removal of its causes. Thus the miner may be protected from explosions; and to a large extent from underground injuries by greater care on his own part and on the part of the managers and proprietors. He may be saved from the excessive fatigue of ladder climbing; and if the mines were well ventilated, he would not break down by so early and premature an old age. The publican has only to abstain from excesses in spirits and other strong drinks to live as long as other people".

No mention was made of local distribution but Dr. Farr, in his evidence to a Royal Commission on the Condition of Mines in 1864, made comparisons between the mortality of metal-miners in Cornwall during 1849-53, and those of non-miners in Cornwall and of coal-miners in Durham and Northumberland. In the Supplement to the 35th Annual Report, the tabulation of deaths in 1871 of males by occupation, age and geographical region was repeated in rather less detail, but although Dr. Farr then extended his comments to six pages the only use he then made of the elaborate regional analysis of occupational deaths was to compare the mortalities of butchers and of publicans in London with those in the rest of England. This comparison, translated for convenience into percentage indices is shown in Table I.

Table I
Relative Mortality of London Butchers and Publicans, 1860-61, 1871

	London Death-rates per cent. of those in the Rest of England and Wales at Ages:						
	15-	25-	35-	45-	55-	65-	75 and over
All Males, 1861-70	97	112	134	142	139	128	113
Butchers, 1860-61, 1871	128	105	123	128	126	111	124
Publicans, 1860-61, 1871	68	117	117	135	130	146	155

Although no general deductions were drawn from these, it is the first demonstration I have found in official records that men following the same occupation suffer a higher mortality in the town than in the country. It is rather surprising that with all the material available in these three Reports for 1851, 1860–1 and 1871, defective in many aspects though it was, no attempt was made to answer the question whether the higher total mortality of towns in the middle of last century could be explained by the effects of certain industries upon the workers engaged in them and upon their families, or whether it was a characteristic of all residents of towns regardless of their occupations. Dr. Farr did not, as far as I know, make any reference either to the question whether the high mortality associated with an occupation could be explained by its location chiefly in places rendered unhealthy by other factors. In no report subsequent to 1871 has a combined tabulation of deaths by occupation or industry and by region or class of area been repeated, except for miners, a peculiar people, from whom it is scarcely safe to make general deductions. ...

In an attempt to ascertain to what extent the mortality in towns increases with the presence of certain industries, I have in Table VI divided up the 83 county boroughs into groups according to their industrial character, and obtained for each group in each period 1911–14 and 1931–4 the average excess of their standardized mortality ratios over those of the rural parts of the counties in which the towns are situated. It was in 1911 that the transfer of deaths to place of residence began to be applied in England and Wales as a whole, and from that date also deaths were tabulated by administrative areas rendering comparison between urban and rural mortality much more reliable. Standardized death-rates expressed as percentages of the corresponding rates for England and Wales were given for 1911–14 and 1931–4 in the Registrar-General's Review for 1934 (Table XCVII) for each county borough and these have been further corrected by the time-comparability factor method which was introduced in the Review for 1935. In Table VI the towns outside Greater London have been divided into the seaside resorts, the Tyneside and Durham towns, South Wales towns, other ports and coastal towns, and the remaining inland towns of England have then been grouped according to the industrial employment of their populations in 1931. Unweighted average standardized mortality ratios are given for each group in columns (1) and (2), the corresponding figure for England and Wales as a whole being 100 in each instance. In the next column is shown the average of the differences between the standardized mortality in 1911–14 of each county borough and that of the aggregate of rural districts of the county in which it is situated, expressed as a percentage of the average S.M.R. of the rural aggregates. The averages used were unweighted, each town being treated as a unit. Column (4) gives the corresponding percentage excess in 1931–34. In column (5) is shown the percentage decline in the standardized death-rate in 1931–34 compared with 20 years previously. The last column gives the unweighted averages of the indices of housing density for each group at the census of 1931, and shows a continuous increase in the average number of persons housed per room with increasing proportion of males employed in mining and manufacture.

In 1911–14 London's mortality was 7 per cent. above, and the average mortality of the neighbouring rural areas was 28 per cent. below the national rate, London's excess above the neighbouring rural areas being 49 per cent. In 1931–34 this excess was reduced to 30 per cent. In the Tyneside and Durham and South Wales towns the excess was 24 per cent. in 1911–14 and 14–16 per cent. in 1931–4, for the seaside resorts it amounted to 12 or 13 per cent. in each period, but for other coastal towns the excess was 42 per cent. in 1911–14 and 30 per cent. in 1931–4. The high rates for the ports arise partly from the fact that the number of seafaring men dying in hospital or at their homes is out of proper proportion to the number employed on shore at the census, since the onset of illness often causes them to remain ashore.

The inland towns of England having half or more of their male population actually at work in the manufacturing or mining industries, excluding building, at the census of 1931 had an average mortality 39 per cent. above the neighbouring rural areas in 1911–14 and 23 per cent. above in 1931–4. In the next group, having a quarter to half of their male population employed in manufacture or mining, the textile towns still have a mortality 27 per cent. above the rural areas, whilst for the other subgroups the excess ranges from 13 to 21 per cent. For the towns with less than a quarter of their males employed in manufacture or mining the excess over the neighbouring rural areas is now no greater than in the seaside resorts. From this it appears that the harmful effect of the smoke-producing heavy or textile industries upon health has diminished somewhat during

Table VI

Comparison of Mortality of London and of the County Boroughs Grouped According to Industry, with that of the Rural District Aggregates of the Counties in which they are Situated

	Average Standardized Mortality Ratio (S.M.R.)		Percentage Excess over S.M.R. of Rural Parts of same Counties		Per cent. Fall in Standardized Death-rate	Persons per Room 1931
	1911–14	1931–34	1911–14	1931–34		
	(1)	(2)	(3)	(4)	(5)	(6)
England and Wales	100	100	—	—	—	0·83
London A.C.	107	104	49	30	30	0·98
Towns of London's Outer Ring	93	99	27	25	24	0·94
Tyneside and Durham coast towns	126	123	24	16	30	1·14
South Wales Towns	113	116	24	14	26	0·88
Seaside Resorts	86	94	13	12	22	0·70
Ports and Coastal towns not included above	115	112	42	27	30	0·86
Inland Towns (except Greater London) of England						
1. With 50% or more of all males over 14 at work in mining or manufacturing industries	121	113	39	23	33	0·96
2. With 25 but less than 50% of all males over 14 at work in mining or manufacturing industries:						
(a) Including 10% or more in textile industry	124	122	35	27	29	0·87
(b) Including 30% or more in mining, pottery, metal, chemical, leather or textile industries	116	109	27	14	32	0·87
(c) Including 15 but less than 30% in mining, pottery, metal, chemical, leather or textile industries	110	109	31	21	29	0·79
(d) Including less than 15% in mining, pottery, metal, chemical, leather or textile industries	99	98	22	13	29	0·78
3. With less than 25% of all males at work in mining and manufacturing industries	94	95	21	12	28	75

the last 20 years, for the excess of mortality in the towns most engaged in these industries over that in the rural areas has fallen from 35–40 per cent. to about 25 per cent. The excess in these towns is still considerably greater than is shown by towns with small proportions employed in the heavier manufactures, where it ranges from 12 to 21 per cent. The towns which grew up around the coal, steel, textile and shipbuilding industries during the early part of the nineteenth century are still those with the least satisfactory mortalities, owing, it may be surmised, to the great difficulties which have stood and still stand in the way of correcting the mistakes then made....

The attempt to separate the direct effects of a man's work upon his mortality from the effects of the industry in which he is working, operating through his general environment, began prior to the 1921 census, when the occupational classification was reconstructed so as to group together men engaged in the same kind of work rather than those employed in the same branch of an industry. The resulting mortality investigation in 1921–3 was consequently more correctly described as occupational than any which preceded it. The separate tabulation of the census population according to occupation and industry also made it theoretically possible to effect some separation of occupational from industrial influences, and for certain occupations, such as that of weaver, where it is known to be of importance, subdivision of the deaths according to industry has been made, but since the localization of industries then leads to the further need for a regional separation, this pathway towards truth loses itself in the wilderness as a rule, because the subdivisions have become numerically so small that their mortality rates are subject to a variation too large to render them conclusive. What is needed is some kind of control population which can be paired off with the men in a given occupation and subjected to the indirect influences attached to it, such as its urban or rural localization, without taking part in the occupation itself. Given such a control, the need for the threefold division into occupation, industry and locality would disappear, and the problem would be simplified. It is extremely fortunate that a control group which fulfils most of these requirements is provided for us in the mortality experience of the wives of the occupied men....

To what extent is the social class gradient of male mortality, which was noticed in 1910–12 and again in 1921–3, attributable to the kind of work done, and to what extent to the accompanying economic environmental and selective factors? ...

The ratios in Table XI show that whereas male mortality at ages 20–65 in 1930–2 ranged from 90 for Class I to 111 for Class V, that of married women had a wider range from 81 to 113, and the figures at 35–65 gave almost the same result. When divided by social class, therefore, married women have a mortality range about $1\frac{1}{2}$ times that of men, a similar result to that found when division of areas was made according to their overcrowding indices, which are fairly

Table XI
Comparison of Mortality Variation according to Social Class amongst Males in 1921–23 and 1930–32 and Married Women in 1930–32

Social Class	Standardized Mortality Ratios at Ages 20–65			Standardized Mortality Ratios at Ages 35–65	
	1921–3	1930–2		1930–2	
	Males (Civilians only)	Males (including Non-civilians)	Married Women by Class of Husband	Males (including Non-Civilians)	Married Women by Class of Husband
I. Professional etc.	82	90	81	90	82
II. Intermediate	93	94	89	95	90
III. Skilled	94	97	99	97	100
IV. Intermediate	99	102	103	102	103
V. Unskilled	124	111	113	112	113

closely correlated with social class distributions of the population. Remembering that the social class mortality of men is influenced by the direct effects of the occupations composing the social classes added to the indirect effects which influence also their wives, it is evident that the contribution made by the actual work done to the men's social mortality gradient from all causes must be very small compared with the contribution made by the accompanying environmental, economic or selective factors.

XLIII

Supplement to the Thirty-Fifth Annual Report of the Registrar-General of Births, Deaths and Marriages in England, London, H.M.S.O., 1875, pp. xiv-xv.

It will be interesting now to give a few illustrative cases of the changes in the marriage, birth, and death rates

(1) where a new industrial enterprise has been suddenly developed, and

(2) where a branch of industry is declining.

As instances of the former, take the districts of Ulverston, Guisbrough, and Stockton; of the latter St. Austell and Redruth in Cornwall, where the works and the population decline.

Ulverston contains Barrow-on-Furness. It owes the increase to a cause thus referred to in the Quarterly Return of the Registrar-General:[1]

"The mortality often augments with the increased prosperity of a district; and this is curiously illustrated by Ulverston, a romantic district extending from Morecambe Bay to Lake Windermere. Ulverston, in the ten years, 1841–50, was one of the healthiest districts of England; the mortality did not exceed 18 in 1000. A change took place, and in the ten years 1851–60 the mortality rose to 20 in 1000. The deaths in the June quarter of 1864 were considerably above the average of previous years, caused, says the registrar of Dalton, 'in part by the increase of the population, and in part by the prevalence of scarlatina and measles'. He adds: 'but there is no distress; work is plentiful, wages good, and provisions cheap. Labourers are earning 3s. 6d. a day; artisans 4s. 3d. and upwards'.

"The population of many of the townships and parishes of the Ulverston district, at the feet of its fells, and round the shores of its meres, is stationary, and in some instances has declined; it is an

---

[1] Quarterly Return No. 62, for second quarter of 1864.

old iron district, which had seen its works decay when coal came into use for smelting, but of late a pure haematite ore has been discovered in the carboniferous limestone of Dalton-in-Furness, for which there is a great demand. The population of the parish rose from 4683 to 9152 in the interval of the two last censuses, and, with the parishes in its vicinity, gave the increase which raised the population of Ulverston district from 30,556 in 1851 to 35,738 in 1861.

"The mortality of the district of Ulverston, exclusive of Dalton, in the last two quarters, was at the rate of 26 and 23 in 1000; while that of Dalton was at the rate of 42 and 31; and it is in this sub-district that the spectacle is presented of 'work plentiful, wages good, provisions cheap', and 'the prevalence of destructive epidemics'. This coincidence is reproduced over and over again. And it must not be supposed on that account that work, good wages, and cheap provisions are in themselves bad things; for they are as salutary as they are attractive to the masses of mankind. But our industrial armies are cut down by the camp diseases which are generated by the inadequate house accommodation and by the want of sanitary arrangements, which are never carried out in the neighbourhood of new works. Impure water, impure air, their own exhalations, kill men, women and children on the spot, and breed the leaven which devastates the towns and valleys in the vicinity. For the sins of a parish are often visited on its neighbours in thousands round. Thus South Wales has been rendered prosperous by the mines, and unhealthy by the negligence of the people. The mining population appears to be even less careful of life than the manufacturing population".

The increase of population went on; for the excess of births exceeded the excess of deaths.

This timely warning was not lost on the energetic authorities of Barrow-on-Furness; and though the mortality in the three decenniads that ended in 1870 increased and was 18, 20, 21, it has gone no further; sanitary measures have been undertaken and are still proceeding. The marriage-rate and the birth-rate, evoked to a higher pitch by the prosperity of the place, rose more rapidly than the death-rate. In cases of this kind of rapid concentration of population the high birth-rate is not the cause of the high death-rate; the first is

Registration Districts	Years	Persons Living at the Censuses of 1861 and 1871	Annual Average Number of			Rates per 1000 Living		
			Deaths	Persons married	Births	Deaths	Persons married	Births
Increasing Populations, Owing to Rapid Development of Industry								
Ulverston (including Barrow-in-Furness)	1860-1-2	35,738	751	485	1313	21·0	13·6	36·7
	1870-1-2	55,083	1150	958	2259	20·9	17·4	41·0
Guisbrough (including part of Middlesborough)	1860-1-2	22,128	449	294	913	20·3	13·3	41·2
	1870-1-2	39,016	966	687	1764	24·8	17·6	45·2
Stockton (including part of Middlesborough)	1860-1-2	57,099	1331	1056	2488	23·3	18·5	43·6
	1870-1-2	99,705	2565	1994	4501	25·7	20·0	45·1
Decreasing Populations, Owing to Decline of Mining Enterprise								
St. Austell	1860-1-2	33,797	673	573	1230	19·9	17·0	36·4
	1870-1-2	31,194	605	437	1007	19·4	14·0	32·3
Redruth (including Camborne)	1860-1-2	57,173	1301	1041	2059	22·8	18·2	36·0
	1870-1-2	53,503	1196	880	1734	22·3	16·4	32·4

caused by the prosperity, the second by the defective sanitary provisions. All the rates had been low in the first healthiest decenniad, quite in conformity with the general law.

Guisbrough and Stockton, including Middlesborough, exhibit a similar series of phenomena; the population became thicker and the mortality increased; the marriages and births also increased.

With a declining copper and tin industry in St. Austell and in Redruth, Cornwall, the mortality slightly declined; but to nothing like the same extent as the marriage and the birth-rates.

XLIV

Forty-Eighth Annual Report of the Registrar-General of Births, Deaths, and Marriages in England, (Abstracts of 1885), London, H.M.S.O., 1886, pp. viii–x

It is a matter of common observation that among working men marriage is not only more general but takes place at an earlier age than is the case among the upper and middle classes; but there do not appear to be any precise statistics bearing on the subject. The following Table, therefore, based upon a large number of marriages of bachelors registered in 1884–85, may be of some interest. It gives the proportion of marriages at different ages per 1000 marriages at all ages in several groups of men following different occupations. It shows, for instance, that in 169 out of 1000 marriages of miners the bridegroom is under age, and in 535 more is between 21 and 25 years of age; whereas among the professional and independent class in only 7 per 1000 marriages is the bridegroom under age, and in only 144 more between 21 and 25 years of age. It is necessary, however, to note that the Table can only be used for such comparative purposes with some caution; inasmuch as the age-distribution of the men employed differs itself very much in different groups. For instance, to take an extreme example, it would be utterly fallacious to compare the ages at marriage of 1000 clergymen with the ages at marriage of 1000 labourers, for there are no clergymen under 23 years of age, whereas a very large proportion of labourers are under this age.

To meet this difficulty, so far as possible, in the professional group have been included students of law, medicine, theology, &c., as also all men returned simply as gentlemen; so also with shopkeepers have been included shopmen; and with farmers their sons or near relatives living with them. By such expedients something has been done to equalise the several groups in respect of age-distribution; still the equalisation can only have been partial, and consequently, as before said, comparison between the several groups in respect of marriage-age distribution must be conducted with much caution, and small differences must certainly be disregarded.

Table C—Marriage Ages of Bachelors in Different Occupations, 1884–5

AGES	Miners	Textile Factory Hands	Labourers	Artisans	Shoemakers and Tailors	Shopkeepers and Shopmen	Commercial Clerks	Farmers and Farmers' Sons	Professional and Independent Class	All Males (1885)
ALL AGES	1,000	1,000	1,000	1,000	1,000	1,000	1,000	1,000	1,000	1,000
Under age	169	144	121	109	172	55	27	31	7	86
21–25	535	558	455	489	477	412	432	253	144	455
25–30	228	205	277	278	232	323	379	349	376	306
30–35	47	58	88	73	76	128	130	217	272	95
35–40	14	16	29	25	23	53	13	75	98	33
40–45	6	12	18	17	6	19	11	47	43	14
45–50	—	5	7	4	8	6	6	14	26	6
50 and upwards	1	2	5	5	6	4	2	14	34	5

The figures, however, show clearly at what very early ages working men undertake the expense of marriage, and how very much later the more prudent classes venture to do so.

The ages, though only given in the Table by quinquennia, were abstracted by single years; and it was found that the year of life in which the largest number of marriages occur among miners, textile factory hands, labourers, and artisans is the 22nd year of life; that is to say, they marry as soon as they are of legal age and can dispense with their parents' consent. After this year of maximum the proportion of marriages in these groups declines very rapidly year by year. In the other groups the year of maximum falls somewhat later, being latest of all in the professional and independent class, where it occurs in the 28th year, and the fall from the maximum in after years is much more gradual. The mean age at marriage in the several groups was as follows:

Miners	23·56 years
Textile hands	23·88 years
Shoemakers and Tailors	24·42 years
Artisans	24·85 years
Labourers	25·06 years
Commercial Clerks	25·75 years
Shopkeepers, Shopmen	26·17 years
Farmers and Sons	28·73 years
Professional and Independent Class	30·72 years

XLV

Seventy-Fifth Annual Report of the Registrar-General of Births, Deaths, and Marriages in England and Wales (1912), London, H.M.S.O., 1914, pp. xxii–iv, xxviii–ix, xxxi.

Fertility in relation to occupation.—The completion of the census tabulation of occupation renders it possible to include in this Report tables showing the numbers of children born during 1911 (as stated in Tables 28A to 28D of the Report for 1911) in relation to the numbers of the parents engaged in the various occupations. These fertility rates will be found in Tables XV–XVIII.[1] Legitimate births are necessarily stated in terms of the numbers of possible fathers, and illegitimate of possible mothers. In many cases, as indicated in the notes to Table XVI, there is reason to believe that the fertility of the single occupational groups shown in this table is misleading, owing to certain characteristic differences in the return of occupations at the census and in the birth registers. As there is on the whole more precision of statement at the census, the numbers tabulated to such indefinite headings as 'general labourer' are relatively greater in the case of births than of population, and the fertility of such occupations is correspondingly overstated, while on the other hand the fertility of labourers attached to definite occupations is correspondingly reduced, in some cases, e.g., that of navvies (XII. 2 (2)), to a very low level. This difficulty has been overcome as far as possible by grouping together, in Table XVII, those headings which experience shows to be liable to confusion entailing overstatement of the fertility of some of them and corresponding understatement of that of others. . . .

The reason for using two methods of statement of fertility in these tables is analogous to that for stating standardized as well as crude death-rates. The constitution of the populations following certain occupations is much more favourable to fertility than that of others for at least three reasons, firstly that occupations differ greatly in the

---

[1] 75th Annual Report of the Registrar-General, pp. xxiii–xxx.—Ed.

proportion of men they contain of an age beyond that at which men's families as a rule cease to increase, secondly that the proportions of married men in the same age-groups differ greatly in different occupations, and thirdly that the wives of married men of equal age are younger in some occupations than others. Occupations having many old men and comparatively small proportions of their younger men married have naturally, other things being equal, a lower fertility than others where the opposite conditions prevail. . . . From some points of view it may be desired to ascertain the rate at which the population engaged in any occupation is reproducing itself, its 'crude' fertility; and from other points of view its rate of reproduction in proportion to opportunity may be the information desired. For this reason two rates are given in Tables XVI and XVII, the first being the crude fertility rate, and the second rate roughly standardized by stating the births in proportion to married men aged less than 55 years.

The accuracy of the standardization obtained by the rough method employed in these tables leaves much to be desired, since the natural limitation of the number of legitimate children born to men is generally formed by the fertility of their wives, which again is closely associated with age. Any refined method of standardization would therefore entail knowledge of the age of the wives of the married men following each occupation. This is obtainable from the census schedules, but has never been tabulated. For the 1911 census however the age at marriage of husbands and wives in combination is being tabulated for each occupation, and this in conjunction with the tabulated statements of numbers of children born and surviving will make it possible to calculate fully standardized families for each occupation or group of occupations. These rates will be free from the weakness of those shown here for the births of 1911 in that due allowance will be made in them for the differences in the age at which men in different occupations marry and for the differences between their ages at marriage and those of their wives. In the absence of such allowance the figures in the second column of rates in Tables XVI and XVII must be regarded as only very roughly comparable, but notwithstanding this the differences between the rates in this column of the tables are so great that no further refinement of standardization could be expected to call for any very serious modification of the conclusions which may be drawn from them.

Table XV summarizes the facts recorded in Tables XVI and XVII into records relating to the same eight social groups as were employed in the section of the Report for 1911 which dealt with infant mortality according to fathers' occupations. The occupations composing the various groups are indicated by the numbers 1 to 8 in the first column of Table XVI. Groups 1–5 are arranged in descending order of the social scale from upper and middle class occupations in group 1 to purely unskilled labour in group 5. It will be seen that in the case of these five groups fertility, like infant mortality, increases progressively from the first to the fifth group. When the total number of workers is considered there is some little irregularity in this increase, but when the births are related to the number of probable fathers alone, the order of the five groups in regard to fertility is exactly the inverse of their order in social status. Thus in respect of fertility as of infant mortality the result of the first investigation on a national scale absolutely bears out the conclusions already arrived at by previous students of the subject, whose material was necessarily less complete. . . .

It will be noted that the gap separating the group of unskilled labourers from that immediately above them in the scale is by far the greatest of the four dividing the five groups. It would seem therefore that the statement that the population is being recruited out of due proportion from its least successful and progressive elements receives confirmation from these figures. It may be of course that there is nothing very novel about this, and that the same tabulation

Table XV—England and Wales, 1911—
Legitimate Birth-Rates in Social Classes

Social Class	Per 1,000 Males aged 10 Years and over (including Retired)	Per 1,000 Married Males aged under 55 Years (including Retired)
I Upper & Middle Class	47	119
II Intermediate Class (excluding scholars)	46	132
III Skilled Workmen	73	153
IV Intermediate Class	70	158
V Unskilled Workmen	90	213
VI Textile Workers	50	125
VII Miners	107	230
VIII Agricultural Labourers	49	161
III–VIII Working Class	76	175
All Classes	62	162

at an earlier date would have revealed a similar result. But the probability is that the causes which have diminished the birth-rate have increased if not created the differences between social classes, and even if this were not so it must be remembered that the differential effect of the much higher infant mortality of an earlier epoch probably had a far greater influence upon the relative increase of the various classes than is produced by this factor at the present time.

The fertility of the sixth group, that of textile operatives, is very little above that of the middle class by either form of statement. As its infant mortality is practically twice as great it can be readily shown that the slight advantage at birth held by group 6 is more than lost by the end of the first year of life, so that the effective fertility of textile workers is really the lowest of the eight groups compared. If it may be assumed that the custom of married female labour in the mills provides special economic inducements to this class to restrict its birth-rate the fact that this is so low in comparison with other workers of similar standing is strongly suggestive of purposeful avoidance of fertility as the cause of the difference. Indeed it seems difficult to account otherwise for the contrast between miners and mill hands, two classes very similarly situated in most respects other than the employment of their womenfolk.

It might perhaps have been expected that the fertility of agricultural labourers would have been higher than it is. In the recently published section of the Scottish census report dealing with fertility, crofters occupy the highest place in the list of occupations and farm servants are highly placed. In England however not only does the agricultural labourer remain unmarried to a much larger extent than the average man (Census Report 1911, volume X Table 20) but when he is married his fertility barely attains the average for all classes, and is eight per cent. below that of the working classes as a whole. The interest of these facts in relation to recent discussion of the adequacy of the agricultural labourer's wages and housing need scarcely be pointed out, but the compatibility of scarcity of house accommodation with high fertility as illustrated by the case of miners must be borne in mind. The advantage of this class in regard to infant mortality was only very moderate in 1911, a year in which, owing to its exceptional climatic conditions, the corresponding advantage of the country over the town was probably almost at its maximum. Using the 1911 rates however, as the only figures available, the 161 infants born to 1,000 married agricultural labourers of less than 55 years of age are reduced to 145·4 survivors at the end of the first year, and the 175 born in the case of the working classes in general to 151·8.

The fertility of miners is a very prominent feature of Table XV. It has long been noticeable that the registration counties in which mining was extensively carried on had high birth-rates, and in 1912 the three administrative counties with the highest birth-rates (pages 133–62) are Glamorgan, Monmouth and Durham. This exceptional fertility of the mining population is also to be noted in the Scottish census returns, and in the statistics of various foreign countries. It may be noted that it exists despite the fact of great scarcity of house accommodation in some at all events of the areas where it is most marked, and that it is accompanied by a heavy excess of infant mortality, the latter however not being nearly sufficient to reduce the number of survivors at one year of age to the average for the working classes.

XLVI

Royal Commission on Population, *Report*, London, H.M.S.O., 1949, pp. 31, 38–41.

74. The fall in the size of the family over the last seventy years, which was described in the previous chapter, is the salient fact in the modern history of population in Great Britain. In examining its causes we have first to distinguish between two distinct kinds of influence, and to measure, so far as possible, the importance of each. These are, on the one hand, the extension of deliberate family limitation, and on the other any changes which may have taken place in what we may conveniently call reproductive capacity";[1] in brief, the distinction between voluntary and involuntary factors....

96. The explanation lies we think in the profound changes that were taking place in the outlook and ways of living of the people during the 19th century. The main features of these changes are well-known. They include the decay of small scale family handicrafts and the rise of large scale industry and factory organisation; the loss of security and growth of competitive individualism; the relative decline in agriculture and rise in importance of industry and commerce, and the associated shift of population from rural to urban areas; the growing prestige of science, which disturbed traditional religious beliefs; the development of popular education; higher standards of living; the growth of humanitarianism, and the emancipation of women. All these and other changes are closely inter-related; they present a complex web, rather than a chain, of cause and effect; and it would be exceedingly difficult to trace how

---

[1] We include under "reproductive capacity" all the conditions contributing to the number of children born to a group of married couples among whom deliberate family limitation is not practised. It is thus affected by changes in the opportunity and desire for sexual intercourse, and by the rate of "reproductive wastage" from spontaneous abortion and stillbirth, as well as by the physiological factors which determine the ease with which conception is brought about.

they acted and reacted on each other or to assess their relative importance. We make no attempt here to do so, but merely to indicate briefly how they severally contributed to the movement for smaller families.

Decline of Economic Importance of the Family

97. In the old domestic handicrafts and in cottage agriculture, women and children joined in the income-earning activities of the household. Children worked at home from very early ages, often as low as 4 to 6 years. As the domestic handicrafts and cottage agriculture decayed, work at home was superseded by factory wage labour, and the family gradually ceased to be an economic unit. Children could no longer share in the economic activities of their parents. In the conditions created by the industrial revolution the employment of children in factories and mines as wage-earners subsidiary to their parents was indeed common in the first half of the 19th century. But this practice was repulsive to the humanitarian sentiment and, with the passing of successive Factory Acts, very young children ceased to be earners. At the same time elementary education was developing, a movement that was carried a great step forward by the Education Act of 1870. By the fourth quarter of the 19th century children had to be fully maintained by their parents at least up to the age of 10 years, which must for many have been more than twice as long as in the days when children helped in the work of the household from their very early years.

98. This change must have altered momentously the ordinary man's thinking about having children. Whereas in the old days children brought income in cash or kind to the household comparatively soon to offset the cost of their upkeep, they had now become, in the economic sense, an unrelieved expense. The contrast between a man who had only his wife and himself to maintain and his neighbour with, say, six children, could not but be conspicuous. As the amount a man spends on his children is related to his own standard of living this contrast must have been very striking in nearly all classes of the community not only among the poor. The contrast would be conspicuous among those who would have to sacrifice "luxuries" to support their children, as well as

among those who had to suffer want. Moreover in the Victorian age the maintenance or improvement of one's standard of living became an important object and ever-present problem to larger and larger sections of the community.

Insecurity and "Social Capillarity"

99. The industrial and agricultural revolutions carried with them a shift from settled, traditional ways of life, in which changes came slowly, to new ways of life in which changes were liable to be frequent and abrupt. The old settled ways of life, in which ties of family and community were strong and in which most persons accepted the station to which they had been born, were passing. They were being succeeded by an intense competitive struggle in which the emphasis was increasingly on the individual rather than on the community. Opportunities for "getting on" were multiplied but, at the same time, it became increasingly necessary to struggle to keep one's job and one's place in the community. The diffused feeling of insecurity was sharpened in 1875 when industrial and agricultural depressions brought a long period of almost unbroken prosperity to an end. The fluctuations in trade and unemployment which followed intensified the struggle for security and brought into public prominence the problems of poverty. Arguments for birth control in this period derived force and point from the condition of the poor in the crowded industrial areas, as brought to light by the investigations of Charles Booth and others, and from the experience of increasing numbers who were conscious in their own lives of the economic and social handicaps of membership of a large family. It seems reasonable to assume that the unsettlement caused by fluctuations in trade and employment, which were both more violent and more noticed than before, contributed to the success of birth control propaganda from the 1870's onwards.

100. In general, it can be said that as the 19th century advanced more and more people were being thrown into the struggle for security and social promotion. There seems no reason to doubt that this process, which Arsene Dumont called "Social Capillarity", helped the spread of family limitation in Great Britain. In the individualistic competitive struggle, children became increasingly a handicap and it paid to travel light. The number of children tended

to be limited also, not merely because the expenditure upon them might handicap parents in maintaining their own standards or achieving their ambitions, but because the fewer the children in the family the more could be spent on each child, and the better start it might have in life. This emerged strongly with the increasing importance of education as a qualification for positions of responsibility. The needs for higher standards of education and technical skills in industry, trade and the public services, the rise of professional bodies demanding higher standards of professional training in their members, and adoption in 1870 of a general system of open competitive examinations for the Civil Service were parts of a process in which material success in life had come to depend increasingly on the sort of education one had had. This process was reflected in the great development of the public school system in the mid-19th century and the later increase of facilities for other types of secondary and higher education and for technical training.

Higher Standards of Parental Care

101. The gradual improvement in the standards of parental care among the mass of the people during the 19th century contributed to this effect. This improvement reflected, among other things, higher standards of living, the development of what is described vaguely as the social conscience, popular education, and, significantly, the wide range of health and social services which began with the great sanitary reforms of the 19th century. Their effect was to deepen and intensify the sense of responsibility of the individual parent.

Growth of Science and New Attitudes

102. In the realm of ideas, perhaps the most important influence was the growing prestige of science in the public mind. The debates on evolution, for instance, which extended through all sections of the community, served, among other things, to diffuse a questioning attitude to traditional views on man's origin and development and to extend the field in which men felt that they need not accept the dictates of tradition. The spheres in which they thought that they could influence, if not entirely control, their circumstances, were widened, and it would have been strange had

this increased sense of personal responsibility stopped short of controlling the numbers of children in the family. The growth of science also was one of the influences that tended to loosen the taboos surrounding the function of sex and to change accepted notions of what was "decent" in discussion and conventional behaviour. The change in outlook and attitude opened the way for the spread of knowledge of the means of controlling conception.

Woman's Status

103. Through this complex, a change was taking place in the status of women. In the old family handicrafts and rural economy, many women enjoyed the more varied life and the more independent status of a partner in the income earning activities of home industry. The rise of the factory system, therefore, in this respect tended to narrow the interests of women, and the movement for equality of sexes was in part a revolt against the conditions that tended to restrict women to the role of producer of children and household drudge. It reflected, of course, other influences, among them the development of education, rising standards of living, and a more refined standard of manners and conduct. This movement, by opening up careers for women, often brought a money-earning career into conflict with motherhood. But its other important effect, in relation to family size, was to weaken the traditional dominance of the husband, to raise the women's status in marriage, with interests outside the home as well as inside, and to emphasise the wife's role as a companion to her husband as well as producer of children. Unrestricted childbearing, which involved hardship and danger to women, became increasingly incompatible with the rising status of women and the development of a more considerate attitude of husbands to wives.

The complex of Causes

104. The above brief review of some of the features of the great transformation in the social environment and outlook that was taking place during the 19th century shows that powerful economic, social, and cultural forces were all tending against the acceptance of an uncontrolled birth rate. With the decay of the family handicraft system, the family was declining as an economic unit, women and children were no longer joining in income-earning activities at home,

and at the same time the age for starting work outside the home was being raised. The period during which children were an unrelieved expense to their parents was being prolonged. For this reason, and because of rising standards of parental care, parenthood was becoming more costly. In industrialism also, the struggle for security and social promotion was intensified and in this struggle parents and children of small families enjoyed an increasing advantage over the large families. An uncontrolled birth rate became increasingly incompatible also with the changing outlook of the people, to which growth of humanitarianism, and the emancipation of women were contributing. Inter-related with these changes was the unprecedented growth of population and the fact that, before family limitation became widespread, large families, because of the lower death rates, were more common than they had previously been. These changes combined to prepare the way for family limitation; they made individual control over the size of family seem desirable or necessary. At the same time the means of control had become more readily available by the invention of new and better methods of contraception and the psychological barriers to their use were being broken down. The widespread adoption of family limitation in the 1870's, in our view, was due to the cumulative effect of these circumstances and to the special jolts which the depression of 1875 onwards and the Bradlaugh-Besant trials of 1877-8 gave to public opinion.

INDEX OF SUBJECTS

Ageing, effect on labour productivity, 183–185; per capita income, 180; saving, 174–175; 185–186; unemployment, 185

Age-structure, 30, 31, 124; effect on demand, 14, 74, 77, 155–156, 185–186; labour-force, 16, 19, 163, 183

Agriculture (food supply), depression in, 125; diminishing returns in, 15, 88, 95–112, 166; productivity in, 13; effect on demand for industrial products, 18–19, 128–135, 141–142; investment in manufactures, 18; mortality, 26; population growth, 21–22, 190, 210, 225–238; population distribution, 244–247; returns to labour, 96, 98–100

Annales de demographie historique, 25

Bills of mortality, 31, 44–46
Birth-rates, 19, 30–31, 43–44, 78–79, 123–124, 153–154, 209, 222–223, 244, 280
Board of Trade, 80
Bradlaugh—Besant trial, 288
Business cycles, 78, 178–179

Canadian Journal of Economics and Political Science, 23
Capital, marginal efficiency of, 159
Capital formation, effect on demand, 76
Celibacy, effect on morals, 39
Census, 26, 80, 120, 127, 212, 215–216, 252, 264, 269, 273, 278–279, 281–282
Census, industrial, 81, 86
Child labour, effect on fertility, 27–28, 199, 284–285
Children, effect on wealth, 42
Children, ratio of to total population, 46
Civil service, 286
Civil registration, 30–31, 261–262
Civilization, effect on returns to labour, 98
Classical economy, 11, 15

Colonies, effect on depopulation, 41
Communications, improvements in, effect on demand, 67–68
Constant return, law of, 107, 111
Consumer taste, effect on demand, 14, 74, 76, 79
Contraception, 28–29

Daedalus, 28
Death, average age at, 262
Death, causes of, 26, 85, 125, 202, 209, 248–250
Death-rates, 19, 23, 28, 30–31, 43–44, 79, 123–124, 153, 202–203, 210, 218–222, 239–240, 244, 249, 267–268, 271–272; of butchers and publicans, 265; of married women by social class, 270; of infants by social class, 280–282
Demand, non-demographic determinants of, 186
Demographic analysis, techniques of, 16–17
Demographic data, 26, 30–31, 127, 212–214, 220–221
'Demographic revolution', 21
Demography, 28
Diminishing returns, law of, 166

Ecclesiastical visitations, 31
Ecomonic growth, non-demographic causes of, 146, 171–172
Economic History, 25
Economic History Review, 17, 18, 26, 31
Economic Journal, 168
Education Act, 1870, 284
Education, economic value of, 84
Emigrants, economic value of, 83–84
Emigration Commissioners, 82
Employment, effect on spending, 157, 174
Employment exchanges, effect on labour-mobility, 165
Engrossing, effect on depopulation, 39–40
Environment, effect on demand, 75
Environmental standards, 24–26

Essay on the Population of England, 1780, 213
Extractive industries, diminishing returns in, 15, 101–102

Factory Acts, 284
Families, composition of, effect on demand, 78–79
Families, number of, effect on demand, 14, 74, 78
Family size, effect on the labour-force, 163; saving, 174–176; decline in, causes of, 283–288
Famine, 86
Fertility, effect on labour-supply, 16; by social class, 278–282
Food prices, 12, 51
Framework knitting, 124
French economists, views of, 97, 233
French Revolution, 105

General theory of employment, interest and money, 1936, 72
Government, methods of, effect on returns to labour, 101

Harvest, quality of, effect on demand, 128–132
Health, economic value of, 85
Health officers, 86
Hearth tax, 48, 212–213
Households, number of, effect on demand, 14; size of, and demand, 74, 78
Households, inhabitants per, 212

Immigration, effect on population growth, 41–42
Income tax, distribution of, effect on demand, 76; and saving, 72, 76
Income tax, schedules of, 80–81
Industrial output, 194–195
Industrial Revolution, 9, 17, 18, 21, 26, 32, 149, 208, 209, 245, 246, 284
Industrialization (manufactures, factory industry), effect on age-structures, 28; child-labour, 197–201, 204, 206, 283–284; demand, 78; families, large, 22; female-labour, 197, 198, 201, 204, 206, 287; fertility, 20, 23–24, 26–30, 199, 222, 271–274, 283–288; food supply, 21; health, 196–197, 251–254, 257, 260, 262; longevity, 251–254; living conditions, 21–22, 24–25, 26; marriage, ages at, 26, 28, early, 22–23, 28, 208, 210, 239, improvident, 191–192, rate of, 21, 271–274; morals, 196–198, 200; mortality, 20, 24–26, 202–203, 218–221, 239, 251–254, 264–274; population density of, 245–247, distribution of, 24, 215–217, 244–247, growth of, 10–12, 20–24, 30, 33–35, 51–56, 189, 191–196, 199, 208–211, 214–215, 218, 223–243, 271–274; positive check, 22; preventive check, 22–23; returns of labour, 95–97, 100–101, 110–112; social mobility, 29; unemployment, 196, 198–199; wages, 55–56; wealth, 33–34. See also, Machinery
Industriousness, effect on Population growth, 2
Inoculation, 26
Innovations, non-demographic determinants of, 168–170
Interest rates, 133, 174, 176
Investment, determinants of, 14, 72–73, 175–177

Journal of Economic History, 27
Journal of the Royal Statistical Society, 27, 150, 166, 216, 218, 264

Keynesian analysis, 72–73

Labour, demand for, effect on population growth, 187–190, 214–215; division of, 91–94, 101; division of, and fertility, 240–241; price of, and demand, 76
Labour-force, non-demographic determinants of, 87–94, 114–121, 178; occupational distribution of, 27
Labour-mobility, non-demographic determinants of, 165
Labour-scarcity, effect on technical progress, 136–140
Life, expectation of, 86; by social class, 262–263
Life Table, 80, 86, 147
'Listings of inhabitants', 31
Literacy, ratio of, 85
Local Population Studies, 21

Longevity, effect on size of labour-force, 163–164; economic value of, 85

Machinery, effect on demand for labour, 204–207; fertility, 23, 240–243; health, 207; length of life, 207; population growth, 23; well-being; 206–207

Malthusians, 15, 146, 149

Manchester School of Economic and Social Studies, 24, 163

Marriage, age at by social class, 275–277; certificates and allegations of, 123; children per, 43–45; encouragement of, 47; rates of, 30–31, 43, 47, 78–79, 123, 209

Matrimony, effect on population growth, 41–42

Maximum return, point of, 110–112

Medicine, improvements in, effect on population growth, 209–210

Middle-class, size of, 143–144

Migration, effect on demand, 74, 79; industrial output, 148; productivity of labour, 82

Miners, fertility rates of, 27, 282

Morals, effect on population, 41–42; returns to labour, 101

New World, imports of food from, 13, 19

Nineteenth Century, 15

Nutrition, standards of, 25

Observation on the state of England, 1696, 211

Optimum population, 112–113

Parents, authority of, effect on marriage, 40–41

Parish registers, 31, 43, 123–124, 212; abstracts of, 127

Poll tax, 43

Poor Law, 86; expenditure on, 12; effect on population growth, 209

Poor rates, 49, 234

Population, distribution of, 12, 215–217, 244–247; economic value of, 80–86; family structure of, 30–31; growth of, 11–14, 17–19, 30–31, 82–83, 124–125, 127–128, 146–149, 151, 164, 169, 171–172, 187, 191, 211–213, 224, 231–232, 272–273; household structure of, 30–31; marital structure of, 16, 30–31, 46; sex structure of, 16, 30–31, 45, 47; size of, 44–46, 151, 156, 163, 191, 212, 272; source-materials for, 9, 30–31— See also, Bills of mortality, Census, Civil registration, Demographic data, Ecclesiastical visitations, Hearth tax, 'Listings of inhabitants', Parish registers, Poll tax, Registrar-general, William and Mary tax, 1694, Window tax

Population, First Essay on, 1798, 11

Population change, economic and social effects of, 66, 171–172

Population, density of, effect on combination of labour, 66; demand, 65–66; division of labour, 65–66; economy of labour, 64; wealth, 64–66

Population growth, effect on agriculture, 15, 18–19, 21, 51–52, 125, 129–135, 150–154, 166, 190; commerce, 36–38, 67–68; communications, 108; consumer purchasing power, 18; demand, 11–14, 16, 18–19, 38, 51, 57–59, 67–71, 74–79, 128–132, 141–149, 155–162, 165, 175–180; division of labour, 37, 57–61, 97; economic growth, 17, 124–125, 128–135, 142–143, 149; emigration, 38; employment, 14, 19, 23, 148, 154, 157, 160–161, 164, 166, 168, 173–174, 177–179, 181; engrossing, 38; export industries, 19; food, imports of, 150–154, price of, 13, 51, supply of, 21, 76, 108, 150–154; industrial development, 9–20, 33–38, 47, 52–56, 70; innovations, 18–19, 61–63, 135–135, 157, 168–169, 182; international economy, 17, 19, 152–154; investment, 14, 18–19, 157, 159–161, 173–178; labour-supply, 10–18, 87, 114–121, 124, 128, 133–134 mobility of, 19, 142, 146–147, 155–156, 164, 177, 179, productivity of, 64–66, 68, 131, 165–166, 180–182, quality of, 12, 14–15, 19; machinery, 62–63, 95, 97; military strength, 38; national strength, 47–51; prices, 154; profits, 14, 70; rents, 51; returns to labour, 15, 95–113, 166; saving, 79, 166, 173–178; standard of living, 125, 148, 152; vassalage (slavery),

Population growth, *continued*
38; wages (per capita incomes), 35, 70, 175, 180; wealth, 69–71, 82
Population Studies, 21, 24, 27, 31, 32
Potato, effect on mortality rates, 26
Poverty, effect on fertility, 192–193; marriage, 192; population growth, 50, 64, 193; ratio of, 48–50
Primogeniture, effect on population growth, 40
Profits, effect on investment, 73
Property, inequality of, effect on returns to labour, 103–104

Regional history, strengths and weaknesses of, 123
Registrar-general, 26, 30, 80, 248, 257, 261, 264, 266, 271, 275, 278
Remingtons, 139
Reports, *Health of Towns*, 255; *Royal Commission on Population*, 180, 185, 283; *Royal Commission on Mines, 1864*, 265; *Sanitary condition of labouring population*, 260

Sanitation, 25, 255–257, 272, 274, 286; economic value of, 85; effect on population growth, 209–210; mortality, 86
Saving, effect on employment, 14, 72–73; non-demographic determinants of, 174, 186
Self-sufficiency, effect on demand, 77–79
Servants, ratio of to total population, 46
Social advance, effect on returns to labour, 101
'Social capillarity', 285
Social change, non-demographic determinants of, 171–172
Sociological Review, 184
Sojourners, ratio of total population, 46
Shipping, tonnage of, 151
'Stagnation thesis', 173–177

State policy, effect on demand, 75; investment, 75, 79
Standard of living, effect on fertility, 29; population growth, 18, 21

Taxation, effect on celibacy, 39
Technology, effect of demand, 76
Textile workers, fertility rates of, 27, 280–281
Trade, effect on population growth, 34–36, 53–54, 226, 229
Trade-unions, 91
Transport improvements, effect on population growth, 208; returns to labour, 99–100

Unemployment, non-demographic determinants of, 72, 176–178
Unemployment Insurance Scheme, effect on labour mobility, 165
United Nations, 74, 114, 171, 244
Urbanization, effect on death-rates, 23–26, 44–45, 85, 188, 202–203, 239–240, 248–250, 265–269; demand, 78, 145; expectation of life, 262–263; fertility, 23, 44–45, 239; health, 255–259; labour-supply, 16; marriage-rates, 44–45; population growth, 23, 226

Vaccination, 26, 209
Vale of Trent, 18, 26, 122

Wages (incomes), 11–14, 16, 18, 25, 29, 70, 80–84, 129–131, 141–143, 145–147; effect on demand, 74–76, 175
War, effect on population, 47, 188; First World, 13, 19
Wealth, effect on population growth, 229–238
Wesleyans, 209
William and Mary tax, 1694, 43, 45, 47
Window tax, 213

INDEX OF PERSONS

Alison, A., 23, 239
Anon, 33
Arkwright, R., 105, 194
Armstrong, W. A., 25, 27, 32
Ashley, W. J., 98
Ashton, T. S., 122, 128, 133, 149

Bagehot, W., 23
Baines, E., 195
Beales, H. L., 11
Bell, A., 22
Bell, W., 22
Benjamin, B., 30
Bentham, J., 210
Beveridge, W. H., 72
Booth, C., 285
Brabazon, Lord, 15
Brownlee, J., 147

Cairncross, A. K., 24, 26
Cannan, E., 15, 110, 164
Carr-Saunders, A. M., 208
Carrier, N. H., 27
Chadwick, E., 260, 261, 262
Chambers, J. D., 17, 18, 21, 26, 122
Charles, E., 163
Chatham, Lord, 211
Clapham, J. H., 139
Clark, C., 147, 163, 170
Cole, W. A., 18, 24, 26, 27, 127, 147, 148
Comber, W. T., 15
Cooke-Taylor, W., 20
Cowan, R., 239
Cox, P. R., 30
Crompton, S., 194

Daniel, G. H., 184
D'Avenant, C., 10, 23, 24, 43
Deane, P., 18, 24, 26, 27, 127, 142, 143, 147, 148
Deering, G. C., 125
Defoe, D., 10, 51
Douglas, P. H., 167
Dumont, A., 285

Eden, W., 214
Edmonds, T. R., 16

Engels, F., 11
Eversley, D. E. C., 17, 18, 25, 31, 43, 141

Farr, W., 261, 265, 266
Fergusson, A., 15
Fletcher, J., 255
Francklin, D., 23
Friedlander, D., 24

Gaskell, P., 20, 23, 24, 200
George, H., 15
George, P., 245, 246
Glass, D. V., 11, 18, 21, 25, 31, 43
Gonner, E. C. K., 216
Graham, Prof., 250
Graunt, J., 23
Gray, S., 15, 57
Griffith, G. Talbot, 208

Habakkuk, H. J., 17, 18, 26, 129, 136, 142
Hajnal, J., 27
Hale, M., 10
Hall, C., 22
Hammond, B. L., 25
Hansen, A. H., 173
Hargreaves, J., 194
Harrod, R., 163, 164, 165, 166, 167, 168, 169, 170
Heer, D. M., 28
Hicks, J. R., 168
Hirst, M. E., 136
Hollingsworth, T. H., 31
Hopkin, A. B., 27
Howlett, J., 20, 24, 214, 232
Hull, C. H., 10, 23
Humboldt, F., 237
Hume, D., 20
Huskisson, W., 195

Innes, J. W., 27

Jebb, Capt., 255
Jeffrey, J. R., 24
Jerome, H., 167
Jewkes, J., 163
John, A. H., 141, 142

Jones, E. L., 141
Jones, R., 23

Kendall, M., 166
Kennedy, J., 20, 23, 204
Keynes, J. M., 72, 157, 159, 161, 168, 173
King, G., 43, 45, 47, 49, 143, 144, 211, 212
Krause, J. T., 26, 31
Krier, D. F., 27

Laing, S., 20, 191
Landes, D. S., 19
Laslett, P., 31, 32
Levine, A. L., 17
List, F., 136
Loschky, D. J., 27

Malthus, T. R., 11, 12, 13, 21, 22 23, 24, 64, 69, 110, 146, 166, 193, 229, 235
Mantoux, P., 211, 215
Marshall, A., 15, 107
Marshall, T. H., 25
Marx, K., 11, 20
Mathias, P., 17
Matras, J., 27
McCulloch, J. R., 15, 20, 22, 23, 33, 195, 202
Meek, R. L., 11
Mill, J. S., 16, 98
Mills, F., 167
Mingay, G. E., 141
Mitchell, B. R., 147
Montgomery, J., 137
Moreton, A. H., 23
Morgan, W., 24, 189, 231
Myrdal, G., 177, 178

Newcomen, T., 133
Newton, I., 111
Newton, M. P., 24
Noble, D., 260

Peel, J., 29
Percival, T., 202
Petty, W., 10
Pierce, R. M., 27
Price, R., 20, 24, 189, 213, 214, 231, 232

Ravenstone, P., 15
Redford, A., 24
Ricardo, D., 110
Richards, J., 139
Rickards, G. K., 15, 23, 64
Rickman, J., 127, 147
Roshier, R. J., 24
Rostow, W. W., 142
Rowntree, G., 27

Sadler, T. C., 263
Saville, J., 24
Saverbeck, J., 150, 151
Schuyler, R. L., 20, 37
Scrope, G. Poulett, 15
Senior, N. W., 23
Shelbourne, Lord, 211
Sidgwick, H., 16, 87
Skinner, A. S., 13, 22
Smith, A., 13, 65, 92, 128, 131, 229
Snow, E. C., 150, 218
Spengler, J. J., 23
Stamp, Lord, 162
Stevenson, T. H. C., 27, 264
Stewart, J., 13, 22, 189
Stocks, P., 264

Temple, W., 10
Terborgh, G., 175
Thackrah, C. T., 251
Thompson, W., 15, 23
Titmuss, R and K., 155
Torrens, R., 95
Tucker, G. S. L., 31
Tucker, J., 20, 37

Ure, A., 25, 145
Usher, P., 245, 246

Wales, W., 214
Wallace, R., 21, 22, 225
Watt, J., 105
Welton, T. A., 26, 30
West, E., 110
Weyland, J., 23
Whewell, W., 23
Whitworth, C., 10, 43
Wilson, C., 143
Wrigley, E. A., 21, 31, 32

Young, A., 20, 126, 144, 187, 213, 214

INDEX OF PLACES

Africa, 71, 82, 167, 189
Africa, South, 84
Alsace-Lorraine, 221, 223
America, *See* United States
America, Latin, 148
America, South, 167, 237
Argentina, 152
Asia, 71, 148, 250
Asia Minor, 84
Australia, 66, 82, 84, 152, 220
Australia, South, 221, 223
Austria, 221, 223

Baden, 221, 223
Barrow-in-Furness, 271, 272, 273
Bavaria, 221, 223
Belgium, 221, 223, 240
Bideford, 53
Birmingham, 52, 54, 187, 200, 217
Bolton, 259
Bradford, 53
Bristol, 53, 216
Bristol, Channel, 216

Camborne, 273
Canada, 82
Canterbury, 188
Canton, 196
China, 167, 211
Cirencester, 54
Colchester, 53, 187
Connecticut, 221, 223
Cornwall, 265, 271, 274
Coventry, 54, 191
Croydon, 215
Cumberland, 191, 216

Dalton, 271, 272
Deal, 53
Denmark, 221, 222, 223
Derby, 124
Derwent, 125
Devizes, 54
Devon, 53
Durham, 215, 216, 265, 266, 267, 268, 282

Edinburgh, 240
Egypt, 84

England, 17, 24, 25, 26, 27, 29, 31, 36, 40, 41, 43, 47, 49, 52, 53, 67, 82, 83, 85, 86, 99, 100, 102, 105, 109, 122, 127, 130, 136, 137, 138, 139, 142, 146, 148, 150, 151, 163, 202, 209, 211, 212, 213, 214, 215, 216, 219, 220, 221, 222, 223, 231, 232, 239, 240, 266, 267, 281
England, Midlands, 215
Essex, 53
Europe, 21, 69, 71, 189, 220, 231, 237, 240, 246
Exeter, 53

France, 33, 39, 41, 221, 223, 240
Frome, 52, 53

Germany, 36
Glamorgan, 282
Glasgow, 187, 191, 203, 239
Gloucester, 54
Great Britain, 27, 31, 37, 39, 61, 63, 137, 142, 146, 164, 165, 169, 184, 202, 239, 242, 243, 283, 285
Great North Road, 125
Guisborough, 271, 273, 274

Halifax, 52, 54
Hamburg, 221, 223
Hesse, 221, 223
Holland, 35, 41, 100, 189, 221, 223, 231, 240
Hull, 53
Humber, 215
Hungary, 71

India, 84, 210, 237
Indies, 33
Indies, West, 206
Ireland, 10, 36, 82, 83 86, 127, 192, 209, 213, 237
Italy, 36

Lake Windermere, 271
Lancashire, 27, 54, 145, 148, 191, 215, 216, 217
Leeds, 52, 54, 191, 215, 251
Lincolnshire, 217
Liverpool, 53, 191, 215, 216

London, 44, 45, 46, 53, 59, 124, 125, 200, 212, 213, 215, 216, 240, 250, 265, 266, 267, 268
Lynn, 53

Macclesfield, 52, 191
Malmesbury, 53
Manchester, 52, 54, 187, 191, 202, 215, 255, 256, 258, 259, 262, 263
Massachusetts, 221, 223
Medlock, 256
Middlesbrough, 273, 274
Middlesex, 217
Monmouth, 282
Morecambe Bay, 271

Netherlands, 10, 35
Newcastle, 53, 215
New South Wales, 221, 223
New York, 196
New Zealand, 221, 223
Norfolk, 53, 84
Norway, 221, 222, 223
Northumberland, 215, 265
Norwich, 53
Nottingham, 125
Nuneaton, 191

Paisley, 203
Plymouth, 53
Poland, 71
Portugal, 71
Prussia, 221, 223

Queensland, 221, 223

Redruth, 271, 273, 274
Riding, East, 252
Riding, North, 252
Riding, West, 148, 215, 252
Rumania, 221, 223
Rutland, 217, 262, 263

St. Austell, 271, 273, 274
Salford, 191
Saxony, 221, 223
Scandinavia, 221, 222
Scotland, 37, 82, 83, 86, 213, 221, 223, 240

Severn, 215
Sheffield, 52, 54, 187, 215
Spain, 33, 35, 36, 41, 71, 221
Stafford, 54, 217
Stockton, 271, 273, 274
Stroudwater, 54
Suffolk, 216
Surrey, 217
Sweden, 221, 222, 223
Syria, 84

Tasmania, 221, 223
Taunton, 52
Tedbury, 53
Tiverton, 52
Trowbridge, 53
Turkey, 71
Tyneside, 266, 267

Ulverston, 271, 272, 273
United Kingdom, 151, 185
United Provinces—*See* Netherlands
United States, 36, 37, 63, 67, 71, 82, 86, 118, 136, 137, 138, 139, 166, 167, 187, 189, 220, 250

Vermont, 221
Victoria, 221, 223

Wakefield, 52
Wales, 24, 25, 27, 85, 127, 150, 151, 163, 202, 212, 214, 219, 220, 221, 222, 223, 266, 267
Warminster, 53
Warrington, 52
Warwick, 54, 148, 217
Westbury, 53
West Ham, 215
Westmorland, 191
Whitehaven, 53
Wiltshire, 53, 216, 217
Winchester, 188
Worcester, 54
Wurtemburg, 221, 223

Yarmouth, 53
York, 53, 188
Yorkshire, 54, 215